God Dreams is a rare resource. Pick it up if you dare to dre[...] in ways you didn't think possible.

Craig Gr[...], [...]

Author of *#Struggles: Following Jesus in a Selfie-Centered World*

God Dreams provides a step-by-step approach toward developing a God-sized vision with your team. I highly recommend this book to any pastor or church leader.

Thom S. Rainer, President and CEO, LifeWay Christian Resources

This is no passive book about growing your church, but a bold challenge to take up our God-given ability to dream and accomplish great feats for God's glory.

Ed Stetzer, Executive Director, Billy Graham Center for Evangelism, Wheaton College

Leadership teams positioning their churches for radical obedience to God's call and significant Kingdom impact should look to this book for deep insight and practical help.

Kevin Peck, Pastor, The Austin Stone Community Church

Will Mancini ushers in a new day, bringing long-term thinking and visionary planning back in vogue.

Lee Powell, Founding Pastor, Cedar Creek Church

Will Mancini creates break-through clarity for leaders. He does it again with *God Dreams*.

Larry Osborne, Senior Pastor, North Coast Church, Author of *Thriving in Babylon*

If you are perfectly happy with your church the way it is, then you don't need this book. For the rest of us, *God Dreams* is required reading.

Richard Kannwischer, Pastor, St. Andrew's Presbyterian Church

It's easy to grow weary in the pursuit of our ministry dreams. Let Will Mancini reignite your passion.

Steve Andrews, Pastor, Kensington Church

If you lead anything, *God Dreams* is a must read.

Rob Peters, Pastor, Calvary Baptist Church

Vision—so obvious and yet so fuzzy. Reading this book is like putting on reading glasses—instant clarity.

Sam Chand, Leadership Consultant, Author, *Leadership Pain*

I am a huge fan of the tools created by Will Mancini and the Auxano team. *God Dreams* is the next installment—an incredible playbook for vision and execution.

Eric Geiger, Senior Pastor, Mariners Church

Author Will Mancini is the rare combination of an inspiring leader, an articulate theologian, a submitted Christ-follower and a clear-thinking engineer. So when he speaks of vision in *God Dreams*, you don't get stuck in theory, lost in presumptuous imagination, or overwhelmed by words on a whiteboard. Rather, Will gives all leaders a clear path to discover their God-given dreams and to express those dreams in a way to move the heads, hearts, and hands of people. This book has helped me turn our church's vision into action-oriented plans. *God Dreams* is a gift to every leader. If you will read it with a readiness to act, you can anticipate the future coming into focus.

Bruce Wesley, Pastor, Clear Creek Community Church

Within my career, I've had the privilege of working with some of the most amazing storytellers and visionary leaders in the world, from within the Walt Disney Company, to George Lucas, to kingdom leaders like Max Lucado and Rick Warren. Some have an intuitive knack for articulating and implementing vision, while most of us would benefit from someone that could help us engineer visions into reality. These "Visioneers" are a rare breed, indeed. I consider Will Mancini among the best of them (and one of the few who is actually a trained engineer) because he is not just one of the most experienced "sherpas" on the journey, but because he is literally writing the map. *Church Unique* and *God Dreams* are that map.

Mel McGowan, President, Visioneering Studios

I'm grateful for all that Will Mancini has done to lift the value of strong, clear vision in the church beginning with his earlier book, *Church Unique*. Now *God Dreams* goes a step further by providing simple tools to craft a compelling vision. This book has the potential to reshape the future of your church.

Tony Morgan, Founder and Chief Strategic Officer, The Unstuck Group

Having walked through the process of vision clarity with Will Mancini, I have seen firsthand his personal passion for helping leaders of ministries clarify the unique calling they have so they can lead forward. In a rapidly changing world where more information, ideas, and opportunities are available at our fingertips, having a crystal clear vision for the future of the organization you lead is more critical than ever before. The stakes are too high simply to muddle your way through. *God Dreams* takes vision clarity to a new level and helps leaders and ministries get laser-focused for maximum impact for the kingdom. Your leadership team will benefit greatly from walking through this together.

Tim Niekerk, Pastor, Salem Lutheran Church

Will Mancini helps you do what every church leader wishes he or she could do but isn't sure how; he shows you, step by step, how to create a clear and compelling vision for your church. Not a generic vision. Not a copy cat vision. Not an uninspiring vision. Your vision. *God Dreams* will not just motivate you; it will help you.

Carey Nieuwhof, Pastor, Connexus Church,
Author, *Lasting Impact: 7 Conversations that Will Help Your Church Grow*

Read *God Dreams* to find how your church can be the canvas on which the Spirit draws your destiny of dreams and writes the story of God's love for the world.

Leonard Sweet, Author, *From Tablet to Table,* Professor (Drew University, George Fox University, Tabor College), and Creator of preachthestory.com

The principles in *God Dreams* have helped shape the work of our church for the next decade and beyond—allowing us the freedom to know who we are and where the Lord is leading us with wonderful clarity. Every leader who wants to help shape the future for God's glory must read this book!

Ryan Rush, Pastor, Kingsland Baptist Church

I love when a resource comes along that helps unlock a leader's God-given potential and then brings clarity to the calling that God has put on their heart. *God Dreams* is that kind of resource. This book will be an invaluable tool to church planters, pastors, and churches to help keep them strategically honed in and focused on the vision and mission that God has put on their hearts to reach their communities for Jesus Christ.

Brian Bloye, Pastor, West Ridge Church

Vision without clear, strategic action is impotent. *God Dreams* provides a much needed frame for church leaders to help translate vision into practical impact.

Charles Lee, CEO of Ideation, Author, *Good Idea, Now What?*

The power of stunning clarity can't be overstated. In *God Dreams,* Will Mancini not only challenges us to think beyond the relentless approach of Sunday, he gives us new tools and techniques to focus our best on the most important kingdom work we are called to do. This is a brilliant and compelling read. My copy is already marked up and making a difference in my leadership. It will fuel the vision conversation for years to come.

Vince Parks, Executive Pastor, Summit Community Church

Will Mancini is a visionary who helped us gain clarity and focus at Bellevue. I highly recommend this book.

Steve Gaines, Pastor, Bellevue Church

I wish I had known about his process thirty years ago. We now have razor sharp clarity.

Gary Singleton, Pastor, The Heights Baptist Church

GOD
DREAMS

GOD
DREAMS

12 VISION TEMPLATES FOR FINDING AND FOCUSING YOUR CHURCH'S FUTURE

WILL MANCINI
AND WARREN BIRD

B&H
PUBLISHING GROUP

NASHVILLE, TENNESSEE

978-1-4336-8845-4

Published by B&H Publishing Group
Nashville, Tennessee

Dewey Decimal Classification: 253
Subject Heading: LEADERSHIP \ PASTORAL WORK \ VISION

5 6 7 8 9 10 • 23 22 21 20 19

This book is dedicated to my beloved wife, Romy. She is my beautiful reminder that God's dreams are always better than our own. She is my soul mate and life partner on my mission to help church leaders experience meaningful progress for God's glory.

—Will Mancini

ΞXPONENTIAL⌐

About the Exponential Series

The interest in church planting has grown significantly in recent years. The need for new churches has never been greater. At the same time, the number of models and approaches are expanding. To address the unique opportunities of churches in this landscape, Exponential launched the Exponential Book Series in partnership with solid partners like B&H.

Books in this series seek to:

- Tell the reproducing church story.
- Celebrate the diversity of models and approaches God is using to reproduce healthy congregations.
- Highlight the pioneering practices of healthy reproducing churches.
- Equip, inspire, and challenge kingdom-minded leaders with the tools they need in their journey of becoming reproducing church leaders.

Exponential exists to attract, inspire, and equip kingdom-minded leaders to engage in a movement of high-impact, reproducing churches. We provide a national voice for this movement as we seek to champion multiplication and equip church multipliers.

The Exponential Book Series is part of a growing library of church multiplication resources that include the Exponential Conferences, learning communities, eBooks, courses, webcasts, and audio training. The Exponential Book Series is an important element in our mission to equip church multipliers with thought leadership.

For more information about Exponential visit exponential.org.

Other Books in the Exponential Series

AND: The Gathered and Scattered Church, Hugh Halter & Matt Smay

Barefoot Church: Serving the Least in a Consumer Culture, Brandon Hatmaker

Discipleshift: Five Steps that Help Your Church to Make Disciples Who Make Disciples, Jim Putman & Bobby Harrington with Dr. Robert Coleman

Exponential: How You and Your Friends Can Start a Missional Church Movement, Dave Ferguson & Jon Ferguson

For the City: Proclaiming and Living Out the Gospel, Darrin Patrick & Matt Carter with Joel A. Lindsey

It's Personal: Surviving and Thriving on the Journey of Church Planting, Brian & Amy Bloye

Missional Moves: 15 Tectonic Shifts That Transform Churches, Communities and the World, Rob Wegner & Jack Magruder

On the Verge: A Journey into the Apostolic Future of the Church, Alan Hirsch & Dave Ferguson

Planting Missional Churches, revised edition, Ed Stetzer & Daniel Im

Sifted: Pursuing Growth Through Trials, Challenges, and Disappointments, Wayne Cordeiro with Francis Chan & Larry Osborne

Transformation: Discipleship that Turns Lives, Churches, and the World Upside Down, Bob Roberts Jr.

More Titles Forthcoming! Visit exponential.org/books for more information.

Contents

Important Note on a Key Feature of *God Dreams*

The Edge Marker for the
Twelve Vision Templates of Part Three

As you use this book in your ministry, you will most likely have opportunities to gain feedback from broader leadership groups. These groups include elders, deacons, small group leaders, teachers, volunteer team leaders, committees, and so on, depending on your church's unique culture.

In order to gain broader support from these leaders in an efficient way, *God Dreams* comes with edge markers in chapters 7-10 of part three only, clearly evident on the page edges of the book. This key feature enables you to gather feedback from leaders without requiring them to read the entire book. Leaders can simply read the overview of the twelve templates (about 20 percent of the book itself), engage the assessment questions in this section, and contribute their opinions. In addition, this helps every reader quickly return to the twelve templates overview for continued reference in the future.

Foreword

Creaturely reality in the Bible is ek-centric: to find one's center in God is, paradoxically, to be freed to be uniquely and oddly one's self. Gathered around the divine throne, the tongues of all creatures are loosed to find their own peculiar parts in the cosmic song.

—Systematic theology professor Joseph Mangina[1]

Reflect on the building you are now in as you read this book. While you might be tempted to question various aspects of its aesthetics, design, or functionality, you can be sure that it could not have been erected unless there was an original blueprint of sorts. Even the crudest buildings require *some* forethought and conceptual preparation. In other words, the building must have "existed" in the mind of the designer or builder before it existed in concrete reality. The same is the case for all artistic expression, but it is also as true for the social structure of human communities as it is for the mission of God's people in the world.

Stephen Covey, in *The Seven Habits of Highly Effective People*,[2] talks about what he calls "first and second creations." The first creation must take place at the level of vision before it can take place at the level of actual realization. The second creation must follow the first, or it cannot be done. Covey incorporates this aspect under the overall habit of what he calls *beginning with the end in mind*. The end, insofar as it is in the future, can only be accessed by an exercise of the vision and imagination—by that God-given ability to dream up the world we want to live in and the organization we wish to lead.

I believe that is one of the fundamental jobs of human imagination: to be able to produce out of the society, we *have* to live in a vision of the society we *want* to live in.

One of the best working definitions of poverty is not just the lack of money or options but the lack of a dream, a vision, a hope. It is the leader's task to rouse the imaginative abilities that lie at the base of the human soul and awaken the possibilities for a new gospel future and thereby activate the deepest sources of human motivation—faith, love, pleasure, and hope. Before we can do it, we need to dream and envision it.

Similarly authentic vision for a particular group of God's people—or what Will Mancini calls a "church unique"—is not something you can simply download from some generic vision store on the Internet, as some seem to suggest. There is no one-size-fits-all vision. Vision, if it is to be powerful and compelling, has to be unique and awaken the latent energies of a group of people.

In *God Dreams*, Will and Warren provide us with precisely the kind of process and framework that can unlock the breakthrough potential God has invested in His church. Strap on your belts and take the journey to becoming genuinely outstanding . . . *ek-centric.*

After reading *God Dreams*, you will have a much clearer understanding about why vision is important and how it can be imagined, planned, and delivered.

God Dreams will do something else for you: It will help you "cultivate an internally generated pressure for movement." I describe that idea of building momentum in my book, *Permanent Revolution.* There I explain gifting like the apostle Peter's: one that retains an entrepreneurial orientation but stays close to the established organization. I see this in Will and his fellow team members at Auxano. He knows how to guide you through a "mining" and "mobilizing" work.

May God use Will Mancini, Warren Bird, and this book to refound and unlock your church's pioneering spirit and missional heartbeat.

Alan Hirsch
Dreamer, Visionary, Eccentric
www.alanhirsch.org

Preface

If the iron is blunt, and one does not sharpen the edge, he must use more strength, but wisdom helps one to succeed.

—Ecclesiastes 10:10

God Dreams is about visionary leadership in the local church. More specifically, it's about articulating a visionary plan in a way that's compelling, measurable, and marked by stunning clarity.

Imagine that the role of vision in your church is like an axe. When skillfully used, it makes a path clear. It removes obstacles. It broadens the path for others to follow. It enables greater accomplishment.

Most pastors regularly pick up the axe of vision in their ministry. Some quickly set it back down, having never been trained in its effective use. Others swing like crazy, unaware that they wield a dull edge. Too often they become frustrated or confused by too little return for their tireless work.

This book is your whetstone. It will sharpen your axe of vision; it will help you gain new competencies in planning and communication. Life is too short and ministry is too hard to swing all day with a blunt-edged vision.

What will your church's ultimate contribution look like in your community or city? Who are you becoming as a congregation? What will guide your most important priorities along the way? And what singular impact will your church have as the years unfold? These vital questions are all informed by vision.

> This book will sharpen your axe of vision; it will help you gain new competencies in planning and communication.

Today's commonly followed menu for becoming a visionary church leader is pretty straightforward: Be a person of prayer and a student of God's Word. Then get additional help: digest a Patrick Lencioni business book, be inspired by a rapid-growth church story or the next edgy missional dude at this year's conference, and sift through your Twitter feed for some strategic ministry gold.

But this wealth of excellent resources is not leading to visionary planning marked by stunning clarity. Today's training diet for pastoral leaders does not automatically or even naturally result in the skills and practices of visionary leadership.

In fact, *God Dreams* will argue that the typical pastor doesn't get close to a basic competence level in visionary leadership. Instead, despite our best efforts to keep our eye on the ball of vision, we get tackled by Sunday's-a-coming busyness, we get distracted by the next how-to-church book, and we stay addicted to "done-for-you" resources. If all those challenges aren't enough to trample our imagination, the needs of a spiritually messy congregation pile on.

> The ultimate goal of *God Dreams* is to make a game-changing difference in your life as a visionary leader.

Whatever your situation, our experience suggests this: the majority of a church's senior team resonates with the idea of visionary leadership but doesn't feel competent enough in it. The ultimate goal of *God Dreams* is to make a game-changing difference in your life as a visionary leader.

More specifically, *God Dreams* gives you new tools to inspire people and focus your congregation, from staff and lay leaders to members and new attenders. If you wholeheartedly work the process in this book, you will have a beautiful and powerful picture of your church's future, and crystal clear next steps to get there.

My Own God Dream

The early years of my journey don't stand out for clarity of vision or visionary leadership. Much of this book comes from my life experiences. ("I," "me," and "my" in this book always refers to Will Mancini, even though in the creation of this book, every sentence was a team effort with my coauthor Warren Bird.)

While my parents took me to church as a kid, the gospel wasn't clearly proclaimed until my middle school years. I came to Christ in eighth grade at a Christian school run by a Presbyterian church. Our family moved every couple of years as my dad climbed the corporate ladder, and I went to Penn State University to pursue an engineering degree. While there I got involved in Cru (then known as Campus Crusade for Christ) and felt called to ministry. I came to Texas and worked in the oil industry a couple of years. Then I went to seminary and served in a broken, declining twenty-year-old Baptist church.

Along the way I bumped into someone who impressed me, not just with his Christlike leadership but also with his clarity of vision. His name is Bruce Wesley, and he had founded greater Houston's Clear Creek Community Church in 1993. You'll hear more of his story in the pages to come (and yes I enjoy the ironic but coincidental humor in the "Clear" part of the church's name).

When Bruce hired me in 1997 to join Clear Creek staff, he literally drove me around Clear Lake and shared his dream of reaching a people far from God by showing me the community. Looking out the windows of his car, I wasn't thinking consciously about vision; I was simply being caught up in the one God had given Bruce.

I served on staff at Clear Creek as it grew from an attendance of six hundred to twenty-five hundred. My family and I are still members there as it pushes past an attendance close to five thousand today.

During my days on staff, the more I learned about visionary leadership, the more I realized the limitations of our best books and tools on the subject. Eventually, God directed me to invest my life in facilitation, consultation, and tool making. Helping church leaders achieve breakthroughs with clarity and vision is what gets me out of bed. Originally my plan was to start a church out of Clear Creek. But instead of planting a church, I planted a consulting group.

That initiative became Auxano, an organization I lead to this day. The word means *to cause to grow*. Luke used it to describe the growth of the early church in Acts. Auxano now includes more than a dozen full-time thought leaders and consulting practitioners who serve alongside me. (Learn more at Auxano.com.)

As far as I can tell, Auxano is the only nationally based nonprofit consulting group dedicated solely to working on the vision process in the local church. Our mission is to create breakthrough clarity with church teams to realize their vision.

Three Benefits of God Dreams

If you apply this book and clarify your own God Dreams, the benefits will be manifold. I am most excited about three outcomes. First, I hope *God Dreams* provides you with a deeper sense of meaning personally as a leader. Many pastors seem to be missing the sense of freedom and confidence that is possible with a vision marked by increased clarity.

Second, I would like you to experience significant improvement in your ability to inspire others. With so much to distract us, the local church leader has a special role to show people the kingdom of God invading the everyday. People need to see what God is up to, or as Eugene Peterson

> Many pastors seem to be missing the sense of freedom and confidence that is possible with a vision marked by increased clarity.

translates so finely, "If [they] can't see what God is doing, they stumble all over themselves" (Prov. 29:18 *The Message*).

Finally and perhaps most urgently for church leaders today, I hope to see your team focusing in a new way. Focusing, that is, on *God things* not just *good things*, resulting in a forced multiplication of every decision, every dollar, and every mobilized saint. The church has a desperate need to learn how better to focus its attention and resources.

Every predictor says the church in North America will continue to have worship services and small groups. We will keep passing the offering plate and paying our utility bills. But if we are to make a noticeable difference in our lifetime, we will need to name, define, and focus everything we have on the specific kind of dramatic good God gives us to do. We are simply too busy and scattered in our best organizational efforts.

> If we are to make a noticeable difference in our lifetime, we will need to focus everything we have on the specific kind of dramatic good God gives us to do.

Coattail Effect with Church Unique

One of my previous books is *Church Unique: How Missional Leaders Cast Vision, Capture Culture, and Create Movement*. *Church Unique* is primarily about your church's *identity*. Think of it as your church's culture, DNA, ministry philosophy, or ministry model. It shows church leaders how to identify and unlock their congregation's individual identity as a tool for unleashing their one-of-a-kind potential.

To do so, *Church Unique* covers the big ideas of what I call "the vision framing process." In *Church Unique* I introduced an important tool called the Vision Frame (see figure 0.1). The Vision Frame has four sides, each representing an essential question that must be answered in order to "frame" who you are as a church. If you're curious about the Vision Frame or want a refresher course on it, see appendix B.

God Dreams is primarily about your church's *direction*. Think of it as the picture of your church's future or your church's ultimate contribution; it's all about your long-term plan and resultant short-term priorities.

Figure 0.1 next shows the central icon for *God Dreams*. The square area in the middle contains four "rows" that represent four aspects or time horizons for describing your church's direction. These four horizons, when put together, make up the Horizon Storyline.

Figure 0.1 also shows how these two images fit together, with the Vision Frame "framing" the Horizon Storyline picture inside. In fact, you could say the Horizon Storyline "snaps into" the middle of the frame and now takes your plan for the future to new levels of clarity.

God Dreams is primarily about what's inside the frame. But many of the graphics in *God Dreams* include the Vision Frame around it. The reason for including the picture frame is to be a reminder that if you don't know what God has uniquely called you to be (your church's Vision Frame), then having clarity of direction (your church's Horizon Storyline) is not as easy.

In short, *God Dreams* is a journey to understand and use a master tool called the Horizon Storyline. This dynamic tool will help you build a visionary plan that integrates the best practices of long-term thinking and short-term execution. It acknowledges that achieving competency in visionary leadership requires the ability to zoom in and out of the

> *God Dreams* is primarily about your church's direction.

future. Sometimes you need to clarify a specific goal in the next ninety days, and other times you need to dream big about the next decade.

In order to help you build your church's Horizon Storyline, I introduce the use of templates, which represents a shift in my thinking and writing. Ten years ago I prided myself in starting churches with a blank slate. Now I am more excited to start with templates because they will bring more speed to your team collaboration without bypassing the imaginative process or short-circuiting ownership of any final decisions.

If you've read or used *Church Unique*, you'll discover a continuation of many ideas it touches upon. However, if you know nothing about *Church Unique*, this book has a stand-alone quality from which you can derive full benefit. You can also work through *God Dreams* and *then* read *Church Unique*.

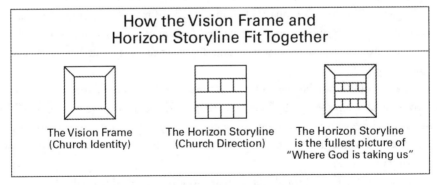

How the Vision Frame and Horizon Storyline Fit Together

The Vision Frame
(Church Identity)

The Horizon Storyline
(Church Direction)

The Horizon Storyline
is the fullest picture of
"Where God is taking us"

Figure 0.1

Visual Walk-Through

The purpose of *God Dreams* is to lead your team to breakthrough clarity by zeroing in on a picture of your church's long-term future. By giving you specific tools, team exercises, and illustrations, your skill as a visionary leader will not just be enhanced, but it will be recreated for a lifetime of leading with greater freedom and impact.

> Your skill as a visionary leader will be recreated for a lifetime of leading with greater freedom and impact.

Figure 0.2 offers a visual walk-through of the book. Part 1's metaphor of churches stuck in a jar comes from a story about farmer who grows a pumpkin in a mason jar. In the end the pumpkin can't express its God-given DNA and full shape due to the invisible glass barriers of the jar. Instead it becomes a deformed orange mass filling the unnatural shape of the jar. In the planning context the pumpkin-jar story is a constant reminder to look, before the vision process begins, for barriers and obstacles that limit what God is doing. It also includes debunking mediocre approaches to vision that also limit good thinking.

As we restart the vision conversation, I want to smash the pumpkin jars in three ways. First I want to reintroduce you to the topic of vision, leaning into the importance of imagination every day (chapter 1). Second, I want to challenge you to make a trade—that is, to exchange your generic idea of your church's future for a vivid picture (chapter 2). Third, I want to warn you about the leader's "obsession with now." If you fixate on next week's programming only, you miss the tremendous opportunity of master planning your gospel impact and inspiring people to heroic contribution.

In part 2, "Discover Visionary Planning," the icon features a Vision Frame and a picture of the future under construction. *God Dreams* offers a dynamic way to think about the future. It represents new tools and new ways to engage our role as cocreators of the future.

Part 3, "Find Your Future," introduces the core resources of the book—twelve vision templates represented by four basic shapes. Through these templates you'll be able to accelerate your conversation, bring great synergy and clarity to your leadership team, and press through your challenges to form something unique, specific, and powerful for your church.

Parts 4 and 5 walk through the primary tool offered in this book: the Horizon Storyline. Part 4 develops the long-range vision and how to use it. Part 5 shows you how to build and execute your short-range goals. Each of the "rows" in the Horizon Storyline icon symbolizes how to articulate the right amount of vision at the right time in the future.

God Dreams Visual Overview

| Restart the Conversation (Part 1) | Discover Visionary Planning (Part 2) | Find Your Future (Part 3) | Focus Your *Long-Range* Vision (Part 4) | Execute Your *Short-Range* Vision (Part 5) | Lead with Freedom (Part 6) |

Figure 0.2

In part 6 our final image is a reminder of why this conversation about vision needs to become personal. My passion for you is that you would know the kind of extraordinary freedom I believe God wants you to have. True freedom is not doing anything you want to do but giving all of yourself to what God has called you to do.

An unexamined look at the part 6 icon seems to be a snapshot of a sign, road, mountains, and then the mountain beyond. It actually represents total clarity for you and your team of God's next dream for your church. The primary benefit of this book is not the visionary plan itself; it's the freedom you experience when you know you've really captured God's vision for your ministry.

When you have worked your leadership team through the journey represented by this visual overview, you can experience a kind of progress you didn't know was possible. All the different personalities and gifting of your team will be on the same page, from dreamers and schemers to the detailed achievers. You will finish the book with a model, a plan, and a pathway forward.

Are You Ready?

I've taken more than five hundred churches through a vision-clarification process, and our hope is that as you read this book, I can be your guide as well, helping your church release greater potential. My own vision—and ours together at Auxano—is to help churches and Christian ministries experience the incredible benefits of leading with stunning, God-given clarity. It begins with the ability to share the story of your life and ministry every day, becoming what I call "the everyday visionary." It ends with experiencing redemptive movement as a church—seeing more men and women and boys and girls following Jesus for the first time and for a lifetime.

You are more of a visionary than you realize. Are you ready to build a visionary plan? Turn the page and let's get started.

PART ONE

Restart the Conversation

Chapter 1
Pursuing God Dreams

Imagination is the voice of daring. If there is anything Godlike about God it is that. He dared to imagine everything.

—Writer Henry Miller

I dream, you dream, we all dream God Dreams.

If you were ever excited about something that's yet to be, then you are a visionary. In its elemental form, being a visionary is simply sharing about an event or development that you are looking forward to.

As it turns out, God is a visionary too. He has dreams that include an extraordinary plan for your church (Eph. 3:20). And I believe His better future for your ministry is meant to be discovered and expressed. When these ideas come alive in your imagination and bring wonder to others, that's vision.

If God does have dreams for your church, how do you really know what they are?

Let's explore this question under four banners: vision as a human thing, vision as a God thing, vision as a relationship-with-God thing, and vision as a church thing. I hope these four perspectives bring you some new insight on an increasingly neglected topic in church leadership today. Let's kick-start our thinking about vision!

I'll offer a fuller definition of vision in chapter 3, but for now think of vision simply as a dream of a better future.

Vision Is a Human Thing

What are you looking forward to? Please personalize the question. Maybe it's . . .

- Taking a vacation next month?

- Sleeping in this Saturday?
- Completing the semester at school?
- Buying a bigger house?
- Seeing your first grandbaby?
- Watching the big game?

If you can identify with one or more of these questions, then you reveal an important dimension about being human: we are by nature future-oriented people. We live in the present, but we think about time in front of us.

With few exceptions, we all have things we look forward to. It's a standard feature that came with your God-created body and brain. More than that, it's a natural part of getting through any day and of anticipating another day to come.

We all hope for, dream of, look forward to, and even count on a better future.

Welcome to the human race. Or maybe I should say, welcome to the humans racing into the future.

Now consider this: Why is it a gift from God that we can look forward to something?

I have asked this question to hundreds of church leaders. It really is an interesting question to ponder. Here are some of the responses I've heard:

Looking forward . . .

- Creates energy on a team.
- Provides hope in difficult times.
- Pushes us to be our best.
- Deepens our dependence on God.
- Reminds us of the payoff of hard work.
- Defines the significance of our lives.
- Leverages the power of focus.
- Gives meaning to the mundane.
- Fuels progress toward our goals.

> It is essential for ministry leaders to develop a top-of-mind competency to apply vision into their daily ministry.

The list could keep going. Looking forward offers endless benefits.

But why is the exploration of this question so important as you and I kick off a book with a title like *God Dreams*? Because experiencing vision is foundational to what it means to be human. Therefore, it is essential, not optional, for ministry leaders to develop a top-of-mind competency to apply vision into their daily ministry. Here are six reasons:

1. **Vision serves people.** Spending time on vision embodies servant leadership. It is a humble act of service—even caring—to help people look forward to what God wants to happen.

   Can leaders use vision for selfish means? Of course. But that doesn't diminish the human need for hope and progress when appropriately addressed by spiritual leaders. Don't let abuse by the few cause you to reject visionary work as being either elitist or arrogant.

2. **Vision is for everyone.** Having vision is natural for everybody. It doesn't require some super gifting to approach the subject. It's not just for advanced-level leaders. It's for you and me and Maria and Joey. It's for our first-time guests at church. It's for small groups in crowded living rooms or coffee talks just between two people. It's something to explore with the kids.

3. **Vision is for every day.** Vision is always relevant. It's not a special-occasion annual message. It's not even a scheduled thing. It's a vital part of every day. Just as we breathe, eat, and sleep, we also pray, hope, and dream. Vision works when I am at work. It comes into play when I'm playing.

4. **Vision is fun.** Vision is actually a lot of fun. It's not something we must do; it's something we get to do. It brings a bounce to your step. It brightens a room with smiles. Who doesn't want to climb a ladder to slide down a slide? Who doesn't want to put gas in the car to drive farther or faster? Who doesn't want to talk about the future in order to look forward to it even more?

   Okay, maybe one time you had to sit through a boring lecture on organizational leadership. Or maybe you endured a crusty strategic planning process. It might not have been fun. Don't fault vision itself. I bet the problem was something else.

5. **Vision makes us better.** When we imagine things better, we are better people. Vision improves us in ways we can readily recognize. Vision is instinctively noble. It connects with God in a mysterious way.

   Sure, we have bad days. We all grumble and complain at some point. We have weak moments when we overrate the past. But most of the time we're looking up and looking ahead. Most of the time we want to win. A sense of vision makes us want to be our best both individually and together.

6. **Vision is ongoing.** Finally, the work of vision is never done. If vision is so closely tied to being human, it's also tied to time. And time keeps moving. Most days build on yesterday's vision. We are constantly moving, evaluating, progressing, and recalculating. The view in a moving car is always changing. Just because we talked about vision last week, last month, or last year doesn't mean we are done talking about it.

These six simple attributes of vision remind us that vision is an inherent part of being human and therefore something everyone can relate to—whether they believe in God or whether they are part of a church.

Now let's consider another angle: the idea of vision from God's perspective.

Vision Is a God Thing

The first moment the concept of vision really grabbed me had nothing to do with organizational leadership in ministry. It was simply about God.

I was taking a theology class (it was named "Trinitarianism," a word I haven't used since!) at Dallas Theological Seminary. Dr. Lanier Burns, one of my favorite professors, blessed me immensely by expanding my view of God. One night a burning question melted my mind. The next day I sought relief in class. With my foot tapping and mind racing, I raised my hand to launch my question. "Dr. Burns, is Adam's situation after the fall *better* than before the fall?"

That's it: a simple question about Adam and Eve messing things up. What was God actually up to with His grand plan to redeem humanity? And would the final result be better than the original state? I had a hunch that God was doing something bigger than returning back to Eden's "business as usual," even if it was perfect there. But how do you improve on perfect? Dr. Burns then confirmed my hunch. He immediately replied, "Redeemed Adam is *better off* than pre-fall Adam."

After hearing that statement, I have never been the same. From that moment on, my thoughts of vision for the local church always push me back to the heart of God.

Here's how my professor's answer translates: In every circumstance of our lives and every sentence of Scripture, our God is a visionary God. He can turn the worst dilemma into eternal victory. That's just what God did with Adam's fall: "For if many died through one man's trespass, much more have the grace of God and the free gift by the grace of that one man Jesus Christ abounded for many. . . . For if, because of one man's trespass, death reigned through that one man, much more will those who receive the abundance of grace and the free gift of righteousness reign in life through the one man Jesus Christ" (Rom. 5:15, 17).

For Adam and Eve as well as for you and me, God gives us a taste of grace and takes us to a better place, better than if we had never sinned. Wow.

God's plans scan every detail of our lives, starting before our birth. As the psalmist says: "For you formed my inward parts; you knitted me together in my mother's womb. . . . Your eyes saw my unformed substance; in your book were written, every one of them, the days that were formed for me, when as yet there was none of them" (Ps. 139:13, 16).

God describes creation as something "very good" (Gen. 1:31) only later to recreate a more dazzling future. He prioritizes the unfolding of something even better: God plans our transformation in this world and our resurrection in the world to come.

Scripture shows the pattern of redemptive history: creation then fall then redemption. But we often don't emphasize that new creation is better than first creation. Or to spell it out exactly: the promises of God and the faith of God's people take us from creation to better-than-creation restoration. As the Bible says, this transformation makes us new creatures, a new creation: "Therefore, if anyone is in Christ, he is a new creation. The old has passed away; behold, the new has come" (2 Cor. 5:17).

The Message interprets this same verse: "Anyone united with the Messiah gets a fresh start, is created new."

In the interim God even allows evil so that He can make an end run around evil's best strategy and then transform it into a greater good. You might call it a divine-crazy good.

Do bad, awful, and painful things continue to plague planet Earth? Of course they do. But God is still a visionary. And in the final day, as J. R. R. Tolkien so beautifully voiced in *The Lord of the Rings,* "Everything sad is going to come untrue."[1]

As Revelation 21:4–5 summarizes: "'He will wipe away every tear from their eyes, and death shall be no more, neither shall there be mourning, nor crying, nor pain anymore, for the former things have passed away.' And he who was seated on the throne said, 'Behold, I am making all things new.'"

The grand finale of the first created universe becomes a most glorious "Revelation 21 day." It's a wedding day but not just any couple's celebration. It's the wedding day of all wedding days and the one that every wedding day in history points toward. It's the presentation of God's people—as a holy and purified bride—to Jesus Christ, the worthy and eternally handsome groom. It comes with a new house as well; we will dwell in the new heavens and new earth. Genesis started with a marriage in a perfect garden between Adam and Eve; Revelation will end with a perfect marriage reimagined beyond our imaginations, between God and humanity.

So the bookends of Scripture, the two utopias of Genesis 1–2 and Revelation 21–22, reveal the visionary nature of our God. And only God could create the final utopia better than the first.

We just can't escape the fact that God is a visionary in this sense: He is always describing, creating, and leading us into a better future.

> The utopias of Genesis and Revelation reveal the visionary nature of our God.

Vision Is a Relationship-with-God Thing

It's one thing to propose that God has a vision and wants each church to make progress toward it. But it's even more amazing to imagine that God invites us into His world of creating that progress.

If you have ever had a dream of a better future, it was probably an idea first in the mind of God. Let's call it a God Dream. And you and I dream because God dreams.

> God invites us into His world of creating that progress.

- Have you ever looked forward to a vacation as a time of refreshment and recreation? Maybe that was a God Dream.

- Did you start a missional community to reach people most churches were overlooking? Maybe that was a God Dream.

- Did you ever imagine a moment of compassion for someone before you acted? Maybe that was a God Dream.

- Did you project an 8 percent increase for next year's ministry operating budget? Maybe that was a God Dream.

Think about what it means to bear the image of God: "So God created man in his own image, in the image of God he created him; male and female he created them" (Gen. 1:27).

Because God is a visionary and human beings are visionaries in His image, the idea of vision becomes a powerful and practical thing to our daily lives. When we walk with God, two visionaries are walking and talking, cocreating a better future.

What is God prompting you to do? What is He teaching you and showing you? What hope is He providing? What picture of the future is He giving?

The reality of our cocreatorship with God is made plain in Genesis 1, when God blessed Adam and Eve and commanded them to "be fruitful and multiply and fill the earth and subdue it, and have dominion over the fish of the sea and over the birds of the heavens and over every living thing that moves on the earth" (Gen. 1:28). With nothing short of five imperatives fired with machine-gun-like repetition, God drives the first command into the heart of first humans. It could not have been a more visionary command.

God expected His human creation to name things, make things, and dream things. And He gave them a pretty big sandbox!

Or consider the faith-filled and future-oriented text of Ephesians 2:10, "For we are his workmanship, created in Christ Jesus for good works, which God prepared beforehand, that we should walk in them."

Imagine what the Holy Spirit is doing for us through the authorship of Paul. Have you ever told someone you have prepared a surprise for them? Why do you tell them? You want them to feel value, of course. Maybe you want them to feel anticipation. Maybe you want them to feel loved.

That's exactly what Paul wants believers to feel. Is it possible that God has prepared in advance good works for us to find and fulfill? Yes! If anyone is fully awake to this promise of God, each day takes on new visionary meaning.

When it comes to God Dreams, let's think for a moment about the difference between God's point of view and ours. Although God can see all of human history (not to mention eternity past and future), we cannot. You could say our partnership with God comes with a limited point of view. He sees all progress from today forward, all the way to eternity. But we see progress unfolding in time, one day at a time. We see only the present. As physical creatures we are prisoners of time. And at first glance that appears to be a bum deal.

But what if this limitation—being constrained within time—actually creates exciting possibilities?

For starters it's not entirely true that we see only the present. We actually see only the present with our physical eyes. With a different set of eyes—our mind's eye—we can see a myriad of future possibilities. While our eyes are limited to snapshots of today, our mind's eye rolls a film reel into the future.

In fact, our holy aspirations reveal a wonderful part of what it means to be human: we imagine. Dogs and cats don't imagine anything. But we imagine all day long. We can skip time and space at any moment and stay there for as long as we want. When was the last time you drifted to the beach during a boring meeting? Imagination is the key that unlocks the prison of time.

Has your heart ever longed for relationships that didn't yet exist? For brotherhood when enemies flourished? For romance when betrayal was vivid? Have you ever hoped for restoration where you could see only brokenness? For a beautiful home where there's a dilapidated shack? For flowing fresh water when all you could see was desert?

> Imagination is the key that unlocks the prison of time.

Imagination makes us powerfully human. It makes us inventors, planners, and lovers. It makes us knowers of the unseen God. Albert Einstein once said that imagination is more important than knowledge. Even the writer of Hebrews connects faith with imagination: without faith—being certain of what we do not see—it is impossible to please God (see Heb. 11:1–6). We could say that faith is being certain of what we can only see with the mind's eye. In the end faith demands imagination, just as breathing demands air. The idea of hope itself would be a hopeless concept if I couldn't close my eyes and imagine a better future.

So to be in fellowship with God is to be in an inherently visionary relationship. We get the thrilling opportunity to activate what is uniquely and powerfully human: the imagination. Our time-bound experience requires faith and brings into the story of our lives the textures of hope and fear, the surprise of the unknown and the ever-revealing flow of time.

> Imagination makes us knowers of the unseen God.

It brings the reality of both pain and joy through the time-marked progress of life. The pain reminds us that we were created for something better. The joy keeps us looking forward.

Could we be describing one of the greatest invitations anyone can receive? Absolutely. It's the opportunity to partner with God! It's an invitation coupled with the corresponding capacity to dream. To dream and then build, to imagine and then initiate, to think and then renovate—this is what you were created to do. God is saving the day and paving the way for you to see and seize a better future.

> To be in fellowship with God is to be in an inherently visionary relationship.

That future is not distant by the way. It is close enough to be really real, as accessible as the location in which you now read. It is a better future in your time and place and based on your gifts and passion. It emerges from the present place and the now moments.

God is a visionary God. And you, God's servant, have been given the profound ability and responsibility to dream.

Vision Is a Church Thing

It's one thing to explore the fun and imaginative aspects of vision. But the tone changes as soon as you put the words *vision* and *church* in the same sentence. Church leaders generally have different ideas, some good and some bad, when it comes to vision.

> You, God's servant, have been given the profound ability and responsibility to dream.

At a recent keynote address for executive pastors, I was asked to speak on "What's after Church Growth, Strategic Planning, and Missional?" The title resonated with many of the pastors attending. And for good reason: we have been overwhelmed with different opinions about the need for vision and planning in the church.

What goes through the minds of most pastors I meet? They affirm that vision is important, but they lack clarity on what it really looks like. Strategic planning is nowhere on their radar. They are as likely to read a blog post making fun of vision statements as they are on getting vision right. They are anxious to get their hands on anything that will bring breakthrough to their thinking and practice.

Why are church leaders generally uncertain about the whole category?

Let's scan the history of "vision" and "planning" over the last few decades.

Strategic planning in corporate America grew out of the application of strategic warfare in World War II. As a new era of management developed in the decades following the war, the practice of strategic planning increased and hit its peak in the 1980s and 90s. Popular expressions of the Church Growth Movement during this time seized any methodologies from the business sector that promised to grow the church, including marketing, management techniques, and, of course, strategic planning.

In the early 1990s *vision* become a hot topic. Business books that put vision on the map include:

- *The Leadership Challenge* by James Kouzes and Barry Posner in 1987
- *Built to Last: Successful Habits of Visionary Companies* by Jim Collins and Jerry Porras in 1994
- *Visionary Leadership* by Burt Nanus in 1995

Church leaders followed suit with titles including:

- *The Power of Vision* by George Barna in 1992
- *Developing a Vision for Ministry in the 21st Century* by Aubrey Malphurs in 1999
- *Visioneering* by Andy Stanley in 1999

Even though books were being written on vision, church leaders by and large didn't find much value in the statements that vision retreats and committee meetings produced. More importantly, church leaders during the nineties were looking for successful models, not vision processes. The decade would see the height of the two largest conferences designed to emulate a proven church strategy: The Purpose Driven Church by Saddleback Church and Rick Warren, and The Prevailing Church conferences of Willow Creek Community Church and Bill Hybels.

By the turn of the century, two developments had happened. First, strategic planning was being left behind by the corporate ranks. Second, conferencing around church models was beginning to slow down. Both Saddleback and Willow Creek (among others) began to see dramatic declines in their enrollments.

The resulting "vision" for local church leaders on a practical level mirrored these two issues. Churches either had an outdated strategic plan, with too much information that paralyzed action. (See my chapter in *Church Unique*, "The Rise and Fall of Strategic Planning," GodDrea.ms/churchunique.) Or they had photocopied another church's vision without much thought and, therefore, without adequate meaning or application.

Between 2000 and 2015 we witnessed a shift in emphasis in both the business world and the church world, but this time with little overlap. In the corporate sector the long-range planning emphasis steered toward strategic *thinking* and short-term goal setting. As the pace of change increased with technology and communication, leaders began focusing on how to adapt quickly, innovate continually, and execute efficiently.

But in the church space the emphasis steered in other directions, most notably the missional conversation. A new breed of writers, thinkers, and practitioners has moved away from improved church methodology to a reenvisioned church identity. In a nutshell they called the church back to evaluate its very nature from a theological perspective (Christology and ecclesiology). The big deal was no longer creating a church mission statement but the church seeing itself as the creation of "missioning" God. The church of God doesn't have a mission as much as the mission of God has a church.

> The church of God doesn't have a mission as much as the mission of God has a church.

Where does that leave church leaders today? The missional conversation continues with mixed reviews. Pastors are writing more and more books on how to do church: *Hybrid Church, Barefoot Church, Total Church, Deep Church, Sticky Church,* and *Slow Church,* to name a few. And the emphasis on short-term goal setting and disciplined execution, found widely in the corporate world, has been largely ignored.

In the end the last twenty-five years of training on vision leaves many pastors in one of the following postures:

- **The skeptics** have endured meeting after meeting, year after year with fruitless retreats and reports that make little difference in the name of vision.
- **The bored** feel the topic of vision is irrelevant and dated.
- **The abused** have abandoned the concept all together, having been overworked and neglected by a "great visionary leader."
- **The busy** are too tired to think about vision while drowning in the priorities of "Sunday's coming" every week.

- **The comfortable** enjoy the peace and well-being of a cruise-control ministry where the status quo is pleasant and perhaps retirement is on the horizon.

But there is one more posture: **the hungry.** This book is for you. You believe God is a visionary, and you know without faith it is impossible to please Him (Heb. 11:6). You believe a better future exists because you have seen it in your mind's eye and you have felt it in your spirit. God is with you, working in you, wanting to cocreate through you; and you know it.

As we move forward, I invite you to reconsider that simple yet profound list of why clear vision for your church is a gift from God.

Looking forward . . .

- Creates energy on a team.
- Provides hope in difficult times.
- Pushes us to be our best.
- Deepens our dependence on God.
- Reminds us of the payoff of hard work.
- Defines the significance of our lives.
- Leverages the power of focus.
- Gives meaning to the mundane.
- Fuels progress toward our goals.

Which benefits from this list get you most excited?

Remember, vision serves everyone, every day. It's fun and makes us better. And it is always continuing and unfolding.

If you are still struggling with the concept of vision, this is still the right book for you. Remember that if you're human, you have a built-in capacity for vision. And if you adopt the tools in this book, your competency as a visionary leader will reap a surprisingly fruitful return.

> If you're human, you have a built-in capacity for vision.

The Double Meaning of *God Dreams*

So far I've spoken of *God Dreams* as a noun, an idea birthed first in the mind of God. I've called it a God Dream.

But *God Dreams* is also a verb. The subtitle to this book contains the words *Finding and Focusing Your Church's Future*. Vision is a human activity wrapped up in the incredible privilege of partnering with a God who dreams.

Now the next step is to ask whether your current vision is generic, and if so, why that's a big problem. That's what the next chapter is about.

Chapter 2
The Problem of Generic Vision

We are kept from our goal not by obstacles, but by a clear path to a lesser goal.

—Blogger Robert Brault

Vision is probably the most talked about and least understood term in the church's leadership lexicon. Churches today miss their potential not because they lack vision but because they embrace a lesser kind of vision, unaware of doing so. That lesser vision is a *generic* one.

Most churches have a generic sense of their vision rather than a clearly defined and contextually crafted vision. In the world of vision, generic is an enemy. Specific is your friend. Settling for generic will suck the life out of a church, and the people won't even know it.

Generic means "to have no distinctive quality." It's predictable, common, unoriginal, nondescript, plain, undecorated, and mediocre.

> Settling for generic will suck the life out of a church, and the people won't even know it.

Is Someone with a Scalpel a Friend or an Enemy?

In this chapter I want to be both your friend and your surgeon. I can't be both unless you agree that you have a problem. Someone in a white coat approaching you with a scalpel seems like your enemy unless you know you have a desperate medical need, like an artery in your chest that is 90 percent blocked.

The challenge for too many people with a blocked artery is that they're oblivious to it. Life may seem just fine. Or maybe they noticed shortness of breath, dizziness, nausea, and sweating, but they haven't connected the dots back to symptoms of a blocked artery.

The most important fact about coronary artery disease is that every person is at risk—literally. Almost sixteen million people in America know they have it, but millions more are unaware. It is the number one killer of Americans, accounting for one-third of deaths for those older than thirty-five.[1] The second most important fact about this disease is that 80 percent of the cases are preventable.

For church leaders the challenge is similar, but the blockage is not in an artery. It's in your mind. In particular it's in your *imagination*. Some have called imagination the organ of meaning. Philosopher Immanuel Kant said that happiness is not an ideal of reason but of imagination. The imagination blockage, which is severe in far more churches than realize it, is generic vision.

> For church leaders the blockage is in your imagination.

Like heart disease in people, every church is at risk of generic vision, and there are thousands of undiagnosed cases. If left unchecked, generic vision won't exactly kill you, but it will keep your church body from being fully alive. It will hold you back from your God-given potential. It will limit your joy.

It's time to stop this plague of generic vision. And the good news is that 100 percent of cases are preventable.

How Generic Vision Shows Up

Generic vision is the outcome of voicing only a *general* sense of your church's future. The opposite of generic vision is leading with a *vivid* picture of your church's future. The lack of a clearly defined vision will cut your church's effectiveness in half. Sometimes it will exact an even higher toll.

Generic vision shows up all over. Consider the phone call I received recently from someone I'll call Javier. He's a real-estate guru for churches and ministries, helping them find the most strategic location and facilities to fulfill their vision. Javier has helped churches of all sizes and types, including many nationally prominent churches whose names you'd recognize.

> The opposite of generic vision is leading with a *vivid* picture of your church's future.

He called me because he keeps running into church teams he describes as "fuzzy" in their focus. In today's case Javier had spent the entire day with a church team gearing up to make a big relocation. As he described his day, I jotted down some of his exact quotes:

- "The church's leadership team had lots of discussion about the potential move but little buy-in."
- "They understood their history and legacy as a church, but they had not translated it into their DNA moving forward."
- "They were not on the same page in how the move would help them reach the next generation."
- They resisted the idea that their vision was not clear because, in their own words, "We are a highly qualified team, we all get along, and our church has a great history."
- "They were oblivious to what they were missing."

What Makes *Generic* So Harmful?

A fuzzy team is one that is not clear about the future. Sometimes it's obvious that the team's vision is fuzzy, such as when there is visible disagreement about the next big dream among staff or elders.

But most times the problem is harder to identify. Everyone is happily going on with their various week-to-week responsibilities, completely unaware that they are missing a fundamental leadership tool.

In fact, you can have great team dynamics and still be leading with only a generic sense of vision. You can deeply love Jesus. You can have the smartest leaders in the world. And you can have a detailed plan while still leading from only a general or fuzzy sense of your church's future.

My years of work with hundreds of churches affirm that Javier's experience is all too typical. Most teams are fuzzier than they realize. This reality creates a massive opportunity because most of these teams are filled with passionate, gifted, called, and visionary team players. When teams like that get vivid, their clarity changes everything. They experience new confidence, new togetherness, new focus, and better-than-ever momentum.

Consequences if *Generic* Is Not Addressed

Why is generic so bad? Using my axe metaphor from the preface, a generic vision is not like wielding a blunt instrument; it's refusing to pick up the instrument to begin with.

Language is itself a tool. One of the first human tools was words. Adam expressed dominion by naming the animals. If you're using generic words, you haven't picked up your available tool set yet. You're swinging with your hand but not an axe.

Instead of being marked by vivid vision, most church leaders are addicts of generic vision, and they don't even know it. That's strong language but appropriate if:

> If you're using generic words, you haven't picked up your available tool set yet.

- Generic is robbing you.
- Generic is the enemy.
- Generic is a deadly poison.
- Generic is the elephant in everyone's room.
- Generic keeps the emperor naked.
- Generic is sucking the life out of your church, and you don't know it.
- There is a demon named generic, and he is near.
- You may live in the United States of America but could be leading in the divided ministries of generica.

God doesn't do generic. There is no such thing as a generic sunset, a generic snowflake, or a generic human being. Likewise there should be no such thing as a generic church or a generic future.

> God doesn't do generic. There should be no such thing as a generic church or a generic future.

Look at the ten contrasts in figure 2.1 to see what's at stake:

Vivid Vision Always Trumps Generic Vision	
Generic Vision	**Vivid Vision**
Escapes notice	Stays unforgettable
Lacks importance	Provides meaning
Dims enthusiasm	Creates energy
Prolongs passivity	Incites action
Limits contribution	Unlocks sacrifice
Excuses mediocrity	Inspires greatness
Scatters attention	Aligns perspective
Enables division	Generates synergy
Dilutes impact	Maximizes achievement
Aids consumerism	Promotes disciple making

Figure 2.1

Three Biases That Contribute to Generic Vision

Generic vision is usually an unintended consequence. Perhaps the greatest irony is that in our efforts to be biblical we have failed to be imaginative.

I opened this chapter with the analogy of an artery in need of surgery, saying that for church leaders the vital organ being starved or blocked is their imagination. Three positive motives, if misplaced, can actually work to block leaders' imagination. Let's call them the biases of accuracy, growth, and efficiency.

> The greatest irony is that in our efforts to be biblical we have failed to be imaginative.

Misplaced Accuracy Bias

1. A bias toward accuracy can unintentionally lead us to confuse biblical statements with biblically informed vision. The story of church vision in the last two decades could be described as the great misuse of the Great Commandment (Matt. 22:34–40) and the Great Commission (Matt. 28:19–20). Most people have heard some variation of the following as a vision statement for a local church:

- "Our vision is to love God and love others."
- "Our vision is to make disciples of Jesus Christ."
- "Our vision is to glorify God."

These biblical imperatives should apply to all churches but not as a vision statement. Why? When Jesus summarized the law, for example, He was not giving churches a vision statement. This is a meaningful summary of the law, but it's not an answer to the question: If we're a church, what should our vision be for the next three to twenty years?

What does Jesus' summary of 613 commands spoken in the context of a lawyer, who is trying to trap Jesus in His words (Matt. 22:34–39), have to do with what your church is going to look like in the next decade?[2] It has very little in terms of particulars.

Yes, your vision must be anchored to the mission and functions of the church that are revealed in Scripture. And yes, your vision must be attuned to the motives and metaphors for leadership revealed in the Bible. It must also align with the disciple-making outcomes revealed in God's written Word. And everything any church does must first and foremost bring glory to God.

God tells you to increase in love, to make disciples, and to give Him glory, but He lets you decide how to translate your church's resources and opportunities to do so.

God gives us a biblical wire frame, and then He leads us by the Holy Spirit to imagine a picture for our time and place of how that fleshes out and colors in.

If you try to make the biblical imperatives themselves into a vision statement, the generic result is impotent. Rather than parroting key Scripture texts, you get to weave the revealed Word into a locally grown, genuinely discerned vision. As much as we'd love it to happen, the Bible's commands don't spell out a specific picture of your church's unique future for this particular season of its ministry.

> God gives us a biblical wire frame, and then He leads us by the Holy Spirit to imagine a picture for our time and place of how that fleshes out and colors in.

Just like a visionary restaurant needs a more specific focus than "serving food," a visionary church needs something more than biblical generalizations like "loving God, loving people" or "making disciples and serving the world."

Imagine that you are excited to start a new restaurant and believe it has potential to be a successful franchise. To get off the ground, you want to attract investors and talented leaders to join your ambitious dream. How successful do you think you'll be if you state your vision as "to make food and serve the community"? Not very. Why? The language of vision does nothing to differentiate you from the thousands of restaurants that already exist. Nor does it guide your thinking, planning, and communication for practical next steps.

You need to decide whether you are casual Italian tapas or fine-dining seafood.

Likewise, when a pastor doesn't move beyond this broad sense of where the church is going, momentum is hard to achieve and sustain. The vision statement lacks meaning, and people don't feel empowered to support it. Howard Hendricks, my former professor at Dallas Theological Seminary, liked to say that when there's a fog in the pulpit, there's a mist in the pew.

Cocreators with God: Instead, following my argument in chapter 1, God invites us to cocreate and coshape the future with Him. God invites us into the possibility of influencing tomorrow. When He does, we experience what it means to be fully human, bearing the image of God (Gen. 1:27) and becoming conformed to the image of Christ (Col. 1:15–28). The ability to imagine a better future that has not yet arrived is our Godlike capability.

If you refuse to engage this picture possibility process, you are robbing yourself and your people of something deeply human. In fact, if God had given us an *already completed* picture of the future, I believe He would have neutered our very humanity.

One analogy is the parent-child relationship at a playground. A parent provides a few guidelines of behavior—when to come home, don't talk to strangers, don't bully other kids, etc.—as framework for how to play. But for children to thrive on that playground, they must have a degree of autonomy, joy, and creativity of choosing where to play, how to play, and with whom to play. Charlie chooses the slide first, but Grace opts for the swings.

In that analogy God tells you how to treat others, but He doesn't tell you to spend two hours on the monkey bars and fifteen minutes on the teeter-totter.

Likewise a marriage is anchored by a lifetime commitment of the Bible-based vows. It is attuned by how husbands and wives should treat each other (love, respect, tenderness, etc.). But each couple also authors together the story of their lives.

In that comparison God anchors the meaning of marriage in Scripture, but no verse names the city and hotel where you should go on your honeymoon.

We can't just extract Bible verses and label them as our church's vision. That's a misunderstanding of God's Word, of using it accurately, and of the nature of vision.

Misplaced Growth Bias

2. A healthy bias toward growth can lead us unintentionally to substitute a grow-only vision for a growth-minded vision. Some church leaders equate growth with vision. "If we experience momentum, we must have vision," they reason. Here are three examples of how growth becomes an end in itself as generic vision statements for a local church:

- "Our vision is to reach more people for Christ."
- "Our vision is to build a bigger facility or launch more campuses in order to take the gospel to more places."
- "Our vision is to change the world."

Every church should be reaching more people and multiplying disciples. And an increased response can certainly lead to more facilities and more campuses.

A healthy bias for growth might undergird a vision, but statements like these are weak by themselves. "Reaching more" and "changing the world" are too vague. And facilities and campuses might be important tools, but they are means to something greater, not an end in themselves.

This same limitation shows up often through consultants who help churches raise money in capital campaigns. Too many fund-raisers limit themselves to a generic vision. Too often the traditional campaign model simply validates the goals of the campaign—land acquisition, building, debt reduction, or multisite expansion—as the church's vision. Capital needs like these, by themselves, don't convey the substance and sustainability of a well-articulated vision.

This limited diet of vision is like trying to run a marathon on junk food. An underdeveloped vision always leads to underrealized resourcing.

> An under-
> developed
> vision always
> leads to
> underrealized
> resourcing.

I once posted a blog stating that many standard capital campaigns are driven by an anorexic vision rather than a healthy one. I'm good friends with many in that industry, and I particularly remember a conversation with Anthony. He confronted me at a conference, "Will, why can't you be more positive and stop saying negative things about the industry?" he asked. After thirty minutes of dialogue, I finally decided to ask him, "Anthony, can you tell me the vision of any church you have raised money for?" (Since he had been fund-raising for over twenty years, I figured at least one might have stuck.) He responded by telling me about one of his best experiences, a church he's been helping for over eight years. "Their vision hasn't changed during that time, and I have helped them with fund-raising several times." I replied, "Great, so what is the vision of that church?" "Their vision is to reach more people," he replied.

Anthony had made my point, at least from the way I saw it. Anthony was so stuck in generic that he wasn't listening. (And by the way, that's why I finally decided to launch Auxano Campaigns.³)

When it comes to multisite churches, which have become the "new normal" for larger or growing churches, it is remarkable how many of them are driven by the "grow-only" kind of generic vision. What is your vision? "To launch multisites." Why are you doing that? "To reach more people."

Keep in mind that "growing bigger" is not a compelling vision for the people who attend your church. And today more than ever, you can't expect people to salute its generic form. Bigger can be viewed as prideful. Bigger can be spun as egotistic. Bigger can be viewed as less personal, less meaningful, and less caring. The key questions that "bigger is better" leaders must answer are: Why will we be better if we get bigger? How will we become better as we get bigger? And what does our kind of bigger mean for people both inside and outside our church?

Another form of grow-only vision is the common phrase of "changing the world." First, let me affirm why I like this phrase. I do believe people can change the world. I think God raises up churches as "the light of the world" (Matt. 5:14) and "the salt of the earth" (Matt. 5:13) to make a dramatic global impact. But no one ever changed the world with a generic vision of changing the world. Rather, visionary leaders define what kind of world-changing value their organization will bring. That requires getting vividly clear and totally focused. While Steve Jobs led Apple, he led with a "change the world" passion, but his vision was concrete and observable in the transformational products that captured the attention—and a massive user base—around the globe.

Misplaced Efficiency Bias

3. A bias toward efficiency can unintentionally lead to a done-for-you vision that neglects do-it-yourself vision ownership. Church leaders across the centuries have been drawn to learn from other churches where good things seem to be happening. Often this happens with the best of motives: they suspect God is at work, and they want to be part of it. They appreciate the encouragement, the ideas, the tools, and the training from the other church's leadership. They follow the spirit of 1 Corinthians 11:1 where the apostle Paul said, "Be imitators of me, as I am of Christ." A noble intent for sure.

> Visionary leaders define what kind of world-changing value their organization will bring.

But the passion that says, "We don't want to reinvent the wheel," while wisely seeking to improve efficiency, can lead to a debilitating blockage of the imagination. Who wants to leverage the learning of others to the point of sacrificing the thrill of having a God-given, handcrafted vision?

This bias shows up in several approaches to vision. But unlike the accuracy bias and the growth bias, the efficiency bias doesn't usually express itself in a written vision statement but in the mind-set of the leaders. I would label three expressions of this intent as follows:

- Serve as a franchise.
- Offer the most.
- Be the best.

Franchise: The franchise identity is sometimes enhanced by also "being first to market." Even if not the first, the idea is to bring an established model into a new geographic area.

The model shows up in many different ways. For example, it may emphasize denomination (our community doesn't have our "brand" so we'll launch as First Baptist or First Methodist), or theological distinctive (we're the first Pentecostal, Reformed, or Peace church in this area), or a combination of cultural nuances and relational affinity of the newer networks, including but not limited to networks like representing Acts 29, NewThing, ARC, City-to-City, Sojourn, Multiply Group, 100 Movements, or Stadia. For example, NewThing highlights the value of multiplication, and Acts 29 emphasizes missional practices within a Reformed, complementarian framework. Finally, the model itself may be a fully adopted church brand and model that has expanded as translocal multisites (we're a campus or affiliate of LifeChurch.tv, North Point, Hillsong, or Christ Fellowship, for example).

The bottom line is this: the gravitation toward being one of the new "franchise" churches can become a generic form of vision. (In chapter 10 I will introduce a cultural replication vision template for these situations.) The primary reason I label franchises as generic is that they risk a diminished imagination and ownership of the vision. Every model was initially formed to solve a problem. The further one is removed in time and context from the problem the founder(s) addressed, the more likely leaders are to lead with what I call second-generation passion. Where the problem is less clear and the passion is less felt, the imagination is more likely to be inactive. Also the further one is removed geographically from the problem context, the less value the model has. I love how North Point pastor Andy Stanley reminds leaders to "marry their mission, but date your model."

The day I'm writing this paragraph, for example, I spoke with a pastor who planted a church in 2001 in Tennessee as part of a church network. This church had just opened its first building, and worship attendance had doubled in several months, from three hundred to six hundred. When the pastor talked about vision, he shared how positively excited he had been in the mid-1990s when he served with the founding church of the network in Arkansas. I could sense that his love for the church model itself was empowering a generic vision in his mind, fifteen years after starting his church.

If he were to state his church's functional vision as a statement (again, it's not often stated this way) it would read:

Our vision is to extend the ministry model of _____ *to a new location.*

Most: The "offer the most" approach is a church that tries to aggregate as many ministries as possible, drawn from the existing programmatic offerings available to the church at large. It's a "more is more" mentality that unfortunately defines success by the number of ministries it offers and by getting as many people as possible on the church campus throughout the week. This mind-set was widely popularized in the eighties and nineties. Lyle Schaller's 1992 book, *The Seven-Day-a-Week Church*, gave words to this form of generic vision.

Expressed today, churches become a "house of brands" providing ministries ranging from recovery ministry (Celebrate Recovery, Grief Share, Divorce Care) to Bible study (Community Bible Study, Bible Study Fellowship, Beth Moore Studies, Men's Fraternity) to outreach ministry (Upward Sports, MOPS) to focused spiritual outcomes (Financial Peace University, Perspectives). The epitome of this mentality is captured by one billboard I drove by in one of our larger US cities that promoted a local church with the promise, "129 Ministries for You and Your Family."

Again there is no stated vision per se but a mind-set that follows the false assumption that more programs will reach more people. I remind churches all of the time that the church in North America is overprogrammed and underdiscipled. And in case you are wondering: programs don't attract people; people attract people. Having too many programs is a common predicament for a church (one reason books like *Simple Church*, which I highly recommend, have become so popular). Your church will need *some* programs—those best coordinated to fulfill your mission and vision. But no church can offer every option to every person and also do it well, much less doing it in alignment with a distinct sense of vision.

To be clear, this is not a commentary of the benefits of any of the programs listed. In fact I am a big fan of all that I just mentioned. What I am suggesting is that one kind of generic vision is seeking to have a ton of plug-and-play ministry activity, running efficiently. Where the first franchise seeks efficiency by using an existing church model, the program-aggregation approach seeks efficiency by using existing church programs.

> The church in North America is overprogrammed and underdiscipled.

The functional vision in such a church would read:

"Our vision is to have as many programs as possible."

Best: The final form of "done-for-you" generic vision is the intent to be the best. It's a done-for-you mode in the sense that it doesn't require imagination; it's simply building on the past or emulating the best as presently defined. This is almost never stated in a ministry culture because it would sound a bit prideful. But it has been a common expression of vision in the secular world.

Several years ago, I was on a Continental flight that the president of that airline happened to be flying on (and it was the best customer service I have ever had). As he walked the aisles, we had the chance to chat a little and came upon the subject of organizational vision. Before leaving the conversation, I asked about Continental's vision. What he didn't share was a vivid picture of the future. Rather he said that Continental's vision is to be the best airline in the world.

And there it was. A little snapshot of the last kind of generic we are talking about: to be the best. Now there is certainly nothing wrong with being the best you can be. It's totally noble to be a model others can follow.

But a vision to be the best, as the loftiest idea of the organization's contribution, is a bit elusive at best and hollow at worst. Why do you want to be the best? How will you know when you have become the best? What specific impact reflects being the best? Simply wanting to be the best always begs for something more substantial to fill it! It also risks sounding prideful.

How might this perspective express itself in ministry? There are two primary ways. I have been with some churches where the functional yet unstated vision is to maintain the leading reputation in the denomination. Churches aspire to be a flagship church, well respected and highly admired.

Another form is being a part of the "top list" in a grouping of churches. In one denomination it's called "tall steeples" group; in another it's the "1000-club," and in another it's the "mega-gathering." Again, I am a big fan of these special learning environments. But when the association with them starts to define the vision (usually unspoken), then a form of generic sets in. No amount of bravado changes the fact that casting a vision to "be the best" is the emotional equivalent of firing a blank round. It's just not inspiring for most people.

When you round up the possibilities of the done-for-you vision, the real problem isn't primarily the "serve as a franchise," "offer the most," and/or "be the best" motives driving the leader; it's the temptation to bypass a meaningful visioning process that pushes through to the personally specific. One feature of the best models we see: no one came up with a great model merely by attending a conference or reading a book. It takes blood, sweat, and tears in a meaningful journey. Only through do-it-yourself ownership is vivid vision really lived out. Vincent Van Gogh purportedly wrote, "Do not quench your inspiration and your imagination, do not become the slave of your model."

This chapter has outlined nine common forms of generic vision. Before we leave this discussion, let me encourage you to use figure 2.2 to rank where you and your church team are tempted to go generic.

Generic Vision Summary: Rank Your Top Three		
Bias	**Example of Generic Vision**	✓ **Check Those Your Church Uses**
Accuracy	Love God, love others	
	Make disciples	
	Glorify God	
Growth	Reach more	
	Launch more	
	Change the world	
Efficiency	Be the first	
	Offer the most	
	Be the best	

Figure 2.2

In summary (see figure 2.3), you don't want a generic vision empowered by misapplied biblical statements, grow-only hype, or done-for-you ease. Rather you want a specific and vivid picture of where God is taking your church, one that is biblically informed, growth minded, and marked by a do-it-yourself ownership.

Three Ways Churches Get Stuck without Knowing It		
Bias	**Generic Misuse**	**Visionary Application**
Accuracy	Exact biblical statements	Biblically informed
Growth	"Grow-only" statements	Growth minded
Efficiency	Done-for-you intention	Do-it-yourself ownership

Figure 2.3

There's More than Generic, Fuzzy, and Copycat

How would you feel if your child came home from college and announced, "Dad and Mom, I finished my résumé," but the document is simply a regurgitation of a form résumé from *Résumé Writing for Dummies* or a cut-and-paste of a best friend's résumé? Think about it: God doesn't stand in heaven with a photocopy machine every time a local church is started. Your church was born an original; don't let it become a carbon copy on your watch.

I've yet to meet a ministry leader who doesn't want to be more visionary. But going forward, you must identify generic as the enemy. You need more than a general sense of your church's future to realize your vision. And I can't wait to show you that it is not only doable; it's also a fun, energizing process to engage with your team.

Your church was born an original; don't let it become a carbon copy on your watch.

The next chapter will explore another obstacle that thwarts your leadership as a visionary: obsessing with the "now." Then the chapters following will show how both these problems can be powerfully addressed through a practical vision and planning tool called the Horizon Storyline.

Chapter 3

Obsessing with Now

Our society has reoriented itself to the present moment. Everything is live, real time, and always-on. . . . It's more of a diminishment of anything that isn't happening right now.

—Media theorist Douglas Rushkoff[1]

I've had fun over the years suggesting that you don't need a vision *statement*; you need a visionary *state of mind*. Now I'll take it a step further: you need a visionary *storyline*.

Specifically you need a tool that I've named the *Horizon Storyline*. It's simple yet powerful. It restores meaningful engagement, even enthusiasm, to the planning process. Most importantly you will use it to wage war against generic vision.

But the Horizon Storyline also takes on another problem that thwarts visionary leadership: the tendency to obsess with "now" to the point that you don't plan. The goal of this chapter is to challenge you to trade an obsession with now for a mind-set that values thinking long. In fact, I hope to lead you to discover twelve compelling benefits in the value of thinking long.

Let's Start Really Long-Range

Like the beginning of a good fairy tale, we will begin work on your church's Horizon Storyline far, far away—not another place on the planet but another place in time. We might say your storyline begins "once upon a *future* time." In this case we are talking about five to twenty years into the future, depending on your life stage and context as a church. We'll get to the exact time for your church later. For this chapter I will use ten years as your imagination-stretching time frame.

Like stretching muscles before you go running, you need to stretch your mind's time frame before you go imagining. I refer to this as your ability to *think long*.

I want to help you anchor your visionary plan with a biblically based long view. I believe God wants church leaders to think long so you can dream even bigger and attempt even greater things for Him. That requires thinking far beyond the next few sermon series and next year's budget. I make my argument for thinking long around biblical revelation, practical wisdom, and human motivation.

> God wants church leaders to think long so you can dream even bigger and attempt even greater things for Him.

The "think long" principles of this chapter lay the foundation for the upcoming chapters, which formally introduces the visionary planning tool I call the Horizon Storyline.

Think Long, Dream Big, Attempt Great

Danny Hillis is a computer engineer and inventor who thinks all types of leaders should care more about the long-term future. He is so committed to that end that he designed a 10,000-year clock. He explains why: "I want to build a clock that ticks once a year. The century hand advances once every 100 years, and the cuckoo comes out on the millennium. I want the cuckoo to come out every millennium for the next 10,000 years."[2]

Danny's motivation in building the clock is to inspire people to take more responsibility for the future. He hopes the clock will raise the question, "Are we being good ancestors?" and cause people to start projects that will outlast their lifetime.[3]

For many reasons long-range thinking is harder and harder to come by these days. Steward Brand, who is working on the same 10,000-year clock project, writes: "Civilization is revving itself into a pathologically short attention span. The trend might be coming from the acceleration of technology, the short horizon perspective of market-driven economics, the next election perspective of democracies or the distractions of personal multitasking. All are on the increase. Some sort of balancing corrective is needed."[4]

The Bible Challenges Us to Think Long

This "think long" clock is consistent with God's view of time. As the Bible says, "For a thousand years in your sight are but as yesterday when it is past" (Ps. 90:4), and "For the LORD is good; his steadfast love endures forever" (Ps. 100:5). Since God's love endures for all of eternity, and if love is to be our number-one goal in life (Matt. 22:34–40; 1 Cor. 13:1–13), then our love needs to affect this world for generations to come.

For church leaders, thinking long is a way to love people beyond your lifetime.

I've always loved Bible charts and overviews. In seminary I mapped most of the sixty-six books of Scripture in order to get the time-related relationships right. How do Genesis and Job fit together? Are Paul's writings placed in chronological order? (In case you are wondering, most of the New Testament letters are arranged by their size—largest first—not their date of writing.) However specific one gets with studying the time stamps in the Bible, it doesn't take more than a casual understanding of God's Word to realize that it was written and revealed over thousands of years.

> For church leaders, thinking long is a way to love people beyond your lifetime.

God chooses to reveal Himself through redemptive history. Time is His canvas. This simple fact by itself challenges us to think about the future in epic chunks of time.

So think long because that's how God reveals Himself.

In addition, you probably have years and perhaps decades of service ahead to God's kingdom. The fact that you're reading this book implies that you are a leader, and in all likelihood you will still be leading a decade from now if Jesus doesn't come back first.

> Think long because, most likely, you will lead for a long time.

If that's not enough, Scripture explicitly links the consequences of generations three and four generations deep. In Exodus 34:6–7, God reminds Moses that sin can affect "the third and the fourth generation"—not just children but grandchildren and great-grandchildren. If God designed the universe with generational cause and effect like this, doesn't it make sense that God's people today should think and plan in generational time frames?

Even when we run into the not-so-exciting genealogies of Scripture, we get a sense of the sweepingly long arc of God's story. We see this clearly in Matthew 1:17: "So all the generations from Abraham to David were fourteen generations, and from David to the deportation to Babylon fourteen generations, and from the deportation to Babylon to the Christ fourteen generations." It's as if God is painting a beautiful picture on the canvas of time, in this case with three sets of fourteen-generation brushstrokes. Elsewhere we see an even longer arc of how God loves to love. "Remember his covenant forever, the word that he commanded, for a *thousand* generations" (1 Chron. 16:15, emphasis added).

Think long because God thinks generationally.

Perhaps the most compelling reason we should think long-range is that our ultimate shared vision as God's people is beyond time itself. One example is the way the writer of Hebrews walks through the "faith hall of fame," describing the great faith of people like Abraham, Noah, Moses, and Rahab. Then he breaks into an epiphany summary of God's people longing for a better future on earth and beyond earth:

> And what more shall I say? For time would fail me to tell of Gideon, Barak, Samson, Jephthah, of David and Samuel and the prophets—who through faith conquered kingdoms, enforced justice, obtained promises, stopped the mouths of lions, quenched the power of fire, escaped the edge of the sword, were made strong out of weakness, became mighty in war, put foreign armies to flight. Women received back their dead by resurrection. Some were tortured, refusing to accept release, so that they might rise again to a better life. Others suffered mocking and flogging, and even chains and imprisonment. They were stoned, they were sawn in two, they were killed with the sword. They went about in skins of sheep and goats, destitute, afflicted, mistreated—of whom the world was not worthy—wandering about in deserts and mountains, and in dens and caves of the earth. (Heb. 11:32–38)

The end of this passage is stunning. Despite the highs and lows of the greatest people of faith, the best future and highest vision is yet to be attained. "Yet none of them received what had been promised" (v. 39 NIV). Why? Because you and I are still alive. You and I are still pressing forward in time. We are now on the planetary stage, surrounded by a great cloud of witnesses. And someday, together with these faithful, we will realize something far better than our best plans on Earth: God's perfect ending when time itself winds down.

Why should we take the long view for now? Because people of faith always take the eternal view, the longest view possible. Eternity itself is calling us and drawing us to look into the future as far as we can.

> Think long because you will live forever.

Think long because you will live forever.

Practical Wisdom Invites Us to Think Long

It has been said that humans tend to overestimate what we can accomplish in one year and underestimate what we can accomplish in five. It seems that shorter time frames tempt us to bite off more than we can chew, and our pathologically short attention spans don't help. But by forcing ourselves to think through a longer time frame, we can raise our sights. When we think in longer time frames, we can literally get more done.

Have you ever thought about the relationship between your ability to imagine and your ability as a leader? The words of James Lane Allen, an American novelist, are as haunting as they are instructive: "You cannot escape the results of your thoughts. Whatever your present environment may be, you will fall, remain or rise with your thoughts, your vision, your ideal. You will become as small as your controlling desire; as great as your dominant aspiration."[5]

Think long because how big you think guides how much you accomplish.

If you own stock in Amazon, you get a letter from founder Jeff Bezos each year, reminding you of Amazon's commitment to think long-term. In his 2015 letter to shareowners, Bezos opens: "A dreamy business offering has at least four characteristics. Customers love it, it can grow to very large size, it has strong returns on capital and it's durable in time—*with the potential to endure for decades*" (emphasis added).[6]

Bezos founded Amazon in 1994, and his commitment to long-term thinking got him to thirty-fifth on the global Fortune 500 list in just twenty years. Each year he reprints his first letter to shareholders at the beginning of the annual report. It's a simple, symbolic act to highlight his value for the long view. The original 1997 letter outlines nine ways Amazon will demonstrate their long-term approach, including the statement: "We will continue to make investment decisions in light of long-term market leadership considerations rather than short-term profitability considerations or short-term Wall Street reactions."[7]

What is true of Jeff Bezos is true of many other business leaders. The wisdom of long-term thinking can make a huge difference. Every church leader would be wise likewise to consider, Am I building a ministry with the potential to endure for decades?

Think long to build a ministry that will endure.

The challenge isn't typically our ability to think long; it's our availability to do so. Chapter 1 established that imagination is the birthright of every human being. Anyone can begin dreaming about the farther-away future. When you do, it's like blowing more air into the balloon of your poten-

> Think long to build a ministry that will endure.

tial impact. Like the air you breathe, it's free. Stretching your minds doesn't cost your team anything but time.

I recently completed a personal vision journey called "younique" with fifteen church leaders.[8] It was my first cohort to work with leaders on their personal rather than organizational vision. The most surprising observation of the cohort came when we discussed long-range planning. Most of the group had never considered the idea of writing down personal aspirations for the next three years. And yet they all readily acknowledged how easy, satisfying, and valuable it was to do so. The opportunity to think long is always available but rarely grasped.

Think long because it costs you nothing.

Master Planning Your Church's Ultimate Contribution

How exactly does thinking long help you do more? The easiest way to explain is to think about creating the master plan of a neighborhood. After days of traveling to consult, I enjoy walking with my wife through our suburban Houston neighborhood nestled in a twenty-seven-hole golf course.

On one walk I was surprised that a secluded forest area that normally feels like a quiet oasis had become a playground for an army of bulldozers. Within weeks new roads were outlined with fresh brown earth and concrete sewer pipes. A few weeks later construction began on the first few houses of what was to become a forty-home subplot.

Right after construction began, I looked differently at the design of the golf course itself and surrounding geography. Even though I've walked here for years, I didn't realize that the design of the course accounted for this additional expansion. What is being constructed today had been built first in someone's mind over ten years ago. That's known as a master plan. Master planning organizes, sequences, and designs all of the action steps necessary to build something meaningful over a long period of time.

A brick-and-mortar kind of master plan is relatively easy to understand. But the same kind of dynamic applies—even though it's harder to see—with your future contribution as a church. Your church is not fundamentally about buildings. It's fundamentally about a disciple-making mission. Is it possible to shape the kind of disciple-making influence your church might have on your city in the next ten years? Is it possible to picture a specific kind of life-changing effect on, in, and through your congregation? I believe so. While only God holds the future, you hold an imagination to help wield it into existence. You can master-plan not just your church's children's building and parking lots but also its footprint of spiritual legacy and influence.

Think long to master-plan your disciple-making impact.

I want to encourage you with an imagination exercise that clarifies the practical wisdom of master planning. When my boys were young, we loved to play Legos. It was fun to buy a small box with a Lego monster truck or Lego X-wing fighter. If they wanted, they could follow the instructions to make the exact vehicle pictured on the box, with a step-by-step guide. Or they could use their imagination to build their own design.

One year my mom and dad took our kids to Legoland in California, an amusement park showcasing some of the largest Lego models in the world. They were blown away by the scope and scale of so many life-size and larger-than-life

> You can master-plan not just your church's children's building and parking lots but also its footprint of spiritual legacy and influence.

Lego creations from automobiles to dragons. That "wow" factor took months and years to plan. In fact, we learned that building creations on a Legoland scale involved an international team of thirty-two full-time master builders. One of their creations was the world's largest Lego model—a twenty-three-ton Star Wars X-wing fighter made up of over 5.3 million Lego bricks. The lead designer, Erik Varszegi, noted that designing it was relatively easy because the model is simply forty-two times the size of the real Lego Starfighter set #9493. Yet it took more than 17,336 man-hours to take the project from vision to reality, which included a team of designers, structural consultants, engineers, model builders, and logistics personnel.[9]

At your church your master planning could address the question, What do you really want to build with your ministry? My guess is that whatever it is, it's worth thinking long. It's a God Dream after all.

What usually happens in a church is the equivalent of working on small Lego projects in random succession. By planning a few sermon series and budgeting for one year, you build some coffee-table toys. You build with the best intentions but without a master plan. There is no overriding picture of the future that organizes and sequences thousands of action steps necessary to build something meaningful over a long period of time. As novelist and cultural observer Mark Twain said, "You cannot depend on your eyes when your imagination is out of focus."[10]

If you want to increase your disciple-making impact, one essential ingredient is to think long enough to warrant a master plan.

Human Motivation Begs Us to Think Long

Most pastors want more motivated church members. I believe the ability to think long holds a key to motivation many leaders are missing. It speaks to the idea that every person in your congregation is defining life by some overarching story. Your privilege as a leader is to help them get out of bed every day motivated that their lives have a larger purpose and role through God's plan.

A book that influenced me significantly in answering this question as a spiritual formation pastor is *The Sacred Romance* by John Eldridge. In particular, he wrote a chapter titled "A Story Big Enough to Live In." The central theme of the chapter is that we are all immersed in a "tournament of narratives"—that is, many kinds of stories that compete for the central way we define our lives. In some way we all choose stories that "control us"—how we think about events and relationships and how we define meaning and success. Eldridge makes the point, that in the absence of the "larger" story of God we settle for the "smaller" stories of our own making.

Some of these smaller stories are broader ideas of a culture. For example, there is the story of consumerism: "My success is determined by how much I possess." Or the story of relativism: "My experience alone tells me what is true."

At other times the stories in our tournament of narratives are personal and specific, such as, "All bosses are jerks, and I will never get ahead in life," or "My life is happiest when my children are good at school and sports."

Listen to how John Eldridge describes our drift to the smaller stories without a larger one:

> In the postmodern era all we have left is our small stories. It's not Pentecost; it's time for spring training. Our role models are movie stars and the biggest taste of transcendence is the opening of ski season. Our best expressions are on the level of "have a nice day." The only reminder we have of a story beyond our own is the evening news, an arbitrary collection of scenes and images without any bigger picture in which they fit. The central belief of our times is that there is no story, nothing hangs together; we all have bits and pieces, the random days of our lives. Tragedy still brings us to tears and heroism still lifts our hearts, but there is no context to any of it. . . . Our heart is made to live in a larger story; having lost that, we do the best we can by developing our own smaller dramas. Look at the things people get caught up in: sports, politics, soap operas, rock bands. Desperate for something larger to give our lives transcendence, we try to lose ourselves in the smallest kind of stories.[11]

The assertion that "our hearts were made to live in a larger story" would take on more significance as I moved from spiritual-formation pastor to a church-vision consultant. I now see this as an essential reason your church needs a long-term vision.

God's Word reveals the overarching story of God with Jesus as the central hero. You preach and teach this every week. Mature believers already define their life based on the gospel. More times than not you continually correct the faulty "smaller stories" people are tempted to believe. As stewards of the gospel, armed with the Sword of Truth, you do daily battle—helping people see, feel, and experience the bigger picture of God's revealed Word. You play an unending game of connect-the-dots, showing them that each day their lives fit in God's unfolding eternal plan. (And at the end of each day, we always seem to find again the need to preach this gospel to ourselves.)

But there's one big problem.

Your preaching, ministry messaging, and programming are delivered in a context of a tournament of narratives, as the John Eldridge quote explains. People need all the help they can get to see God's bigger picture for their lives.

What if a stunningly clear, long-range vision could be a powerful stepping-stone to God's big picture? What if, by thinking long, you create a personalized, local window to transcendence? It's a story that is much bigger than the smaller stories that stifle our lives, but it is relatable, accessible, and foreseeable—an on-ramp to the universe's biggest story!

Think long to connect people to God's big story of redemptive history.

Before leaving this line of thought, let me make one more point from my Lego illustration. I stated earlier that without a long-range vision your church staff or volunteer leaders are rebuilding small Lego projects every summer, fall, and spring. After a few weeks all the Legos go back into the box, so to speak.

> By thinking long, you create a personalized, local window to transcendence.

The same thing is true for your church members. Each person who calls your church home represents someone working with another box of Legos. They too are building small things each week based on the smaller stories that define their lives: from soccer practices to sales quotas.

So now imagine what happens when you proclaim a vivid long-term vision. It becomes an invitation for every church member to be a part of a bigger God-sized project. It's as if a bigger vision reveals and gathers a much larger collective Lego set. Now God's people work together for a longer time with more resources. Now we don't rebuild lots of little projects week after week, but we build one giant project for a decade's worth of weeks. It's the master plan for local gospel impact. May I ask, "How big is your church's combined Lego set?"

Think long because it focuses a broader resource base.

When you review all of the reasons to put on a long-term lens, the case becomes pretty compelling, don't you think? For me it compels me to revisit one of the most amazing verses of Scripture and one of the key verses for this book. Paul's prayer in Ephesians 3 is about a God who is able

> "How big is your church's combined Lego set?"

to do immeasurably more, not just a little more, than all we ask or imagine, according to His power that is at work within us. To Him be the glory in the church and in Christ Jesus throughout all generations.

Think long so that God can do more than you think.

If we stretch our imaginations, maybe God will superstretch His provision!

At this point I have highlighted twelve reasons to *think long* under three board categories. We think long first because the Bible challenges us to do so, second because practical considerations invite us to do so, and third because it's a key for unlocking the motivation of people. These twelve reasons will be continued fuel for you to build out the top half of your Horizon Storyline—the long-range part. Here are our *think-long* principles summarized as a table in figure 3.1:

Twelve Compelling Reasons to Think Long		
Biblical Reasons	1.	Think long to love people beyond your lifetime.
	2.	Think long because that's how God reveals Himself.
	3.	Think long because, most likely, you will lead for a long time.
	4.	Think long because God thinks generationally.
	5.	Think long because you will live forever.
Practical Reasons	6.	Think long because how big you think guides how much you accomplish.
	7.	Think long to build a ministry that will endure.
	8.	Think long because it costs you nothing.
Motivational Reasons	9.	Think long to master-plan your disciple-making impact.
	10.	Think long to connect people to God's big story of redemptive history.
	11.	Think long to focus a broader resource base.
	12.	Think long so that God can do more than you think.

Figure 3.1

Our Church, Our City, Our Lifetime

What if a ten-year master plan of unique impact locally opened up a new appreciation for God's biggest story of redemption globally? It's not just about what happened in Acts 2. It's not just about what is happening with church-planting movements in faraway places like India. Rather, it includes what *our* local church is doing today, in *our* community, in *our* lifetime.

I believe your church's five-, ten-, or twenty-year vision is something your people are desperately searching for. If you don't have one, it's a motivational miss of epic proportions. Without it the larger story of the Bible seems so distant. Practically speaking, it gets swallowed up by the urgency of now; it gets slain in our culture's arena of smaller stories.

Pastors wonder why people seem less committed today. Ministry leaders wonder why people attend less frequently. It seems like years ago a committed church leader came at least three times a week, but today that same leader may come only three times a month.

I don't wonder why any more.

The answer seems pretty simple. People go to places where they are given a larger story to live in. At work the larger story is quarterly profit reports, annual raises, and beating the competition. In social spaces the story is fueled by juicy gossip and the latest romance. You name it: from extreme sports to porn addiction, from leisure pursuits to Netflix binging, everyone is chasing the biggest story they can.

Consider the power of sports as a smaller story for men—from watching college bowls and March Madness to playing weekly golf and fantasy football. Let's not even mention the temptation to live vicariously through their children's sports. Our stadiums today are the worship centers of choice.

Please let me apply that to your church through some probing questions. I bet your church has either a strongly inspiring choir or a really good band. Right? Check. Your church probably has solid teaching and quality programs. Check. My guess is that your church rallied people to serve the community this past year. Check. Finally, I bet your church sent people on mission trips this past year. Check.

Here is where my challenge begins: What makes you think weekly participation of your programs is helping people experience God's larger story? Do the weekly patterns of involvement and sporadic service opportunity *by themselves* unveil the beauty of God's work through your church? Or do these ministries need to happen in the context of a meaningful and memorable picture of the next decade?

Are your church activities a random series of events that report the distant story of God in history, or master-planned programming to engage people in a specific story of God today?

Do you really think another "serve the community day" by its disconnected self is going to inspire people to something big, or is it just adding another thing on their church to-do list? Does adding another women's weekday Bible study by itself compel people to see the dramatic potential of your church? Probably not. The problem is not the program; the problem is a lack of overarching, long-term vision.

Do you really want to inspire people? Don't flood your church with more programs and events. Rather, blow their minds with new context. Give them something that blows up the smaller stories. Disrupt the casual week-to-week worship routine with a real, visible, and dramatic picture of the specific difference your church will make ten years from now. Give people something epic!

That's why we need to take your imagination beyond the horizon.

If you think long, you are more likely to dream big and attempt great.

Armed with these perspectives, you're ready to wrap your mind around a distant reality that doesn't yet exist. In short, how can you meaningfully picture the future? The answer I propose is a visionary planning tool named the Horizon Storyline, which I'll introduce over the next several chapters.

PART TWO

Discover Visionary Planning

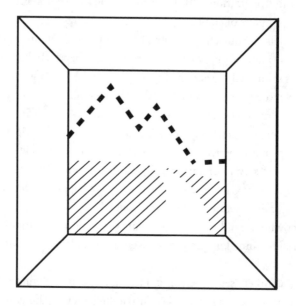

Chapter 4
Solving Your Planning Problems

If people can't see what God is doing, they stumble all over themselves; but when they attend to what he reveals, they are most blessed.
—Proverbs 29:18 *The Message*

To help lay a conceptual foundation for the Horizon Storyline tool, I would like first to look more deeply at the topic of visionary planning from a biblical perspective. Also I want to show you how this tool solves ten big obstacles that can thwart your team's planning efforts. From there future chapters will define the tool itself as you then launch into building your own Horizon Storyline.

Vision, Plan, or Visionary Plan?

To get started let's first clarify the difference generally between having a vision and having a plan. *Vision* is about the picture of your church's future. A *plan* is about the steps to get there. The vision answers the question, Where is God taking us? The plan answers the question, What are the best next steps, and how do they relate?

Suppose a church has a vision to see the spiritual revitalization of a nearby apartment complex over the next three years. The plan might involve sending three couples to live in the apartments to start a missional community. The series of steps or goals to get this missional community off the ground could be one component of the plan.

> *Vision* is about the picture of your church's future. A *plan* is about the steps to get there.

With these simple definitions it's not hard to see that you can have a vision without a plan. Some churches have an action plan on paper with no vision. It's been said that vision without execution is a daydream, and execution without vision is a nightmare.

Recently I met with a leader at one of the fifty most recognizable churches in America. The team there had asked me to help them refine their vision. When our meeting started, the executive pastor opened an eleven-by-seventeen summary of their plan. It included mission and vision statements, seven strategic objectives, and a total of twenty-five detailed goals. As soon as he rolled it out, I recognized that the mission and vision were generic and that the number of objectives and goals were far too many. I sensed immediately that the document probably had little meaning to leaders in the organization, including him.

I was with one of my Auxano teammates who asked this executive pastor, "What are you most excited about on this page?" Watching him respond was like the proverbial cat grabbing his tongue. After an awkward pause, he said, "I don't really know." The pause continued. Finally he said with a sigh, "I'm just responsible for the whole thing." Our conclusion? The church had a plan but no real vision. There was no excitement and no focus—just a long list of stuff to get done.

> Vision without execution is a daydream, and execution without vision is a nightmare.

But more commonly a church has some form of vision, albeit generic, with no plan. Almost four times more people type "church vision" into Google every month than they do "church planning." My conclusion is that vision is more of the felt need than planning. Plus, it's maybe a thousand times cooler to be considered a *visionary leader* than a *planning leader*. But both are real needs, and as you will see in this chapter, we will fuse them together.

Another important distinction between the vision and the plan is that the future picture can stay the same while changes and updates are made to the plan through implementation. In the case of my apartment example, one of the couples dropping out due to illness, a delayed missional community launch, or the complete failure of the missional community altogether does not mean the vision failed. It just means the plans must be revised. Andy Stanley captured this distinction in his classic 1999 work on personal vision entitled *Visioneering: God's Blueprint for Developing and Maintaining Vision,* when he wrote, "Visions are refined—they don't change; plans are revised—they rarely stay the same."[1]

The design of the Horizon Storyline makes it simultaneously a "vision and planning" tool. Both ideas are at play, as you will discover in the next chapter. Rather than repeating both of these ideas separately, I call this combined approach a "visionary planning" tool. It's fundamentally about planning, but it embeds visionary essentials in its structure. Here is my promise: if you take this tool to heart, you will be surprised how it covers all of your needs for vision and planning at the same time.

The Horizon Storyline blends long-term and short-term vision as well as qualitative thinking (vivid picture) and quantitative thinking (goal setting). It keeps the entire plan on one page and focuses the number of ideas for the church's future down to ten or fewer. Finally it links those ideas into a story.

> If you take this tool to heart, you will be surprised how it covers all of your needs for vision and planning at the same time.

Church Unique Meets God Dreams

Many readers may be familiar with a core tool from *Church Unique* called the Vision Frame. Or you may have bumped into it through seminars, church-planting networks, denominational leadership, or trainers Auxano has certified. I want to share in a nutshell how *God Dreams* stands on the shoulders of that previous writing.

Simply put, I have spent more time facilitating on the *identity side* of vision than the *planning side*. While *Church Unique* covered many vision competencies, the primary focus was defining your church's culture. My earlier passion focused on applying a dynamite plunger to casually "photocopied" and hastily written mission, values, and strategy statements. These statements about "who we are" populate many websites and membership classes but never make it into the minds and hearts of most leaders in those same churches.

The primary way I facilitated a better conversation is with the Vision Frame, which asks five irreducible clarity questions and can be drawn on a whiteboard or napkin. While *Church Unique* did define vision and provide tools for vision-based communication and vision-based alignment, I did not unveil a vision-based *planning methodology* until now. For an extensive look at the behind-the-scenes story and Vision Frame definitions, see appendix B. For a free digital summary of the Vision Frame, created just for *God Dreams* readers, go to GodDrea.ms/visionframe.

Why has the planning piece waited to come until now? Simply because it was more difficult to create. The nature of balancing simplicity and complexity within a good plan that *anyone can engage* has taken additional time to hammer out and extensively field test.

The Bible's Take on Planning

My starting point for God's view on planning is Scripture. If you are an experienced church leader, you will be familiar with the following "planning passages." Nevertheless because Scripture warns us not to be presumptuous about the future, it's paramount to build on what God teaches.

The way I like to organize God's direction on planning from Scripture is in four categories: foundations from Proverbs, directives from the New Testament, expectations of "guidance metaphors," and insights from narrative history.

When you add up all the Bible teaches on the subject, I believe a practical summary boils down to this: Scripture establishes the wisdom of planning as a God-dependent, assessment-based, collaborative process for seasonal rhythms and special reasons. Let's take a close look with a brief scan of God's Word.

> Scripture establishes the wisdom of planning as a God-dependent, assessment-based, collaborative process.

Foundations from Proverbs

The thirty-one chapters of Proverbs richly root the concept of planning as a wise activity. On the one hand, wisdom reminds us that God is ultimately in control and that our planning must flow from Him and for Him:

- "Commit your work to the LORD, and your plans will be established" (Prov. 16:3).
- "The heart of man plans his way, but the LORD establishes his steps" (Prov. 16:9).

And on the other hand, we are warned about laziness and a spirit which refuses either to plan or to work. In Proverbs 6:7–8 (NIV) the ant is elevated as a planning model for the sluggard as "It has no commander, no overseer or ruler, yet it stores its provisions in summer and gathers its food at harvest."

In Proverbs we also see planning as both a reflective process requiring time to think and a collaborative process that seeks wise input from others:

- "The simple believes everything, but the prudent man *gives thought* to his steps" (Prov. 14:15, emphasis added).
- "Plans are established by counsel; by wise guidance wage war" (Prov. 20:18).

Directives from the New Testament: Three passages leap off the pages of the New Testament when it comes to planning. The first is Jesus' well-known teaching, the Sermon on the Mount, which beautifully reminds us that planning should not be motivated by worry or fear. Rather, we are to trust God for everything we need: "So do not worry, saying, 'What shall we eat?' or 'What shall we drink?' or 'What shall we wear?' For the pagans run after all these things, and your heavenly Father knows that you need them. But seek first his kingdom and his righteousness, and all these things will be given to you as well. Therefore do not worry about tomorrow, for tomorrow will worry about itself" (Matt. 6:31–34 NIV).

Indeed, we may assert again that worry is the misuse of the imagination. And fear must never drive our visionary planning work.

The second passage is James 4:13–16 (NIV). This specifically warns us to avoid presumption or arrogance when it comes to the future:

> Indeed, we may assert again that worry is the misuse of the imagination.

> Now listen, you who say, "Today or tomorrow we will go to this or that city, spend a year there, carry on business and make money." Why, you do not even know what will happen tomorrow. What is your life? You are a mist that appears for a little while and then vanishes. Instead, you ought to say, "If it is the Lord's will, we will live and do this or that." As it is, you boast in your arrogant schemes. All such boasting is evil.

Part of the corrective in this text is the visible and vocal signal to say, "If it is the Lord's will" when people are discussing the future. I prefer to take this literally.

Years ago I consulted for Laney Johnson, a senior pastor then in his seventies at Mobberly Baptist Church, Longview, Texas. He invited his entire staff to get on their knees as we prayed for that day's planning session. I left that meeting, early in my consulting career, with the conviction that I should personally kneel in every "consulting prayer."

Another pleasant reminder of James's admonition is my wife, Romy. Originally from Chile, she speaks with a rich Spanish accent and flavors any talk about the future with the words, "With God's favor." It's so embedded in her mind-set that she could never talk about the future without a reverent spirit that is verbally signaled almost daily. "With God's favor let's spend a few hours at the beach this afternoon."

In the third passage, Luke 14:28–32 (NIV), Jesus uses explicit planning illustrations when teaching about the cost of being a disciple:

> Suppose one of you wants to build a tower. Won't you first sit down and estimate the cost to see if you have enough money to complete it? For if you

lay the foundation and are not able to finish it, everyone who sees it will ridicule you, saying, "This person began to build and wasn't able to finish."

Or suppose a king is about to go to war against another king. Won't he first sit down and consider whether he is able with ten thousand men to oppose the one coming against him with twenty thousand? If he is not able, he will send a delegation while the other is still a long way off and will ask for terms of peace.

Jesus implies here that planning is not only good but will spare someone significant embarrassment, massive stewardship problems, and even life-threatening situations. The idea of sitting down to estimate (v. 28), and as the proverb mentioned earlier that a prudent people give thought to their steps (Prov. 14:15), is my basis for describing planning as an "assessment-based" process. It requires reflection, analysis, inventory, and imagination of possible scenarios.

In addition, Jesus' teaching uses both positive and negative causes for the planning process. It might be an opportunistic project like a building campaign. Or it might be a tragedy or crisis—in this case the threat of an attack.

In contrast Proverbs uses the ant as a model for seasonal planning. So the Bible references planning for both "seasonal rhythms and special reasons."

Expectations of the Guidance Metaphors

The Bible is saturated with pictures and promises that guide God's people. It's worth not missing the obvious: God is not trying to hide His will but is always revealing Himself. That fact should shine like the noonday sun over all of our planning efforts!

One of my seminary professors, Dr. Ramesh Richard, categorized many guidance metaphors in his book *Soul Vision*:[2]

- The Lord as light (Ps. 27:1; 1 Pet. 2:9; Mic. 7:8; Pss. 97:11; 112:4)
- The Lord as shepherd (Ps. 23:1; 1 Pet. 5:4; John 10:11; Heb. 12:20)
- The Lord as mother eagle (Deut. 32:11–12)
- The Lord as path maker (Ps. 27:11; Prov. 3:6)
- The Lord as a guiding hand (2 Chron. 30:12; Pss. 32:4; 37:25; John 10:28)

These images are both heartwarming and soul strengthening for the work of discerning God's future for your leadership team. The Lord is with you. God is for you.

Insights from Narrative History

Finally, the Bible is filled with countless insights for planning from the historical narrative. Let me highlight one of the most prominent themes: God delights in both providing the way and delivering the strategy. Consider Joshua's unlikely march sequence to bring down Jericho's walls (Josh. 6:1–27) or Gideon's surprising success with the tiny army of three hundred (Judg. 7:1–25) or Paul's imprisonment that counterintuitively becomes a catalyst for gospel progress (Phil. 1:11). We should never forget that our all-powerful God stands outside of time and rules over it.

> God delights in both providing the way and delivering the strategy.

Running prominently like a Mack truck through each of these four biblical sources is the centrality of God dependence. The primary feature I have built into my definitions to anchor the beauty of God dependence is the often-referenced, shorthand question for vision as, Where is God taking us? The question is not, Where do we want to go? Rather the God-centered question explicitly asserts that He has a vision for us already and that all planning efforts must seek to know it.

> Our all-powerful God stands outside of time and rules over it.

That's why I opened this section with this summary of a biblically informed view of planning: Scripture establishes the wisdom of planning as a God-dependent, assessment-based collaborative process for seasonal rhythms and special reasons.

The Visionary Planning Problems We Must Solve

May I ask you to do an experiment through a quick-time assessment? Most pastors, as I have observed them, will spend more time on preaching preparation for the next month than on vision preparation for the next five years. How about you?

I've never had a pastor disagree with my simple time analysis, at least to my face. In fact most of them quickly nod with agreement. They also understand that something is not quite right about it. My questions are: Why is this the case? Why is it so easy and natural for pastors to spend ten hours working on what to say this weekend, but they can't find thirty minutes to pray through, think about, write down, and communicate what is going to happen in the next five years? I could easily list a dozen reasons. One of the most important reasons is that no one has shown the pastor *how* to spend time on vision planning. That's what this book is designed to do. And the process isn't that hard if you have the right tools.

As I write these sentences, I am really excited to share this tool with you. It has literally taken me over a decade to develop. Sharing it with you reminds me of the epic movies of our generation like *Star Wars* or *The Lord of the Rings*. Every hero requires special tools to fulfill their calling and destiny. Who would Luke Skywalker be without his light saber? Who would Frodo be without Sting, the famous Elvish-made dagger that would glow blue when the Orcs or goblins were close by? If every senior team needs special tools, the Horizon Storyline is the equivalent of your magical dagger, essential for fulfilling your God-given calling as a visionary leader.

As we begin to unveil the Horizon Storyline, I want first to reveal many of the problems the tool is designed to solve. Every tool solves some problem, whether it is a fundamental tool like a wheel or a hammer or a sophisticated tool like a garage-door opener or a microwave oven.

See if you can relate to these everyday challenges when it comes to vision and planning. For each problem I will make a quick comment and provide an observation as to how the Horizon Storyline will help. I consider this a top ten list: the greatest challenges to vision and planning in the church.

The Ten Biggest Vision Planning Problems in Today's Church

1. **You craft a vision statement, but it's not meaningful enough to talk about after it's been written.** As crazy as it seems, this is a common experience. The words become "caged" on paper after the vision retreat or committee meeting. The problem is that vision transfers through people not paper. *The Horizon Storyline, on the other hand, will encourage people to use vision every day.*

2. **You articulate vision without defining the time frames involved.** Sometimes a vision statement is a short phrase with no time frame attached to it at all. I call that a "lofty one-liner" (see appendix C). Sometimes a plan has a list of goals with no meaningful sequence or relationship to time. *The Horizon Storyline, in contrast, will clarify the different time frames from which to lead.*

3. **When you do create goals, you create too many and try to do too much.** This is a massive predicament in almost every church I visit. It's the primary problem with all of the classic strategic plans I have evaluated. One of management expert Peter Drucker's primary observations about the nonprofit sector is that the organizations try to do too much. Most experienced church leaders will attest to this problem. *The Horizon Storyline, therefore, intentionally limits how many goals leaders should have.*

4. **People who like to dream and people who like to execute are rarely on the same page.** The fact that most primary leaders in the church communicate for a living amplifies this problem. Sermon development is intuitive, creative, and idea oriented. It's often hard to get conceptual thinkers like that sitting down with the operational leaders who manage, budget, and make decision after decision, day after day. These two staff functions usually pass like ships in the night hardly recognizing the other is present. *The Horizon Storyline will fuse the big-picture vision with next week's priority in a way that activates the dreamers and the implementers at the same table together.*

5. **People don't see the vision as pertinent to their ministry area.** It's easy for staff or volunteer leaders to reject a vision statement or planning document because they can't see the immediate connection to their favorite area of ministry. *But the Horizon Storyline and the recommended process to create it naturally generate support from all ministry areas involved.*

6. **The planning tool is so complicated that few people want to revisit it.** If I ask, "What is your vision?" or "What is your plan?" too many people scramble to look for a supporting document. Most of the time it becomes obvious that the plan isn't referenced on a regular basis. People just don't care about it. Not because they don't care about the future but because the plan itself is overwhelming. *One feature of the Horizon Storyline is that it dramatically simplifies planning, making it easy to remember and revisit.*

7. **The vision rarely creates an exciting organizational focus.** At the end of the day, a plan that doesn't get people excited has little value. A plan that doesn't channel resources is worthless. *Therefore, an essential feature of the Horizon Storyline is the ability to focus everyone on one thing at a time without being too simplistic.*

8. **The plan is too rigid and can't account for changes in the ministry environment.** Many classic strategic plans assume that the immediate future will resemble the recent past. Anyone alive in the twenty-first century knows that this assumption is no longer valid. We simply must be ready to adapt to major changes in our world from culture and politics to communication and technology. *The Horizon Storyline allows for unforeseen changes.*

9. **The planning events happen randomly (not rhythmically) with little follow-up.** Aside from a few things that *have* to get done—like budgeting and sermon prep—few church cultures embed a process of planning from a thirty-thousand-foot vision to a thirty-foot execution. Until now. *The Horizon Storyline was designed to help you create your own rhythm and pace of planning and follow-up.*

10. People can resist being accountable for goals. The average church leadership team has surprisingly little accountability. As long as families don't complain and the bills get paid, most staff and volunteer leaders do what they want to do. Enter a new vision or plan into the equation and people can become a little resistant. The good news is that their resistance is usually not an accountability issue but a process issue. That is, people don't support what they didn't create. *So the Horizon Storyline and the process to build it form a useful way to introduce nonthreatening accountability.* I think of it as positive accountability.

In short, what is this powerful new tool all about? The Horizon Storyline is about your church leaders being pumped up about the future and enthusiastically sharing the vision everywhere they go. It's about focused effort as they work together with adaptability and accountability. It's about a ministry plan that involves every ministry engaged in a repeated process that people actually like. It's about feeling progress and celebrating it together.

Would you like that for your church? If so, please turn the page.

Chapter 5
Introducing the Horizon Storyline

Why is it important to have a clear vision? Because leadership is about going somewhere. If you and your people don't know where you are going, your leadership doesn't matter.

—Author and management consultant Ken Blanchard

In the final season of the hit television series *Mad Men*, Don Draper, played by Jon Hamm, continues his struggle for meaning on the inside while indulging the fruits of career success, good looks, and marketing savvy on the outside. In the episode entitled "Forecast," Don is handed an urgent work assignment from his mentor Roger; he must write a thirty-five-hundred-word speech that Roger can use to outline their agency's future in a high-profile meeting with their parent company.

The episode is driven by an immediate problem: Don, the golden-tongued wordsmith, is at a loss for words. As he stares the future in the face, he quickly realizes that he doesn't have a vision—partly due to his remarkable success (he has achieved everything he's ever wanted) and partly because life has never felt emptier. So he begins asking coworkers and subordinates about their aspirations for the future. They are oblivious to the fact he has been given this assignment, which puts Don in a Sherlock Holmes-like posture. He begins looking for clues in every conversation in an effort to complete his assignment: What should the future of the agency really be?

Throughout the episode Don finds excuses to talk about the future. At one point he walks into a peer's office and blurts out, "What do you want us to do next as a company?" Ted spouts out in reply, "My goal is to land a big pharmaceutical company." "That's it?" Don responds, disappointed with the small scope of his aspiration.

In another scene Don is reluctantly giving a performance review to Peggy, a copy-writer and longtime protégé. He decides to use the interview to get her ideas about the future, "What do you dream about, Peggy?" he asks. She shares her dream to be the first female creative director in New York. "What next?" Don replies. She pauses for a moment and then reports her hope to land a really big client. "What next?" Don replies. He repeats his questioning several times to the point of frustrating Peggy. At the end of the conversation, her responses don't go far enough to add any new insights to Don.

Toward the end of the episode, Don starts talking about the future with his teen-age daughter and her friends. At one point his daughter hints that her biggest aspira-tion is just having dinner because she's hungry. Don's several-day journey to explore the future comes up short. In a closing line he jokes about his daughter's comment: "She has always had very practical goals."

The episode is relatable, albeit a bit sad. It reflects the vortex of life: many times we are just too busy to reflect well about the future. Other times the generic vision of "reaching more and being bigger" is simply not enough. In Don's case the common answer to "get a bigger client" for the agency just seemed too hollow. At all times dif-ferent people project different views of the future, from career dreams to what to order for dinner.

While *Mad Men* doesn't offer much by way of biblical edification, Don's unsuc-cessful conversations on forecasting are reminiscent of church planning conversa-tions—widely different motivations and widely different opinions all swirling around. Church leaders rarely "land the plane" in discerning the next big dream. It is rare for a leadership team to see the future together with crystal clarity.

Don Draper's need is the same as what most church leaders need: a simple way to have a meaningful conversation with their team. For most episodes I want to reach through the flat screen and give Don Draper a Bible. But on the just-described episode, I wanted to give him the Horizon Storyline.

> What most church leaders need: a simple way to have a meaningful conversation with their team.

The Horizon Storyline

The Horizon Storyline is a simple and powerful vision-ary planning tool developed over more than a decade of church consulting. It's the result of my reluctance to do plan-ning in general due to my deep dislike for lifeless plans and fruitless results. It is the product of countless mistakes, numerous mentors, and thou-sands of Expo-marker hours at the whiteboard. It also wouldn't be possible without the brain-cell stretch of my diverse training outside of seminary and pastoring—chemical engineering and ad agency leadership to name two. Most importantly it was birthed as a labor of love just for church leaders. My God Dream is that you can use it to better find and focus your own God Dreams.

In a nutshell the Horizon Storyline is a tool to develop the right amount of vision content for the right time in the future, for the entire leadership team. That way it helps a church achieve all the merits of a vivid vision in a way the whole team engages. It does this by providing four time frames to plan around and by showing how many goals each time frame needs. Quickly you will begin to see how it solves the problems identified in the previous chapters.

The breakthrough of the Horizon Storyline is the development of a planning tool that fits human experience. It's natural to grasp, using the way we already see, think, and communicate. What if we could forever remove the "it's just too complicated" barrier stated as number 6 in the previous chapter's problem list? What if your planning tool would intuitively and immediately make sense? What if it would actually be fun to revisit over and over again?

> The Horizon Storyline is a tool to develop the right amount of vision content for the right time in the future, for the entire leadership team.

What makes the Horizon Storyline so accessible? Five key features stand out, as figure 5.1 summarizes.

Five Key Features of the Horizon Storyline

Principles	Benefits
1. How our eyes see different distances (up close and far away) will relate to different time horizons or "distances" into the future.	The linking of long-range and short-range planning.
2. How people long for simplicity to get greater impact with fewer goals.	Focus and enthusiasm with one big goal at a time.
3. How people think differently to create better team synergy.	A combining of inspirational and operational abilities on your team.
4. How the brain works to leverage pictures and numbers.	A meaningful and memorable plan.
5. How we communicate to blend planning and storytelling.	An easy-to-share plan.

Figure 5.1

For the purposes of this chapter, I will focus on the first two features—how our eyes see and our need for simplicity. The first observation is what led to the four-part structure of the tool itself: we define vision by looking at four horizons into the future. The other features will be addressed in future chapters as we look more closely at each horizon.

Using How Our Eyes See

The Horizon Storyline is defined by how we see different "horizons" in our field of vision every day. Did you know that of our five sensory inputs (seeing, hearing, tasting, smelling, touching), 80 percent of what your brain "knows" comes from your vision?[1] This fact led A. M. Skeffington, a famous American optometrist, to say, "If a person cannot see 100% they cannot be 100%."[2] Your brain is continually working to decipher and direct your body movement as your eyes perceive what is right in front of you.

A significant insight about eyesight hit me one day watching my wife, Romy, paint a watercolor landscape. (She loves acrylics and watercolors, and our home is filled with her lovely work.) While she was turning some random pigments on her palette into a beautiful autumn forest, I realized that the landscape she was painting had three horizons. After a little digging, I learned that artists refer to these as the background, midground, and foreground planes of the painting. In fact a landscape painting without one of these horizons becomes much less interesting. Why? Because it would fail to engage our depth perception and would be considered a dull work of art.

In a landscape painting (which figure 5.2 represents), the background may be a blue sky, a beautiful sunset, or a mountain range. It's as far away as the eyes can see. Then there is usually a focal point of the piece in the midground that draws and keeps your focus, a deer or a stream or a tree in a field of wildflowers. Finally, you will notice that most painters create a further dimension by having an object in the foreground like a tree branch or the side of a house or a person. These objects are up close, right before our eyes. The artist must intentionally plan and design these three planes to simulate a peaceful or soul-stirring three-dimensional viewpoint.

In fact, the landscape painting simply reflects what is happening every moment your eyes are open. The ability for the human eye to focus in and out of distances is called "accommodation."[3] Your eyeball can zoom out and zoom in—say from looking at the sky, to looking at words on this page—in 350 milliseconds.

Right now your eyes can focus on each of these three horizons—background, midground, and foreground. Try it wherever you are reading this book. Look up from the book and notice what is in your midground—a desk and chairs, other people?

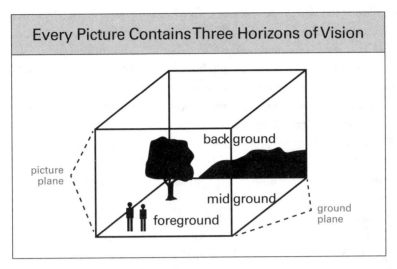

Every Picture Contains Three Horizons of Vision

Figure 5.2

Now look to the background and note what you see. A window to look through or a bookshelf? Of course this book itself and your arms and hands are in your foreground. Now, without moving your head, experience the ability to focus in and out of these three horizons going back and forth quickly. That's called accommodation. It's a natural reflex that is happening subconsciously all day long. But it's also a voluntary process. You can consciously control it whenever you want, as you probably did when I asked you to try the exercise.

Now here's the useful factor: what is so natural to your daily life can also be natural to your church's organizational life. We are going to use the three basic distances you are zooming in and out of all day long to build our visionary planning model. In fact, the primary reason for vision in human-body functioning is to guide and direct movement. The same might be said of your visionary plan: it exists to guide and direct movement for the church body as a whole.

To start, we just carry over the simple idea of background, midground, and foreground using those as names for three of our four planning horizons. We will simply see them as horizons, not in three-dimensional space but into the future. They are time horizons.

> What is so natural to your daily life can also be natural to your church's organizational life.

Here's how it works. The near future we will define as ninety days away. That is the foreground vision. The next horizon, the midground vision, we define as one year away. And the furthest horizon we can "see" as an organization is the background vision, defined as three years away. The eyes of your church or ministry should be able to "see" this amount of time into the future.

Now that leaves one more horizon to define. This fourth horizon is just a little farther than you can clearly see. It's just past your visible range. I call that "beyond the horizon" as a reminder that it is far away, just over the next mountain range, so to speak. I define this time frame as anywhere between five and twenty years depending on the church's life stage and context.

We can summarize the names of four vision horizons and the corresponding time frame into the future as follows:

Beyond-the-Horizon Vision	5–20 years
Background Vision	3 years
Midground Vision	1 year
Foreground Vision	90 days

Figures 5.3 and 5.4 create simple and memorable representations of vision in general and the Horizon Storyline in particular. In figure 5.3, I represent vision as a future picture using a mountain in the distance with a road and mile marker. This is the symbolic representation of vision as "where God is taking us." It reminds us that vision is a picture of the future. I like to think of it as our next big dream as a team or the next hill we are going to take for God. The mountain in a distance is farther away than the mile marker just ahead on the road. These images hint to the reality of long-range and short-range vision.

Figure 5.4 represents the Horizon Storyline by "double-clicking," so to speak, on a simple mountain picture, to reveal four rows representing the four horizons. This will be the bridge to a simple whiteboard drawing or napkin sketch you can use at any time. The top row of the simple diagram represents the farthest distance away.

The most obvious feature of the Horizon Storyline is the way it links long-range and short-range vision together in the plan. We will use the top half of the tool, the beyond-the-horizon vision and the background vision, to describe long-range vision. In essence it's anything after one year. Then we will use the bottom half of the tool, the midground and foreground vision, to describe short-term vision. It's anything one year or less.

Using Our Need for Simplicity

Notice in the Horizon Storyline visual that the background and foreground horizons each have four squares. This is a part of the secret of this tool. That means these horizons have up to four separate ideas or goals. The beyond-the-horizon vision and the midground vision will each have only one idea. For now I will reaffirm that the

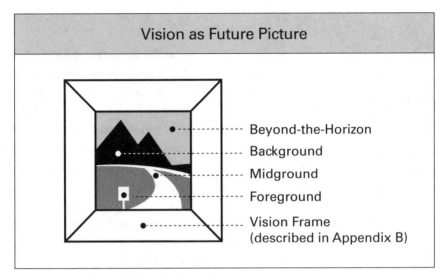

Figure 5.3

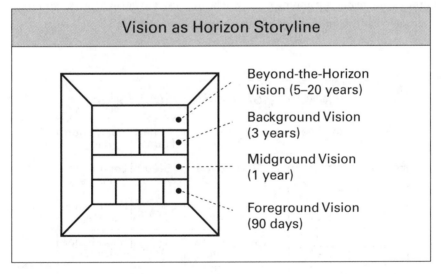

Figure 5.4

Horizon Storyline develops the right amount of vision content at the right time in the future for the entire leadership team.

By counting up the number of ideas represented by each horizon, it would be impossible to have more than ten ideas for the entire visionary plan. It doesn't matter if your church has one hundred, one thousand, or ten thousand people; the plan is built with no more than ten ideas. In addition, no single time frame contains more than four ideas.

Both long-
range and
short-range
visions convey
a single idea
that simplifies
"where we are
going."

Notice that if we count the ideas allowed for the long-range vision, there is a 1:4 sequence starting from the top. Then another 1:4 sequence follows for the two short-range visions. Many of our clients have dubbed the term 1:4:1:4 to describe this simple visual representation of the future.

Essentially the long-range vision has one big idea with four supporting ideas. The short-range vision likewise has one big idea with four supporting ideas. To describe it a different way, both long-range and short-range visions convey a single idea that simplifies "where we are going" (visionary) and four ideas that clarify "how will we get there" (strategic). See figure 5.5 as I continue to present various features of the tool.

As mentioned earlier, other features of this tool will make it engaging and usable. These features, including its use for inspiration and execution, thinking in pictures and numbers, and telling a planning story, will be unpacked in later chapters. For now let's cover some basic definitions for each horizon.

How the Horizon Storyline Works

Horizon Storyline	Horizon Name	Time Frame	Long/Short Range	Max # of Ideas
	Beyond-the-Horizon Vision	5–20 years	Long-Range Visionary	1
	Background Vision	3 years	Long-Range Strategic	4
	Midground Vision	1 year	Short-Range Visionary	1
	Foreground Vision	90 days	Short-Range Strategic	4

Figure 5.5

Defining Each Horizon

While the rest of the book will walk through each horizon, let's finish the chapter with the definitions and benefits of each of the four horizons. We will dive into many illustrations shortly so hang in there for this definition stage.

Beyond-the-Horizon Vision (5–20 years)

The beyond-the-horizon vision is a vivid picture of a church's future five to twenty years away depending on the life stage and context of the church. It is an aspirational sense of destination and clarifies the church's ultimate contribution for the given time frame. It should build from a singular idea that can be stated as both a sentence and a vivid description narrative. It is primarily qualitative and will have a compelling character that feels almost unbelievable to the listener. The primary benefits include:

- Shapes the destiny of the whole congregation.
- Creates deeper meaning for individuals.
- Cultivates heroic sacrifice among people.
- Guides the development of long-term strategy (background).

The twelve templates in this book (featured in chapters 7–10) were created to help you and your team develop a vivid description for this horizon. While we will cover each horizon, my hope is that you will focus immediately on the beyond-the-horizon vision as the import long-range context to everything else you do.

Background Vision (1–3 years)

The background vision contains four ideas, primarily qualitative, that clarify the four most strategic emphases in the next three years in order to fulfill the beyond-the-horizon vision. Each emphasis can be stated in one or two sentences. The background vision is not designed to inspire but to clarify. As such the background vision:

- Creates a broad-level road map to approach the future.
- Directs long-term allocation of church resources.
- Limits blind spots that would inhibit progress.
- Provides context for short-range goal setting (midground).

Midground Vision (1 year)

The midground vision is a single emphasis stated as both a qualitative and quantitative goal in the next year.[4] That means the midground or one-year vision should be both an inspiring picture and a measurable number. They accompany each other. Like the beyond-the-horizon vision, the midground vision is designed to inspire people and stretch their thinking of what might be possible. It can be stated in one sentence and adapted regularly for communication every day. The midground vision:

- Generates excitement for what God is doing in the next year.
- Focuses the attention, prayers, and resources of the church in a dramatic way.
- Reveals progress for celebration (or recalibration).
- Highlights one shared priority for all ministry areas.
- Cuts through the complexity of life and ministry with one focus.

Foreground Vision (90 days)

The foreground vision contains up to four specific initiatives that must be started within ninety days, as needed. The foreground initiatives are typically led by cross-functional staff teams or may be carried by individual ministry departments. Most initiatives support the midground vision directly or indirectly. Think of these as the four most important next steps in order to complete the single, midground vision:

- Clarifies weekly action steps and daily priorities for leaders.
- Sequences short-term projects, tasks, and goals.
- Activates the unique gifts and abilities within the body.
- Provides regular, positive accountability for individuals and teams.

Illustrating the Horizon Storyline

Let me show how this works with a nonchurch example first and then use it with a ministry. The first example is Mouse Free, Inc., a fictitious company I often teach about when facilitating. The mission of Mouse Free, Inc., is to help people experience mouse-free living. Years ago the team developed a new mousetrap that is better, cheaper, and safer than the traditional ones used for years. When the team launched, they articulated their Vision Frame (that is, their mission, values, strategy, and mission measures) to clarify their identity and basic business model. Last month they completed their Horizon Storyline in a two-day retreat. See figure 5.6.

My second example is a four-year-old church plant that is riding the urban revitalization in an unnamed North American city. The year this was developed they were running about 150 on one campus that felt like a large, missional community meeting in a school. They recently launched a second campus running forty people. To get started they relied on significant outside support that they want to continually ramp down to 20 percent of their operating budget within the next three years. During the first year of the church, the leadership developed their Vision Frame to articulate their

The Horizon Storyline of Mouse Free Inc.

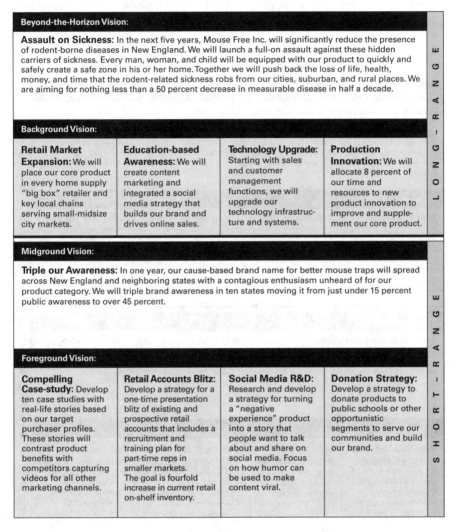

Beyond-the-Horizon Vision:

Assault on Sickness: In the next five years, Mouse Free Inc. will significantly reduce the presence of rodent-borne diseases in New England. We will launch a full-on assault against these hidden carriers of sickness. Every man, woman, and child will be equipped with our product to quickly and safely create a safe zone in his or her home. Together we will push back the loss of life, health, money, and time that the rodent-related sickness robs from our cities, suburban, and rural places. We are aiming for nothing less than a 50 percent decrease in measurable disease in half a decade.

Background Vision:

Retail Market Expansion: We will place our core product in every home supply "big box" retailer and key local chains serving small-midsize city markets.

Education-based Awareness: We will create content marketing and integrated a social media strategy that builds our brand and drives online sales.

Technology Upgrade: Starting with sales and customer management functions, we will upgrade our technology infrastructure and systems.

Production Innovation: We will allocate 8 percent of our time and resources to new product innovation to improve and supplement our core product.

LONG-RANGE

Midground Vision:

Triple our Awareness: In one year, our cause-based brand name for better mouse traps will spread across New England and neighboring states with a contagious enthusiasm unheard of for our product category. We will triple brand awareness in ten states moving it from just under 15 percent public awareness to over 45 percent.

Foreground Vision:

Compelling Case-study: Develop ten case studies with real-life stories based on our target purchaser profiles. These stories will contrast product benefits with competitors capturing videos for all other marketing channels.

Retail Accounts Blitz: Develop a strategy for a one-time presentation blitz of existing and prospective retail accounts that includes a recruitment and training plan for part-time reps in smaller markets. The goal is fourfold increase in current retail on-shelf inventory.

Social Media R&D: Research and develop a strategy for turning a "negative experience" product into a story that people want to talk about and share on social media. Focus on how humor can be used to make content viral.

Donation Strategy: Develop a strategy to donate products to public schools or other opportunistic segments to serve our communities and build our brand.

MID-RANGE

SHORT-RANGE

Figure 5.6

DNA and ministry model as a new church plant. Four years into the launch, they recently updated their Horizon Storyline as seen in figure 5.7.

Before finishing this chapter, please look at one more example. This time the church is a larger church in the suburbs, running approximately twenty-five hundred in worship attendance. The church is twenty years old with a strong, stable congregation. Although they have a high trust culture, the church has grown comfortable and drifted from the practice of personal evangelism. Before getting to their visionary planning work, they developed their Vision Frame, which includes a new mission statement to take personal risks to bring the gospel to every relationship.

The Horizon Storyline of New Urban Church

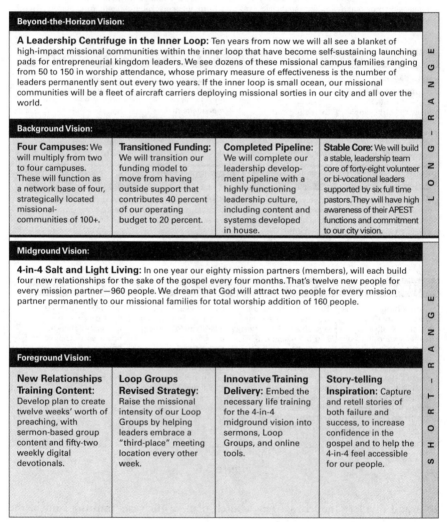

Beyond-the-Horizon Vision:

A Leadership Centrifuge in the Inner Loop: Ten years from now we will all see a blanket of high-impact missional communities within the inner loop that have become self-sustaining launching pads for entrepreneurial kingdom leaders. We see dozens of these missional campus families ranging from 50 to 150 in worship attendance, whose primary measure of effectiveness is the number of leaders permanently sent out every two years. If the inner loop is small ocean, our missional communities will be a fleet of aircraft carriers deploying missional sorties in our city and all over the world.

Background Vision:

| **Four Campuses:** We will multiply from two to four campuses. These will function as a network base of four, strategically located missional-communities of 100+. | **Transitioned Funding:** We will transition our funding model to move from having outside support that contributes 40 percent of our operating budget to 20 percent. | **Completed Pipeline:** We will complete our leadership development pipeline with a highly functioning leadership culture, including content and systems developed in house. | **Stable Core:** We will build a stable, leadership team core of forty-eight volunteer or bi-vocational leaders supported by six full time pastors. They will have high awareness of their APEST functions and commitment to our city vision. |

(side label: LONG-RANGE)

Midground Vision:

4-in-4 Salt and Light Living: In one year our eighty mission partners (members), will each build four new relationships for the sake of the gospel every four months. That's twelve new people for every mission partner—960 people. We dream that God will attract two people for every mission partner permanently to our missional families for total worship addition of 160 people.

Foreground Vision:

| **New Relationships Training Content:** Develop plan to create twelve weeks' worth of preaching, with sermon-based group content and fifty-two weekly digital devotionals. | **Loop Groups Revised Strategy:** Raise the missional intensity of our Loop Groups by helping leaders embrace a "third-place" meeting location every other week. | **Innovative Training Delivery:** Embed the necessary life training for the 4-in-4 midground vision into sermons, Loop Groups, and online tools. | **Story-telling Inspiration:** Capture and retell stories of both failure and success, to increase confidence in the gospel and to help the 4-in-4 feel accessible for our people. |

(side label: MID-RANGE)
(side label: SHORT-RANGE)

Figure 5.7

The exciting news is that fifty thousand new people are projected to be either working or living within ten minutes of the church in the next five years (the church is close to a major highway intersection). Let's call it Stable Suburban Church.

The Horizon Storyline of Stable Suburban Church

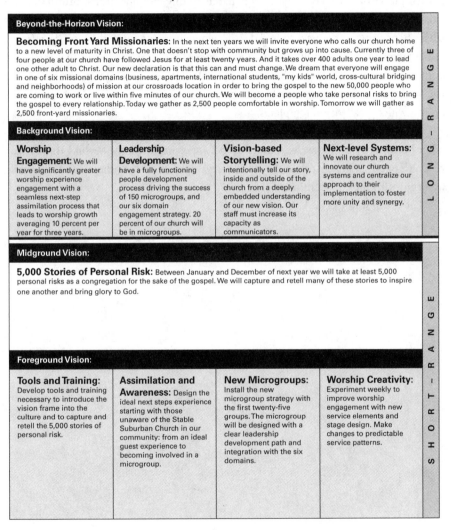

Beyond-the-Horizon Vision:

Becoming Front Yard Missionaries: In the next ten years we will invite everyone who calls our church home to a new level of maturity in Christ. One that doesn't stop with community but grows up into cause. Currently three of four people at our church have followed Jesus for at least twenty years. And it takes over 400 adults one year to lead one other adult to Christ. Our new declaration is that this can and must change. We dream that everyone will engage in one of six missional domains (business, apartments, international students, "my kids" world, cross-cultural bridging and neighborhoods) of mission at our crossroads location in order to bring the gospel to the new 50,000 people who are coming to work or live within five minutes of our church. We will become a people who take personal risks to bring the gospel to every relationship. Today we gather as 2,500 people comfortable in worship. Tomorrow we will gather as 2,500 front-yard missionaries.

Background Vision:

| **Worship Engagement:** We will have significantly greater worship engagement with a seamless next-step assimilation process that leads to worship growth averaging 10 percent per year for three years. | **Leadership Development:** We will have a fully functioning people development process driving the success of 150 microgroups, and our six domain engagement strategy. 20 percent of our church will be in microgroups. | **Vision-based Storytelling:** We will intentionally tell our story, inside and outside of the church from a deeply embedded understanding of our new vision. Our staff must increase its capacity as communicators. | **Next-level Systems:** We will research and innovate our church systems and centralize our approach to their implementation to foster more unity and synergy. |

Midground Vision:

5,000 Stories of Personal Risk: Between January and December of next year we will take at least 5,000 personal risks as a congregation for the sake of the gospel. We will capture and retell many of these stories to inspire one another and bring glory to God.

Foreground Vision:

| **Tools and Training:** Develop tools and training necessary to introduce the vision frame into the culture and to capture and retell the 5,000 stories of personal risk. | **Assimilation and Awareness:** Design the ideal next steps experience starting with those unaware of the Stable Suburban Church in our community: from an ideal guest experience to becoming involved in a microgroup. | **New Microgroups:** Install the new microgroup strategy with the first twenty-five groups. The microgroup will be designed with a clear leadership development path and integration with the six domains. | **Worship Creativity:** Experiment weekly to improve worship engagement with new service elements and stage design. Make changes to predictable service patterns. |

(Right margin vertical labels: LONG-RANGE, NEAR-RANGE, SHORT-RANGE)

Figure 5.8

Next Steps to Your Own Visionary Planning Tool

Can you imagine the excitement at New Urban Church and Stable Suburban Church as they imagine themselves becoming a leadership centrifuge or a gathering of twenty-five hundred front yard missionaries? Can you sense the level of ownership as each player or team not only has a part but readily sees how it fits into the whole? Every player, from new attender to full-time staff, can follow the vision's progress, from what's happening in the next ninety days to where it is leading in the next decade.

As the author of a book titled *Church Unique*, I continue to affirm that the development and phrasing of your church's vision will be as unique as a fingerprint. To help you find that pathway, the next five chapters offer a total of twelve different starting points, which I call vision templates.

Keep in mind that we develop your Horizon Storyline starting with the long-range horizons first. The twelve templates focus specifically on the beyond-the-horizon vision (longest range) that then sets up the development of the others. In other words, we begin with the end in mind.

Let's keep rolling!

Chapter 6
Imagining beyond the Horizon with Four Starting Points

Questions of implementation are of no consequence until the vision can be imagined. The imagination must come before implementation. Our culture is competent to implement almost anything and to imagine almost nothing.
—Old Testament theologian Walter Brueggemann

Let's start this chapter with an imagination exercise. I want you to visualize a sequence of events in your mind's eye as you read the next two paragraphs.

Imagine a church with a steeple on a beautifully sunny day. As your mind zooms in on the steeple, notice the sun reflecting off the brown metal construction. Now zoom in close enough to see the rivets on the sheet metal surface. Zoom back out to your original mind's-eye view of the church.

Keep imagining. Now lift the steeple off the top of the church, making it float above the building itself. Turn the steeple slowly upside down while it's still floating. Imagine that the steeple is a giant ice cream cone and put a giant ball on top. Now remove the ball and turn the steeple right side up. It's still floating above the church. Now expand the steeple like a giant teepee and make it large enough to cover the entire church building. Gently lower the steeple down to the ground so you can't see the church building. Now lift the giant steeple off the ground, and the building is gone. All you can see is people running enthusiastically out from under the floating teepee.

What you just accomplished in your mind was pretty remarkable. Nothing like that probably has ever happened in real life, but you could imagine it anyway.

One tool that guided your ability to do this exercise is the storage file of pictures you already have in your mind. You have seen steeples, ice cream cones, and teepees before.

Aristotle observed, "The mind thinks in pictures."[1] Even though science can now expand on the idea, it doesn't change the enormity of Aristotle's insight. In his book *Ten Steps Ahead*, Erik Calonius summarizes his study of brain science:

> In particular, scientists are discovering that the brain is a visionary device—that its primary function is to create pictures in our minds that can be used as blueprints for things that do not yet exist. They are also learning that our brains work subconsciously to solve problems that we cannot crack through conscious reasoning and that the brain is a relentless pattern seeker, constantly reinventing the world.[2]

Seeing the future—beyond the horizon—is all about relying on your brain's power to create a picture in your mind. Therefore we're going to rely on pictures you already have in your mind. But while we tap into that reserve, we won't be limited by it. Just as we could lift, spin, and expand the church's steeple, we can have fun with different scenarios of your church's future. What will your church look like in ten years?

For several years I worked in a company that owned and operated its own printing press. When it comes to ink on paper, all it takes are four colors—cyan, magenta, yellow, and black, or CMYK for short—and you can print pictures with the infinite color and variety of the universe. Printers call it a four-color process. Likewise, as we look at our primary tool to help you paint a picture of your church's long-term vision, we will use four big categories. These are what I call template types. Think of it as a four-shape process. Your church's unique vision, though distinct from tens of thousands of other churches, will still be defined by one of four starting points.

> You can't be a visionary leader without leveraging your imagination.

This chapter unpacks how vision templates work, inviting you to use them as tools for your imagination. As I've emphasized over and over, you can't be a visionary leader without leveraging your imagination.

Four Quadrants That Define the Twelve Templates

For the last twelve years I have logged more than ten thousand hours sitting with church teams, praying with leaders, and listening to them. They have invited me to facilitate strategic thinking and vision planning. We have talked for long hours about hopes and dreams. The conversations have often burst at the seams with a sense of expectation for what God might do. The journey has been more than meaningful and better than fun.

Something new happened at about the ten-year mark of this work. The patterns of the conversations began to fall into categories. Over time they both solidified and crystallized. The designs became increasingly clear with a particular beauty and completeness, like a geode rock that cracks open to reveal an array of purple crystals.

A historic urban church on one side of the country would share dreams similar to a church plant in another part of the country. A predominantly Asian church in Chicago imagined the future with a similar trajectory as a multiethnic church in San Antonio. A Baptist church would zero in on the same key vision Scripture as a Lutheran church they had never talked to.

Each of these churches was completely unique, but their dreams fit into patterns.

The patterns I observed first settled into four broad categories of vision. Then I gradually came to spot variations within each of those four—three in each one to be exact. That made a total of twelve different vision templates.

This chapter presents those four categories, which I have laid out as quadrants. As I've shared them with church leaders, many have found them to be immensely helpful, and I trust they will be useful in your context as well.

Each quadrant, in turn, opens further to three vision templates, which I develop in the next chapters. Take a look at figure 6.1. Starting at the top right and moving clockwise:

The first quadrant is vision that **advances.** The basic shape is an arrow. Think of a literal arrow released from an archer's bow moving with speed and direction toward its target. Vision that advances is strong, forceful, determined, and moving. Advancing vision says, "Take it!"

The second quadrant is vision that **rescues.** The basic shape is a medic's cross, like the Red Cross. Think of a life preserver flung into the ocean to save someone drowning. Vision that rescues is responsive, resourceful, preparing, and caring. Rescuing vision says, "Save it!"

The third quadrant is vision that **becomes.** The basic shape is a circle. Think fruit of a healthy tree that is fully ripe. Vision that becomes is whole, healthy, authentic, and maturing. Becoming vision says, "Grow it!"

The fourth quadrant is vision that **overflows.** The basic shape is a wave. Think of a glass of water brimming over and splashing out. Vision that overflows is good, bountiful, extending, and blessing. Overflowing vision says, "Let it go!"

Before we take a tour of twelve different kinds of vision grouped by threes within the four basic quadrants—and the combinations of them that might represent your church's God Dream—you might like to know why I call them vision templates.

The Four Basic Shapes
for Each Quadrant

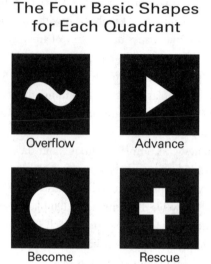

Overflow   Advance

Become   Rescue

Figure 6.1

Why Twelve Vision *Templates*?

First let me comment on the runners-up. One candidate was the word *vectors*. The engineer in me likes the idea of twelve vision vectors. After all, a vector by definition has speed and direction. Perfect! What is your church's speed and direction? I could have used twelve vision vectors, but vector sounds too Star Trekish.

The part of me that likes gardens (I can't really say there is a gardener in me) likes the idea of twelve vision *varieties*. The term *variety* sounds colorful, creative, and organic. Not bad for vision. I imagine that gardens can be well ordered or designed to have a wild feel. Again that gives room for the varying approaches I see with visionary leaders. But the garden image is a bit too static so it didn't make the final cut.

What about twelve *species*? Too extraterrestrial.

And twelve categories? Vision categories kind of box you in. This book is about opening new possibilities, not limiting you.

Likewise, *vision types* is too stiff.

Vision *breeds* has too much bite.

Vision *styles* feels too trendy.

Vision *assortments* is too chocolaty.

The main runner-up was kinds. The term *vision kinds* is plain but accessible. Twelve kinds of vision means that vision is for everyone. Kinds is "kind of" a plain way to talk about it, after all. It's doable and fun.

It is one way I have always thought about the idea of vision. It's a term I could use with my teenage daughter, and it's also a term I could use with a PhD in theology.

The word *kinds* also represents a move away from the language of consultant speak. I thought people would like to know about "twelve kinds" more than they want to know the twelve of whatever else we might call it. Kinds was so close to being the finalist that one of my websites is www.12kinds.com (but for all materials related to this book, see www.GodDrea.ms).

Ultimately, however, I chose the term *template.*

Why?

- It aligns best with how these kinds of vision should be used.
- It connotes design, pattern, and picture.
- It connects to people who remember using templates as a kid; it's warm, artistic, and instructional.
- What I like best about it is that it gets you started and you can continue to be creative.

A template is something you can choose to use and then adapt or combine; it accelerates your start but doesn't limit your art.

You don't use a template to break a mold. Rather, you use a template to get started; and then you generate a unique version with every subsequent step. That's what I want church leaders who read this book to do.

Similar Templates but Thousands of Unique Variations

The deciding factor for using the term *templates* is a story I just couldn't shake. It showed me the relationship between vision and painting a picture.

My wife, Romy, as mentioned previously, is a painter. A few years ago I went to a three-day watercolor class with her. (If you are thinking I am a good husband, I won't disagree.) There were about sixteen of us in the class, some experts and some complete newbies like me. The first thing everyone did, regardless of experience, involved tracing a light pencil outline based on a template. We had no color and no personalization, just an outline as a guide.

When we all finished, every single painting looked completely different! We each started with the same basic object, but our final artistic vision displayed great variation in color and style. (Mine probably not enough.)

That's why I like the idea of a template. *God Dreams* speeds up your team's ability to picture the future through the use of templates. Yet if a thousand churches choose the same template, every picture will be unique.

> *God Dreams speeds up your team's ability to picture the future through the use of templates.*

Those who have read my previous writings or have attended a conference workshop I have led have seen other ways I've been impacted by art. I use painting illustrations in *Church Unique* and whenever I talk about the four horizons of leadership: beyond-the-horizon, background, midground, and foreground.

When I claim that all vision can fit twelve types or a combination of two of them, am I limiting you? Is the guy whose celebrated book with the title of *Church Unique* now backing off and saying, "Nah, you're not that unique"? No, this is no different from saying that the color spectrum is seven colors (red, orange, yellow, green, blue, indigo, and violet). You may be a "yellow" type of church, but maybe you're muted mustard yellow, and the church down the street is sunshine yellow. Infinite varieties exist. Or you may be two "colors" combined into one idea, as chapters to come will show you that many churches combine two vision templates into one idea, leading to at least 132 possible variations (twelve primary vision templates each blended with up to eleven different secondary templates).

One final note about the term *template*: I seriously dislike the "100 percent done for you" resources that remove the need to think or imagine. Yet that is what sells, reminding me that many pastors are anxious to get their hands on how-to resources. The templates strike a great balance; they show you the way, but you do the meaningful work. It's a how-to guide for helping your imagination soar, not checking your brain at the door.

In short, I believe God has bestowed on us and for us twelve kinds of vision templates. And that's the story behind describing these patterns as templates. The role of templates in this book is so important that they're built into its subtitle: *12 Vision Templates for Finding and Focusing Your Church's Future.*

Vivid Vision Makes All the Difference

More energy. Greater resources. Better synergy. Would you like to have that right now at your church? Sure you would. Would you have guessed that the first step toward these improvements is defining your specific vision as a church? Probably not. And that's my point. If you don't have a clear vision, you certainly won't have a culture that matches. And if you don't have a strong culture, then what are people in your church really doing? Why are they there?

Visual Preview

Let's start by imagining what some of the options could look like. In particular, which one of the twelve makes the most sense as the primary template for your church's beyond-the-horizon vision?

It might be helpful to see where the next chapters are headed. Figures 6.2 and 6.3 offer a forecast of where the plane will be landing by the time you finish chapters 7–10. As a quick overview, notice that figure 6.2 contains the four basic shapes at its core. Each shape has a set of three vision templates associated with it. The numbers one through twelve do not signify importance but simply a forecast of their order of presentation. We'll walk through them, one quadrant at a time, in each of the next four chapters.

Then figure 6.3 fleshes out these twelve vision templates a bit more. It's a lot to take in visually, but let me tease your curiosity by saying that not only will they make sense by the time you finish chapter 10, but in all likelihood you'll discern that one or two of them give clarity to the God Dream of the lasting contribution your church can make.

Please turn the page to begin exploring the first quadrant of vision templates.

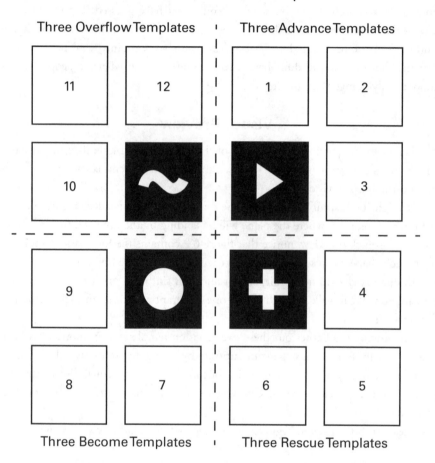

Figure 6.2

Twelve Vision Templates Preview

Figure 6.3

PART THREE

Find Your Future

See page xv for a helpful explanation of edge markers used in chapters 7–10.

Chapter 7
Vision That Advances

The future is not the result of choices among alternative paths offered in the present. It is a place created—created first in the mind and will; created next in activity.

—Animator and entrepreneur Walt Disney

While in seminary I met one of America's leading church architects and asked if I could shadow him for a day. I was impressed with his big pads filled with a myriad of 3-D sketches. One pad was particularly loaded with drawings; it was his largest project ever. When he told me how the design process began for this church, my jaw hit the floor.

The project started with a national tour of America's best facilities. That's right, the architect and three pastors from the church visited seven cities in one week, looking at the marvelous designs—including the breakthroughs and blunders of previous creative work so they could catch the design big idea for their facility. Their goal was not to copy the churches but to glean their favorite attributes.

The purpose of this chapter is to take you on a similar trip—a trip less extravagant but more important: to scan in one whirlwind tour how God's people of all times and places dream about the future. Throughout *God Dreams*, you've seen repeated statements that God "is able to do immeasurably more than all we ask or *imagine*" (Eph. 3:20 NIV, emphasis added) and wants each of us to prayerfully *imagine* the future of the churches we serve. So let's stretch our imaginations by seeing what God is up to!

This chapter, plus the three that follow, are designed as imagination catalysts; as we travel to different locations and times in history, the intent is that you travel ahead to *your* church's future. These chapters offer a series of fly-by templates designed to jump-start your thinking. In total you'll encounter twelve vision templates, three per chapter, each as a potential doorway to your God Dreams. This chapter in particular will review three templates for advancing the gospel: geographic saturation, targeted transformation, and people-group penetration.

Each template is accompanied by a graphic taken from one of four simple images I call basic shapes: arrow (to depict advance), plus sign (to depict rescue), circle (to depict becoming) and wave (to depict overflow), each of which the previous chapter described in greater detail. They are some of the most basic forms found in human existence. They're universally recognized.

> Let's stretch our imaginations by seeing what God is up to!

Which Quadrant and Template Best Represent *Your* Church?

As you read, I'm asking you to identify which specific template best represents your church's beyond-the-horizon vision. Remember, *the beyond-the-horizon vision is the future picture of your church and a declaration of your congregation's ultimate contribution. It is a destination in time more than five years into the future.*

Using the twelve total templates, the goal is for you and then your team to prayerfully pick two at most. Once you select two, you will relate them together to create a single "picture idea" from which to develop further a vivid description of your church's future. Here are some questions that might help you:

- Which of the vision templates is most meaningful to me personally?
- Which of the vision templates best represents our church's most current conversations about vision?
- Which of the vision templates best represents what our church together *should* be pursuing?

Overview of What's Coming

In presenting the vision templates, I'll use the following pattern for each:

- **Quick Definition:** Each template will have a clear and concise definition.
- **Personal Snapshots:** For each template I will reflect on experiences from my "field of vision."
- **Biblical Reflections:** Scriptural teachings, patterns, or illustrations are briefly explored.

- **Metaphors for Communication:** In future chapters I encourage you to "paint a picture" with words. An initial sampling of metaphors is provided to help you envision for communication purposes.
- **Historical Examples:** An illustration from church history is provided for each template.
- **Contemporary Examples:** A sampling of real-time stories is included.
- **Personal Exercise:** As you move from template to template, rate how each one applies to your church with first-impression questions.

Please do take time to fill in the exercise as you finish your review of each vision template. All twelve exercises ask the same set of questions. Then after the final template, we'll guide you to look over your ratings to discern which might be a primary template for your church and which might be a secondary template.

Overview of Advance

In this chapter all the shapes are built from the basic arrow shape to symbolize the idea of advancing (see figure 7.1). Vision that advances is strong, forceful, determined, and moving. Advancing vision says, "Take it!"

Arrow Basic Shape for the Advance Templates

Figure 7.1

As I unfold a total of twelve vision templates, I will present three templates for each quadrant. The three Advance templates are represented as figure 7.2, with the basic shape in the lower left.

Three Advance Templates
with Basic Shape

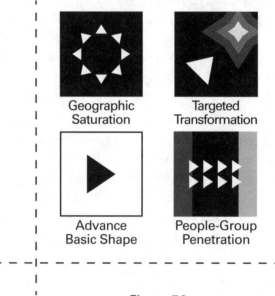

Figure 7.2

Geographic Saturation Vision Template

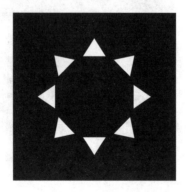

Figure 7.3

Advancing through Geographic Saturation

Quick Definition

Your church's vision is to bring the gospel to as many people as possible in your surrounding geography. You might state it as, "We will define a geographic area around us and take responsibility to personally communicate and demonstrate the gospel to everyone in that area."

Personal Snapshot

I am not sure exactly why I did what I did. No one told me to do it. It wasn't for anyone else but me. Shortly after I learned how to share my faith as a sophomore in college, I found a floor map of my dorm floor—the third floor of Geary Hall at Penn State's East Halls. Not a very glamorous place but my home for my first two years of college. I placed the map on those built-in corkboards they often put in college dorms. On mine you could find mountain biking pictures, snowboarding snapshots, and a diagram of my dorm floor with three of the twenty rooms highlighted in bright yellow. The highlighted rooms marked those with believers: my room, a fellow member of Campus Crusade for Christ (now known as Cru) three doors down, and Chris Urban on the corner. The map was a visual tool for my gospel saturation vision. I had one year to share the gospel personally with forty students living in high proximity to me.

In those days I had cut my teeth on evangelism and Bible study. By God's grace and through strong modeling of a campus ministry, I was passionate about representing Jesus. The map just came naturally. I wanted to pray for my floor. I wanted to strategize relationally. I wanted to see progress. I was vision casting to myself. And several guys came to Christ that year.

The following year I was given responsibility over West Halls by the Campus Crusade leadership. Between 1989 and 1990, my map increased to include more than fourteen hundred students. This time I gathered a small team of guys to blitz West Halls with me. My geographic vision expanded and so did the highlighted rooms on a much larger map as we shared the gospel every week.

Geographic gospel saturation is as special to me as it was most intuitive to me as a younger leader. In fact, if I were to choose a vision to recommend to any group of believers, without knowing their situation, gifts, and passion, I would recommend starting here. That's why it's listed first in this chapter.

Biblical Reflections

In Acts 1:8 Jesus promised that through the power of the Holy Spirit, His disciples would be His "witnesses in Jerusalem and in all Judea and Samaria, and to the end of the earth" (NIV). Jesus calls for intentionality in spreading the gospel geographically from their present location (Jerusalem) to nearby areas (Judea, Samaria)—even if ethnically different—and ultimately to anywhere people reside.

This was also the pattern of Jesus' ministry, according to missionary Steve Addison. In his book *What Jesus Started: Joining the Movement, Changing the World*, Steve maps the ministry of how Jesus went from village to village, spreading the gospel across Israel. Addison writes: "Matthew records that Jesus' ministry touched 'all' 175 towns and villages of Galilee. To reach them all Jesus could rarely have stayed in one place for more than a few days; he would have been constantly on the move. By the end of his ministry, most of Galilee's 200,000 people would either have met Jesus or have known someone who had."[1]

Metaphors for Communication

Figure 7.3 shows the arrows of advancement moving outward in all areas and directions, taking the gospel outward to saturate everywhere possible.

One of the most useful tools available for this template is a map. What does your community look like as you zoom in and out with Google Earth? What is the shape of your congregation's geographic footprint? (That's the geographic area defined by the people who attend your church.) To see this footprint, create a Google map pin drop of your membership with this free tool: https://mapalist.com.

All churches have a unique shape based on natural boundaries or local demographics. One congregation is at an intersection of two interstates making a "crosshairs" while another is tucked away in a suburban neighborhood. One church is wedged between a mountain range and an Indian reservation while another borders an uptown center for the arts. What picture do you see when you map your geography?

In addition to the geographic shape, use demographic information to determine the number of people defined by your footprint. Do you have seventy-five hundred people close by or 750,000? For years missiologists and denominational leaders have used the benchmark of one church per one thousand people as an indication that an area has been "reached" or "saturated."

Other images that convey geographic gospel saturation are a world map with a cloud moving to overtake it just as the Holy Spirit can travel like the wind and go anywhere. Consider also ink spilling across a desk, a flood or flowing water, a tide coming in, a ground-cover plant (like ivy filling a bordered flower bed), a dandelion puffball or "magic grow capsules" children drop into a bathtub and watch them expand to cover the surface of the water.

Think of the images that come from words like *permeate, drench, deluge,* and *douse.* Imagine someone handing an invitation, sharing, singing, proclaiming, speaking, inviting, or telling. Build on phrases like "Go tell it on the mountain!"

Historical Examples

John Wesley, the great eighteenth-century preacher and founder of Methodism, was famous for saying, "The world is my parish." As he explained in his journal, he felt it was his "duty to declare unto all that are willing to hear, the glad tidings of salvation."[2]

This attitude challenged the current thinking in his time where church leaders were assigned a geographic area (parish) as their world to care for. Instead, Wesley sent one of his circuit-riding preachers to wherever people were present. Again the image of "advance" captures the circuit-riding strategy. As a result, the conversion rate and the spread of Methodism was the fastest-growing faith of that century, becoming for a season the largest denomination in the United States, as well as in other countries.

Contemporary Examples

Many churches identify a geographic area or geographic concentric circle they take responsibility for, including the church I'm part of, Clear Creek Community Church in greater Houston. As I'll explain more in Appendix A, our gospel saturation vision involves adopting a 500,000-population area we refer to as the "4B" area. The 4Bs run from the interstate beltway to the Gulf of Mexico beach, from Brazoria County to Galveston Bay. We're advancing the gospel by taking it to the people around us.

Other large-scale examples are McLean Bible Church in metro Washington, DC, and Eagle Brook Church in greater Minneapolis, both of whom are purposely planting campuses all over their respective metroplexes as a way of creating a ring around their cities so hearing the gospel is accessible within an easy commute to all.

Smaller churches have likewise followed an adopt-a-block strategy to take the gospel and the tangible love of Christ to certain blocks they've designated near their church facility. Some churches, like the Dream Center of Los Angeles's Angelus Temple, started with a handful of people and the idea of "instead of reaching the entire city, let's adopt the two blocks right in front of us." Today the congregation is nicknamed the "church that never sleeps" because it has adopted more than fifty blocks representing over two thousand homes.

Jeff Vanderstelt wrote a book entitled *Saturate* encouraging Christ followers and churches to join the vision to see one missional community per 1,000 people in every key population center.[3] Another influential leader for geographic gospel saturation is Dwight Smith, of Saturation Church Planting. He has popularized the language of reaching "every man, woman and child" with the question he poses: What would it look like if the "church" gave every man, woman and child the opportunity to hear and understand the gospel and be reconciled to God through Christ without their coming or going anywhere?[4]

Exercise: Should This Vision Be Your Church's Focus?

1. How closely does this template match **your own vision** for your congregation as a gospel-centered, disciple-making church over the next ten years? Use a scale of 1 (low) to 10 (high):

    1   2   3   4   5   6   7   8   9   10

2. How would you rate your **key opinion leaders' buy-in** at present for this template as the focus of their vision? Same 1 (low) to 10 (high) scale:

    1   2   3   4   5   6   7   8   9   10

3. How would you rate the **entire congregation's buy-in** at present for this template as the focus of their vision? Same 1 (low) to 10 (high) scale:

    1   2   3   4   5   6   7   8   9   10

4. How would you rate the level of **momentum and progress to date** your church has made on this particular vision template? Same 1 (low) to 10 (high) scale:

    1   2   3   4   5   6   7   8   9   10

Now add up these four scores: _____ (You'll compare the tallies after you've reviewed all twelve templates.)

Advancing through Targeted Transformation

Quick Definition

Your church's vision is to identify a specific people, place, or thing you want to see changed dramatically by the gospel. You might state it as, "We will direct our energy toward a specific people, place, or thing in order to see a specific kind of dramatic transformation."

Targeted Transformation Vision Template

Figure 7.4

Personal Snapshot

I arrived late in Manhattan the day before my meeting with Redeemer Church's City to City leaders. I enjoy the city, and I couldn't wait to spend time with these thoughtful leaders who really *love* their city. What impresses me most about this team: their laser focus! Their vision is guided by one thing: church planting in the "great global cities." It's a glowing example of targeted transformation because it targets four specific dimensions: (1) the city as a unique expression of humanity, (2) a specific number of strategically identified global cities, (3) a methodology of church planting, and (4) helping other local churches transform their "missions" investment by helping them engage in City to City's unique strategy. In addition, the intellectually robust nature of the ministry led by Tim Keller brings wonderful nuance to their church's ultimate contribution.

Just in case the scope of fifty global cities seems a little overwhelming, let me offer a different example. I was sitting with about ten leaders under Rick Duncan's leadership at Cuyahoga Valley Church outside of Cleveland. I asked a question to the team and marveled at an idea that would weave its way through our day conversation like a golden thread. It was a moment where a targeted transformation vision would precipitate. The question was, What do you secretly believe you would be great at but never told anyone? One pastor talked about his desire to see an entire street block renovated spiritually and physically for the sake of the gospel. This would eventually lead to the targeting of a specific neighborhood for radical renewal.

Biblical Reflections

Transformation is a powerful and familiar biblical theme. From Jesus' first miracle of turning water into wine to the larger-than-life description of a new heaven and new earth, the Bible is filled with stories and images of transformation. Jesus transforms the disciples' vocation from fishing for fish to fishers of men. Every believer is commanded to "be transformed" as a human being through the "renewing of your mind" (Rom. 12:1–3 NIV).

With the theme of change filling the pages of Scripture, noteworthy glimpses of vision are characterized by transformation.

Jesus wept over only one city: Jerusalem (Luke 19:41). His ministry took Him many places, but He kept circling back to Jerusalem. Could it be that He wanted Jerusalem, more than any other city, to be changed dramatically by the gospel? Even in His most angry moments—using a whip and turning over the tables in the temple—we see Jesus' passion for this city to be different.

Jonah is another stunning biblical illustration of targeted transformation. God called Jonah to be an agent of change to the great ancient city of Nineveh, a town that spanned a three-day walk with a population of at least 120,000 people. As a result of Jonah's preaching, the town repented starting with the king who issued a decree: "Let them call out mightily to God. Let everyone turn from his evil way and from the violence that is in his hands. Who knows? God may turn and relent and turn from his fierce anger, so that we may not perish" (Jon. 3:8–9). And relent God did.

Metaphors for Communication

Figure 7.4 imagines a directional force aiming for and acting on some object in its sights for the purposes of transformation. The change is depicted by a starburst image with a gradient inside to indicate energy release. Targeted transformation is also like an arrow aiming at a bull's-eye, with the target representing a hub of community vitality being impacted by the gospel.

Biblical images of transformation include high-contrast ones: cleansing from crimson stained to white as snow (Isa. 1:18), transferring from the domain of darkness to the saints of light (Col. 1:12–13), and exchanging a heart of stone with a heart of flesh (Ezek. 11:19). Those who would follow Jesus are to be salt of the earth and a city set on a hill; they should go the extra mile and love their enemies, all symbols of dramatic transformation from a "normal way" of life (Matt. 5:13–48).

Other images that convey the idea of transformation include a change in a stem cell that changes the entire body that grows from it, a renewed farmer's field or garden that feeds a surrounding community, a heart transplant that brings new life, and a bonsai tree whose changed roots change the tree itself.

We use all kinds of everyday phrases to signal a transformation:

- Turning over a new leaf
- New Year's resolution
- Extreme makeover
- Night-and-day difference
- Revolutionize
- Reform
- Sing a different tune
- Shifting gears

Historical Examples

Many churches and denominations have prayerfully adopted a town, city, region, or even country, seeking to pour energy and resources into it. One of the Southern Baptist Convention's most celebrated missionaries, Charlotte Digges "Lottie" Moon, went as a thirty-three-year-old single missionary to China. She focused on a certain unreached region in the country's interior both through personal outreach and through a vigorous campaign of letters and articles back home that rallied hundreds of US churches to raise prayers, money, and personnel to support the advance of the gospel in her region. When she died at age seventy-two, thousands of converts and hundreds of churches existed in that area.

Contemporary Examples

Kingsland Baptist in Katy, Texas, envisions the transformation of homes in a city where people obsess over having the best for their kids. The big idea is to reinterpret what true fulfillment looks like in order to restore the image of God in the home.

Good Shepherd United Methodist Church in Charlotte, North Carolina, embeds "radical impact projects" into their disciple-making strategy that focus on specific transformation themes like sex trafficking. In 2013 they evaluated their multisite options that deviated from the typical "start a worship service" pattern of campusing to envision "radical impact sites" to bring local community transformation initiatives before starting worship services. For example, one location focuses on recovery ministry, food distribution, transitional housing, and personal retreating and prayer.

The Bridge Bible Church, Bakersfield, California, embraces a targeted transformation vision that is mobilized significantly through its small-group strategy. Each group is given money from the church's operating budget to unleash on a specific need in the community.

The key to distinguishing the targeted transformation template is the motivation to see a completed change on a person, place, or thing at a level where the entire mind's eye of a congregation is "zeroed in" on that type of transformation.

Exercise: Should This Vision Be Your Church's Focus?

1. How closely does this template match **your own vision** for your congregation as a gospel-centered, disciple-making church over the next ten years? Use a scale of 1 (low) to 10 (high):

1   2   3   4   5   6   7   8   9   10

2. How would you rate your **key opinion leaders' buy-in** at present for this template as the focus of their vision? Same 1 (low) to 10 (high) scale:

1   2   3   4   5   6   7   8   9   10

3. How would you rate the **entire congregation's buy-in** at present for this template as the focus of their vision? Same 1 (low) to 10 (high) scale:

1   2   3   4   5   6   7   8   9   10

4. How would you rate the level of **momentum and progress to date** your church has made on this particular vision template? Same 1 (low) to 10 (high) scale:

1   2   3   4   5   6   7   8   9   10

Now add up these four scores: _____ (You'll compare the tallies after you've reviewed all twelve templates.)

Advancing through People-Group Penetration

Quick Definition

Your church's vision is taking the gospel to a group of people who don't have it yet. You might state it as, "We will engage a specific group of people, usually different from our own congregational makeup, through service and gospel proclamation."

Personal Snapshot

I was meeting with Austin Stone Church's Kevin Peck and his team in the Texas capital city of Austin for a Church Unique certification experience. At a break, in

People-Group Penetration Vision Template

Figure 7.5

Austin Stone's For the City Center, I was blown away by a fascinating billboard in the foyer. It was a visual progress chart for their 100 People Network, a long-range vision initiative the church launched in 2009. The vision is to send one hundred people from their local church to an unreached people group for at least two years. Every person in the church is challenged to play one of three roles: to be a goer, a sender, or a mobilizer. My visit was May 2014, five years after the initiative was launched, and the billboard showed that they had identified more than seventy-five of the one hundred people. Their billboard showed it in a creative way: the faces of those who were signed up. (Check out 100peoplenetwork.org for more information.)

Matt Carter, the lead pastor, says that from the beginning they had asked, "What does God want from us as a church with our limited time and resources?" Their primary answer is sending their people into the six thousand unreached people groups of the world.

Another amazing story of people-group penetration comes from the community of Northwest Bible Church. Approximately three miles from their location off the North Tollway and Highway 12 north of Dallas is Vickery Meadows, the most densely populated area in Dallas and a leading area for refugee resettlement. Technically refugees are persons who have been forced to leave their country in order to escape war, persecution, or natural disaster. The people group, in this case, includes political refugees of more than fifty nationalities and thirty-two spoken languages all living in one square mile, making it one of the leading areas of refugee resettlement in the country. Within two years of clarifying their vision and focusing on reaching this group, Neil

Tomba reported a tremendous surge of increased energy, focus, and resources like he had not seen in his prior decade as senior pastor. You can learn more at Northwestbible. org/vickery.

Biblical Reflections

The apostle Paul said he had "become all things to all people, that by all means I might save some" (1 Cor. 9:22). At the same time, he was clear that he was uniquely called as Apostle to the Gentiles (Gal. 2:7; Rom. 11:13). In particular, Paul sensed a call to take the gospel to Rome (Acts 19:21; 23:11; Rom. 1:15; 15:22).

Others such as Peter served as apostle to the Jews (Gal. 2:8) and sought to penetrate that group with the gospel. In fact the entire book of Acts can be outlined around the biographical emphasis of Peter as the apostle to the Jews transitioning to Paul as apostle to the Gentiles with a pivot point at Acts 13:1. Peter's name is mentioned more than sixty times in the first thirteen chapters and only once during the second half of the book, as the emphasis shifts.

Notice also how the writers of the four Gospels each tried to penetrate a different group. Matthew's heavy emphasis on how Jesus fulfilled various Old Testament prophecies spoke especially to Jewish readers. Mark's fast-moving account appealed to another group. Luke wrote with special emphasis on Gentiles and women. John's angle spoke specifically to the unbeliever, calling for a decision to believe and follow Jesus.

Perhaps the most dramatic example of people-group penetration is the incarnation itself. God became a man as Jesus "though he was in the form of God, did not count equality with God a thing to be grasped, but emptied himself, by taking the form of a servant, being born in the likeness of men" (Phil. 2:6–7). Ultimately God, by sending Jesus the Son, walked across an infinite divide that humanity could not. He penetrated the time-space world as we know it to show us what God looks like in the flesh.

Metaphors for Communication

Figure 7.5 imagines an army of people moving from one sphere to another sphere, penetrating it with the gospel, and carrying the gospel from one people group to another.

Imagine pictures and scenes of people trying to "get into" another group of people. The army image sometimes creates a forceful tone, which might not work for you. Perhaps consider more tender pictures like kids playfully jumping the fence to find new friends or ambassadors skillfully and sensitively negotiating in a foreign country or a business trying to take their strategy international. Imagine ideas of long-term and quiet infiltration like a police officer going into deep undercover or a spy going "dark" for a long time in enemy territory. Envision your own images for "how beautiful are the feet of those who preach the good news!" (Rom. 10:15).

Consider these related terms:

- Fit in, relate to, or walk in another's shoes
- Enter, insert, breeze in, or barge in
- Tunnel, burrow, mine, drill, or sink
- Infiltrate, perforate, or invade
- Impregnate, implant, or fertilize

Other images that depict people-group penetration include a swimming pool full of people with a slide that enables outsiders to be conveyed and perhaps even thrust into the heart of that gathering, a doctor's shot with life-giving medicine in the point of the needle, or a funnel that concentrates the flow into one specific opening.

Historical Example

Americans celebrate Saint Patrick's Day each March, but what many don't realize is that Patrick was a missionary. He was kidnapped as a youth, taken to Ireland as a slave, but he eventually escaped, came to faith in Christ, and then returned to Ireland because he had a burden and calling to share the gospel with the people who represented his former captors.

Contemporary Examples

Just outside Wichita, Kansas, Joe Boyd planted a church to reach a surprisingly unique people group: folks in the aviation community. Started in 2008, Aviator Church has seen more than one thousand people profess new faith in Christ and take the step of baptism. Aviator Church sent people and resources to start seven church plants before their seventh anniversary. Joe Boyd often says, "We are not a church with a mission. We are a mission that has churches."

Russell Cravens planted a church in Houston's midtown to reach busy young dads moving back to the city. He was burdened to bring the whole gospel to this under-reached segment of people in the flux of Houston's urban renewal.

Recently Jim Randall, who helped me start Auxano in 2004, started working with The Cowboy Church of Ellis County. It was founded in January 2000 as an outreach to team ropers, barrel racers, working cowboys, and others who love Western culture and enjoy rural life. More than three hundred attended the first service, many of whom rarely or never attended church.

While these groups represent an entire church reaching a specific people group, Jeff Vanderstelt, formerly of Soma Church in Tacoma, Washington, challenges missional communities to develop their own people-group penetration strategy. He writes in his book *Saturate*:

> We remind one another that we are commanded by Jesus to make disciples of all people groups. So we ask: "What people and place do we believe God is collectively sending us to this year? Who do we hope to see become followers of Jesus Christ?"
>
> Our missional community has identified the faculty and families of Grant Elementary School, as well as the neighborhoods around it. Some groups focus on a neighborhood or region. Some focus on a particular group of people with common interests, experiences or needs. The missional community in which Greg and Mary participate has identified families transitioning out of homelessness. Some of our artists are on mission to the artistic community, which is much more nomadic in nature. We have missional communities reaching out to college campuses, others that partner with Young Life to reach high school students, and some that see the local military base as their missional focus.[5]

A helpful resource to look at people groups from a global perspective is people groups.org. By their analysis the world's 7.2 billion population is made up of 11,511 people groups. Of this wider group, 6,823 people groups or 4.1 billion are technically "unreached" people groups (UPGs) meaning that the evangelical population is less than 2 percent without the capability of an indigenous group to sustain church planting. In addition, 3,213 groups or 210 million people are described as "unengaged and unreached" (UUPGs). This status means there is no "church planting strategy, consistent with evangelical faith and practice underway." Their website enables you to explore UPGs and UUPGs on a map of the world.

Exercise: Should This Vision Be Your Church's Focus?

1. How closely does this template match **your own vision** for your congregation as a gospel-centered, disciple-making church over the next ten years? Use a scale of 1 (low) to 10 (high):

    1   2   3   4   5   6   7   8   9   10

2. How would you rate your **key opinion leaders' buy-in** at present for this template as the focus of their vision? Same 1 (low) to 10 (high) scale:

  1   2   3   4   5   6   7   8   9   10

3. How would you rate the **entire congregation's buy-in** at present for this template as the focus of their vision? Same 1 (low) to 10 (high) scale:

  1   2   3   4   5   6   7   8   9   10

4. How would you rate the level of **momentum and progress to date** your church has made on this particular vision template? Same 1 (low) to 10 (high) scale:

  1   2   3   4   5   6   7   8   9   10

Now add up these four scores: _____ (You'll compare the tallies after you've reviewed all twelve templates.)

How Do You Rate on Vision That Advances?

The three vision templates in this chapter each explored some aspect of vision that advances. At the conclusion of each template, you rated how this model applies to your church. You'll do likewise for all twelve templates, and then I'll ask you to look back and see which one or two you scored as highest.

Chapter 8
Vision That Rescues

And they said to me, "The remnant there in the province who had survived the exile is in great trouble and shame. The wall of Jerusalem is broken down, and its gates are destroyed by fire." As soon as I heard these words I sat down and wept and mourned for days, and I continued fasting and praying before the God of heaven.

—Nehemiah 1:3–4

The previous chapter looked at vision that advances. This chapter will look at three templates all characterized by vision that rescues. The basic shape for rescuing is the image of a cross—like a medic's cross (see figure 8.1). Vision that rescues is responsive, resourceful, preparing, and caring. Rescuing vision says, "Save it!"

All three overflow templates are represented as figure 8.2, with the basic shape in the upper left.

Rescuing through Institutional Renovation

Definition

Your church's vision is to rejuvenate an institution that matters to God, most often a ministry that historically has been significant but has lost a degree of relevance, focus, or momentum. You might state it as, "We will renew a God-ordained institution like marriage, family, or church that has suffered decline, collapse, or neglect." The key is that churches in this template see the concept of institution in a positive way.

Cross Base Shape for the Rescue Templates

Figure 8.1

Three Rescue Templates
with Basic Shape

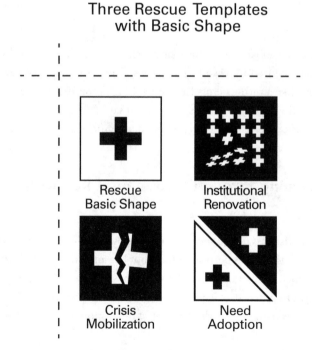

Figure 8.2

Institutional Renovation Vision Template

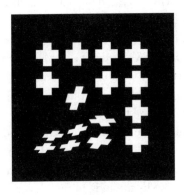

Figure 8.3

Personal Snapshot

It was brisk summer morning in Billings, Montana, and I couldn't wait to meet with the leadership team of Harvest Church led by Vern Streeter. Harvest is a fast-growing, contemporary-styled church with the mission of living life as if Jesus were living through you. Within the first hour with the team, we focused on the story of the church's founding. This "creation story" of the church would eventually influence the team to select the institutional renovation template for developing their vision.

How did Harvest get started? Vern was a youth pastor at an area church of the same denomination. Someone had given money to the denomination for the purposes of starting a new church. The money had a ten-year expiration date. Every year Vern would inquire about the money, asking his denominational leadership if anyone had taken it yet. When the tenth year came on the horizon with no takers, Vern still wasn't sure if God was calling him to plant. Then a local event changed everything.

A large master-planned community was developing in a new area of Montana. To Vern's shock he read a news article stating that city planners were restricting the development of new churches because they said churches represent zero value being added to a community. The news was like a bomb going off in Vern's heart. How is it possible that churches could be perceived that way? Vern decided to start a church that would renovate the value of God's people and God's institution—the local church—in the eyes of people in his corner of the world.

The day I visited I saw the amazing progress the people of Harvest have made. The foyer of the church was decorated with camping and hunting gear (including a dozen elk-head mounts) for a teaching series designed to reach unchurched men who love the outdoors. I also toured the Oasis Water Park that was a gift to the community in 2012 valued at five million dollars. When Warren Bird interviewed Vern, he conveyed his passion with crystal clarity: "We need to be so relevant and so tangible that even the most ardent critic of Christianity would be bummed if we ceased to exist. If our doors close, we want the most vocal atheist to say, 'I never believed a thing they said about God, but they were certainly good for our community.'"[1]

I like this story because it illustrates the versatility of the institutional renovation vision template. At first, it's natural to think about brick and mortar, which certainly fits. But in addition you can think of institution in the most positive way—as God-ordained vehicles—expanding its meaning to the ideas of the local church in general or to families, marriages, and governments as alluded to earlier.

Biblical Reflections

Romans 11 explains how the Gentiles have been grafted into the blessings of Israel, much like a wild olive shoot can be grafted in to "share in the nourishing root" (v. 17). This teaching speaks to the renewal and rejuvenation needed among God's chosen people during the time of Christ. In some ways the movement from Old Testament to New Testament is a "renovation of agreements" between God and men. Hence Jesus speaks of the "new command" in John 13:34 (NIV) and elsewhere. Even the cryptic nature of Jesus' verbal sparring with some Jews hints to this massive renovation in John 2:19: "Jesus answered them, 'Destroy this temple, and in three days I will raise it up.'" They were thinking about the physical temple, and Jesus was referring to His body.

In contrast to the epic "renovation" in God's redemptive plan, we find a more concrete illustration in the days of Nehemiah when the walls of Jerusalem needed rebuilding—as did the vision and hearts of God's people. Nehemiah's amazing fifty-two-day city wall rebuilding project is a perfect example of an institutional renovation vision. In this case the institution is the holy city of Jerusalem.

Starting Point Metaphors

Figure 8.3 shows an established pattern that's now falling down, collapsing, or crumbling—all in need of rescue, rebuilding, and innovation.

Another image to depict institutional renovation is a once-solid wall now in need of attention but buttressed by a new foundation. In the old a few bricks are missing, the sense of freshness is gone, but the new is building on the old, forecasting a sense of fresh start.

Other images that convey this idea are the restoration of the Sistine Chapel (or other historic sites), reconstructive surgery, a stained-glass window being rebuilt, or an antique dealer working on an old stately chair.

Renovation can also carry ideas and images of innovation. Imagine an upgrade of software, installing a new strategy or model or a new invention. Picture the change from filament bulb to an LED bulb or the movement from film processing to digital photography. Imagine a house where every appliance is Internet connected and Wi-Fi enabled.

A great picture of going back and forward is when Volkswagen introduced the new Beetle in 1997. The car was altogether new and updated, yet it was inspired by the original design of 1938 that had become the longest running and most manufactured single design in history. The "bug" design was essentially renovated. Steve Jobs did the same thing to the cell phone.

Use this list of words to expand your idea of renovation that moves from light-duty ideas like "cleaning" to more substantial ideas like "reconstitute":

- Clean, recondition, refurbish, spruce up, face-lift
- Repair, rehabilitate, revamp, overhaul, refit, retreat
- Remodel, remake, restore, update
- Revitalize, rekindle, reactivate, resurrect
- Recreate, reconstitute, renew, reactivate

Historical Examples

The Sunday school movement has been a major instrument of breathing new life into established churches. In previous eras the revitalization of Sunday school was a community-wide event. Typical was Brooklyn, New York. Beginning in 1829, when that area was known as the city of churches, churches began holding rally day parades that were the focal point of community life. In 1905 the state legislature created Brooklyn Day as an ongoing official holiday, closing the public schools in Brooklyn for the day so children could participate in these massive Sunday school parades. Churches pulled out all the stops to recruit children into their Sunday school programs, with those events often forming a trigger point to rejuvenate a long-standing congregation.

Contemporary Examples

There are countless examples of churches that have engaged long-term renovation projects when it comes to location, facility, brand, and mission of the church. For example, Willy Rice took the helm of Calvary Baptist Church in Clearwater, Florida, in 2005. At the time of this writing, Calvary is preparing for its 150th anniversary as the first church in both its city and county in the 1800s. Before Willy arrived, the church had suffered decline in several troubled interim years. But over a five-year period, Willy led through a massive turnaround season including relocation, building, rebranding, and reestablishing a culture of mission. Within just a few years of clarifying their mission of building relationships that bring people to dynamic life in Christ, the church conducted a congregation survey with remarkable results. One open-ended question asked, "What do you like best about the church?" Twenty percent of the people answered that they liked having a clear mission.

Another example of the institutional renovation template is the Church of the Y. David Newman started a church and church-planting network with the vision of using fourteen thousand YMCA locations globally as community gathering points to plant churches. The hub is Antioch Church of the Y in Lebanon, Ohio, where thirty-five thousand residents are associated with the significant YMCA presence. When sharing the vision, David references the officially stated but practically overlooked global mission of the YMCA: "The Young Men's Christian Associations seek to unite those young men who, regarding Jesus Christ as their God and Saviour, according to the Holy Scriptures, desire to be his disciples in their faith and in their life, and to associate their efforts for the extension of his Kingdom amongst young men."[2]

Realizing that the Y has drifted from its vibrant evangelical bearings, the church-planting movement is partnering with the 172-year-old organization to refurbish the original intent.

As Nehemiah began his rebuilding project by spending a period of time inspecting the broken walls of the city, David felt the Lord stir him to spend five years studying the history and mission of the YMCA through a doctoral program that focused on institutional renewal. He also traveled much of the world, meeting with YMCA leaders and seeing God's ongoing work through this global institution. He wanted to have a true sense of God's heart for this institution and the "status of the walls."

When defining renovation as upgrading or innovating, I think of LifeChurch.tv, led by Craig Groeshel, and the investment the church made into the YouVersion Bible App developed by Bobby Gruenwald and the "digerati" team. The popular mobile Bible platform launched in 2008 and currently contains more than nine hundred Bible translations in more than six hundred languages.[3] Having passed 140 million downloads, one church's vision to "renovate" how God's Word is made available (even though Scripture is not an institution per se) is making a dramatic impact across the globe.

Exercise: Should This Vision Be Your Church's Focus?

1. How closely does this template match **your own vision** for your congregation as a gospel-centered, disciple-making church over the next ten years? Use a scale of 1 (low) to 10 (high):

    1   2   3   4   5   6   7   8   9   10

2. How would you rate your **key opinion leaders' buy-in** at present for this template as the focus of their vision? Same 1 (low) to 10 (high) scale:

    1   2   3   4   5   6   7   8   9   10

3. How would you rate the **entire congregation's buy-in** at present for this template as the focus of their vision? Same 1 (low) to 10 (high) scale:

    1   2   3   4   5   6   7   8   9   10

4. How would you rate the level of **momentum and progress to date** your church has made on this particular vision template? Same 1 (low) to 10 (high) scale:

    1   2   3   4   5   6   7   8   9   10

You'll compare the tallies after you've reviewed all twelve templates.

Need Adoption Vision Template

Figure 8.4

Rescuing through Need Adoption

Definition

Your church's vision is to adopt a specific need you identify, often through compassion or mercy, typically triggered by studying the needs and then responding to them. You might state it as, "We will choose to respond to a specific need in our society, locally, regionally, and/or globally."

Personal Snapshot

I was spending the day at LakeRidge United Methodist Church in Lubbock, Texas, with Mike Gammill who serves on the Auxano team. Founding pastor Bill Couch personifies the unique strengths of the congregation; the people blend the rugged, can-do spirit of a West Texas agricultural town with deep dependence on God, the virtue of acceptance characterized by the Methodist denomination, and a passion for helping people. The future picture that would develop from our process focused on the goal to eradicate hunger in their city as the first step of breaking the cycle of poverty. Specifically, they would funnel their resources toward ensuring that no kids of middle-school age in Lubbock go hungry. Their rescue mission became totally clear.

Every city has more needs to be met than one church can be called to address. But it is amazing to watch a team gel around a particular need that God leads them toward. Usually this happens when strong gifts of mercy and helps are evident in the senior leadership team, church council, or elder board.

The first time I ran into an active church culture operating out of the centering gift of mercy was Sagemont Church in Houston. One day during our consulting session, I was offended slightly (working hard to keep it unnoticeable, of course) by how many times the senior pastor, John Morgan, was interrupted by his assistant who would pop in with little notes to give to him. My curiosity deepened with each interruption. At a break I realized that the notes were pastoral care needs on which John wanted to be updated.

A new respect began to grow—pushing aside my shortsighted annoyance—for a leader and a church whose guiding value would be stated as, "Each individual matters." Shortly after my day at Sagemont, I consulted another church in another city where I learned of one of their key volunteers named Morgan after Sagemont's Pastor John Morgan. The story was shared that her parents were attending Sagemont at the time of her birth, but they didn't have the money to pay the hospital bill. When Pastor John heard of the need, he took off his boot in the middle of a sermon, passed it around and took up a financial collection for the family. His act of mercy inspired the parents to name their daughter after him.

This simple story illustrates what is now a community-wide reputation for a church. People in the community know Sagemont is a place that really cares.

Most importantly my story might help you recognize if the need adoption template "runs through the veins" of your congregation.

Bible Reflections

Throughout the Old Testament we see countless expressions of the heart of God toward those in need. In Psalm 12:5 we see Him spring to action: "'Because the poor are plundered, because the needy groan, I will now arise,' says the LORD; 'I will place him in the safety for which he longs.'"

God's wisdom is for His church to be "full of mercy and good fruits" (James 3:17). We are also to be marked by compassion: "Put on then, as God's chosen ones, holy and beloved, *compassionate* hearts, kindness, humility, meekness, and patience, bearing with one another and, if one has a complaint against another, forgiving each other; as the Lord has forgiven you, so you also must forgive. And above all these put on love, which binds everything together in perfect harmony" (Col. 3:12–14, emphasis added). This emphasis came not in teaching alone but was also the practice of Paul and others: "They asked us to remember the poor, the very thing I was eager to do" (Gal. 2:10).

In addition, God highlights people throughout His Word who paid special attention to those in need. In Acts 9:36 Tabitha is honored: "Now there was in Joppa a disciple named Tabitha. . . . She was full of good works and acts of charity."

In Acts 10:4, Cornelius is commended by an angel, "The angel answered, 'Your prayers and gifts to the poor have come up as a memorial offering before God'" (NIV).

Starting Point Metaphors

Figure 8.4 shows mirror images where one side has something identical to what the other lacks. This visualization affirms that a church has some resources and can match or plug into a hole created by clear needs.

Another image to represent need adoption are two hands reaching toward each other. One is in a position of greater strength, able to help the other. Another iconic biblical image is that of washing another's feet.

Think of images that convey the acts of serving, helping, treating, nurturing, fixing, listening, nursing, caring, or supporting. Picture a foster parent, a child being sponsored, a food kitchen, a bandaged knee, or a serving towel around someone's arm. Imagine the tearful storytelling in a support group with listening friends or a construction work crew ready and willing to build a house.

Historical Examples

"Immigration reform" may always seem to be in process, but modifications in 1965 were the most far-reaching revision of US immigration policy in more than fifty years, opening doors to new waves of immigrants. In response tens of thousands of churches championed the idea of sponsoring a refugee family, many from a Southeast Asia country such as Vietnam. This in turn led to any number of need-meeting church ministries, the most popular being classes to teach English as a second language (ESL).

Several years ago when visiting Bethlehem Chapel in Prague, I was moved by a "need adoption" story from before the Reformation, as priest and future martyr John Hus led the congregation. While touring the church building, I was immediately struck by two oddities: the first is a large stone water well in the middle of the sanctuary, and the second is the prominence of babies in the larger-than-life medieval-style murals on the walls. The tour guide shared that in the early fifteenth century the town experienced setbacks due to influence of criminals and prostitutes. Evidently the prostitutes disposed of their unwanted babies in the town's local water source, polluting the water. The horrific acts ignited the people of the Bethlehem Chapel to take up the cause of these murdered children (symbolized in the large mural) and to provide a clean, safe water source for the community. Nonchurch members were invited, even during Sunday services, to come in and draw water from the well.

Contemporary Examples

Although Rick Warren of Saddleback is most known for the widely successful book *Purpose Driven Church*, I wonder if his greatest contribution comes from building a church that meets real needs. Rick has always challenged pastors to know more about their community than anyone else. The first line of Saddleback Church's vision says, "It is the dream of a place where the hurting, the hopeless, the discouraged, the depressed, the frustrated, and confused can find love, acceptance, guidance, and encouragement." Saddleback has developed more than seventy ministries to targeted felt needs within the community like Empty Arms for women dealing with miscarriages or Hope for the Separated for people trying to save their marriage.[4]

But perhaps the church's best-known and widely adapted ministry, Celebrate Recovery, is a fusion of the Sermon on the Mount and the classic twelve-step approach of Alcoholics Anonymous. What started in 1990 has today brought the Christ-centered approach to recovery to more than twenty thousand churches worldwide helping people recover from "hurts, hang-ups, and harmful behaviors" including drugs, alcohol, pornography, anger, depression, and abuse.[5]

Leaders at The Life Church, Memphis, Tennessee, were surprised by a newspaper headline saying their city had the "hungriest zip code in the United States," where 74 percent of children went to bed hungry every night. They focused their outreach efforts on that area and bought an old bread delivery truck to distribute food. The church was able to partner with schools in the neighborhoods with the greatest need—showing up after school on Friday to distribute bags with enough groceries to feed a family for a weekend. Volunteers in the growing ministry do more than hand out food; they do it all in Jesus' name. "Volunteers line up outside the school," explains Pastor John Siebeling. "When the kids come out, they give them hugs and pray for them. They tell them, 'You're a champion' and give them their bags."

Another specific need churches adopt is the opportunity to adopt orphans within their sphere of influence. In Colorado, LifeBridge Church, for example, has set a goal—and invited other churches to participate as well—to zero out the number of kids waiting for adoption through Colorado's child welfare system. Over a six-year period, that number of waiting children has already reduced by 70 percent.[6]

Another way we see the need adoption template expressed is through the starting of separate nonprofits and parachurch organizations to cooperate with the church in meeting particular needs. According to the National Center for Charitable Statistics, more than ninety-one thousand nonprofit Protestant organizations filed tax forms for Christian work last year in the US. Mack Stiles writes, "This dizzying array of parachurch ministries feed the hungry, focus on families, evangelize youth, and send missionaries. They publish, lobby, and educate. They broadcast, fund, clothe, and heal. Parachurch ministries serve the Christian community around the world."[7]

Exercise: Should This Vision Be Your Church's Focus?

1. How closely does this template match **your own vision** for your congregation as a gospel-centered, disciple-making church over the next ten years? Use a scale of 1 (low) to 10 (high):

    1   2   3   4   5   6   7   8   9   10

2. How would you rate your **key opinion leaders' buy-in** at present for this template as the focus of their vision? Same 1 (low) to 10 (high) scale:

    1   2   3   4   5   6   7   8   9   10

3. How would you rate the **entire congregation's buy-in** at present for this template as the focus of their vision? Same 1 (low) to 10 (high) scale:

    1   2   3   4   5   6   7   8   9   10

4. How would you rate the level of **momentum and progress to date** your church has made on this particular vision template? Same 1 (low) to 10 (high) scale:

    1   2   3   4   5   6   7   8   9   10

Now add up these four scores: _____ (You'll compare the tallies after you've reviewed all twelve templates.)

Crisis Mobilization Vision Template

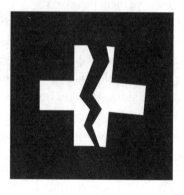

Figure 8.5

Rescuing through Crisis Mobilization

Definition

Your church's vision is to mobilize for crises, or be prepared to mobilize for a future crisis. You might state it as: "We will respond to crisis by rallying our people and resources for immediate relief and/or long-term deployment and development."

Personal Snapshot

I was riveted to the story of Rich Kannwischer as he talked about leading a congregation through the shocking September 11, 2001, tragedy in New York. He said the finest hour for Central Presbyterian in Summit, New Jersey, was in the wake of the terrorist attack. A church traditionally marked with a myriad of activity and even competing agendas at times became totally galvanized around one ministry: rallying for the families impacted by the devastating attack. With many church members working in the World Trade Center's twin towers that day, the church become laser focused first on accounting for missing family members, then on crisis care, and then on long-term recovery.

Some churches are best in crisis. And this template accounts for this not-so-common possibility as a long-range area of contribution for a church.

Bible Reflections

The book of Acts is full of ways God's people mobilized for crisis. Sometimes it was the entire church community banding together. For instance, when a famine arose in Jerusalem, the church in Antioch responded as soon as they heard about it: "The disciples determined, every one according to his ability, to send relief to the brothers and sisters living in Judea" (Acts 11:29). Other times it was individual responses, such as Peter saying to a lame man, "I have no silver and gold, but what I do have I give to you. In the name of Jesus Christ of Nazareth, rise up and walk!" (Acts 3:6).

In fact, God's people from Old Testament to New Testament are marked by mobilized compassion, just as God is: "For the LORD has comforted his people and will have compassion on his afflicted" (Isa. 49:13; see also 2 Cor. 1:3–4). With the psalmist we can say, "I will rejoice and be glad in your steadfast love, because you have seen my affliction; you have known the distress of my soul" (Ps. 31:7).

The recent run of Hollywood-produced Bible movies (some of which have tried to stay faithful to the original text and others have been more creative) remind us that life was full of drama, giving constant opportunity for God's people to rally behind one another in crises. Noah, for example, is a strong example of a crisis preparation. So are Moses and Joseph.

Starting Point Metaphors

Figure 8.5 shows that the cross symbol has cracked or broken, implying a need for help that the church could be mobilized to address. Imagine an earthquake, a building cut open by a tornado, the broken glass of a downtown riot, or a family photograph ripped in half.

Still other images that convey this idea are the Red Cross, an ambulance, an EMT team, a rescue ladder dropping down from a military helicopter, a "jaws of life" machine cutting a trapped person from a smashed car, or a bright orange life-flight helicopter.

Historic Examples

In May 1861, at the dawn of the Civil War, President Abraham Lincoln issued by executive order a call for three-year volunteers to increase the size of the regular army and navy. Plymouth Church in Brooklyn rose to the occasion and defined its vision in light of the wartime crisis for years. The members immediately raised money first for the 13th Regiment to buy clothing, blankets, pistols, holsters, and other equipment. Later the church would adopt two other regiments. The soldiers and their families were supported by special sermons and events. Church facilities were used to store weapons, and the church parlor was turned into a workshop training women and girls how to sew, knit, and pack for soldiers and their wives. The entire community rallied around the special needs of the crisis.[8]

Contemporary Examples

When Hurricane Katrina devastated New Orleans and the surrounding region in 2005, becoming the costliest natural disaster in US history, the greatest army of workers to provide relief efforts came from church teams. Not only did churches from across the country send teams to help with rebuilding efforts, but existing church facilities in the affected area became staging grounds and support bases for those teams. Congregations worked with one another at unprecedented levels to rescue and rebuild these hard-hit areas.

Likewise, for international crises from Rwanda's genocide to Haiti's massive earthquake, churches have been quick to organize a response of prayer, physical resources, and human expertise.

Sometimes the crisis is real but short-term. When racial tension spilled into violence in Ferguson, Missouri, and Baltimore, Maryland, pastors and their congregations were among the first to offer help and be a voice of peace. When the Sandy Hook Elementary School massacre occurred in Newtown, Connecticut, local clergy, backed by other caregivers in their congregations, sprang into action.

Sometimes the crisis mobilization occurs with denominational help, such as the Southern Baptist state convention in Virginia. It created a "ready church" training program.[9] Over the years Virginia has faced college shootings, floods, tornadoes, hurricanes, earthquakes, massive industrial accidents, and more. Its "ready church" process develops teams to respond within the local church when events go wrong in their communities, mobilizing their members to make a difference. Each training offers necessary instruction for volunteers to respond with other Southern Baptists around the world. This concept sounds sticky, something other denominations could develop as well.

UK-based Tearfund works through churches to help the people in the world who are in the greatest need, regardless of race, religion, gender, or nationality. Founded in 1968, they have experience around the world in crisis mobilization. For example, after the Indian Ocean tsunami in 2004, many people lost their homes and were given temporary accommodation in camps. The Pentecostal Mission in Port Blair, the Andaman Islands, listened to, prayed for, and cared for people living in a camp and also served food to more than five hundred people a day. Emergency financial help and support came from Tearfund.

Tearfund's book, *Disasters and the Local Church*, identifies four basic types of disasters. This list, shown in figure 8.6, builds an appreciation for the scope of crisis mobilization opportunities. In addition each kind of crisis provides many different opportunities for the role of a church including immediate response, resource provision, compassion and care, influencing and shaping values, acting as a community peacemaker, facilitating community action, and advocating for marginalized people.[10]

Crisis Mobilization Applies to Many Types of Crises	
Bias	**Examples**
1. Slow-onset disasters	Drought, displacement, water-logging, long-term conflict
2. Rapid-onset disasters	Windstorms (hurricanes, cyclones, typhoons, tornadoes), earthquakes, volcanic eruptions, floods, flash floods, glacial lake bursts, tsunamis
3. Human-made disasters	War, civil strife, displacement, fire
4. Technological disasters	Severe pollution, nuclear accidents, air crashes, major fires, explosions

Figure 8.6

Exercise: Should This Vision Be Your Church's Focus?

1. How closely does this template match **your own vision** for your congregation as a gospel-centered, disciple-making church over the next ten years? Use a scale of 1 (low) to 10 (high):

    1 2 3 4 5 6 7 8 9 10

2. How would you rate your **key opinion leaders' buy-in** at present for this template as the focus of their vision? Same 1 (low) to 10 (high) scale:

    1 2 3 4 5 6 7 8 9 10

3. How would you rate the **entire congregation's buy-in** at present for this template as the focus of their vision? Same 1 (low) to 10 (high) scale:

    1 2 3 4 5 6 7 8 9 10

4. How would you rate the level of **momentum and progress to date** your church has made on this particular vision template? Same 1 (low) to 10 (high) scale:

     1   2   3   4   5   6   7   8   9   10

Now add up these four scores: _____ (You'll compare the tallies after you've reviewed all twelve templates.)

How Do You Rate on Vision That Rescues?

The three vision templates in this chapter each explored some aspect of vision that rescues. At the conclusion of each template, you rated how this model applies to your church. You'll do likewise for all twelve templates, and then I'll ask you to look back and see which one or two you scored as highest.

Chapter 9
Vision That Becomes

Him we proclaim, warning everyone and teaching everyone with all wisdom, that we may present everyone mature in Christ. For this I toil, struggling with all his energy that he powerfully works within me.

—Paul the apostle, Colossians 1:28–29

The previous chapter looked at vision that rescues. Now this chapter will look at three templates all characterized by vision that becomes. The dominant symbol or basic shape for becoming is the image of a circle to represent wholeness, completeness, and purity. The white colors represent God (see figure 9.1).

Vision that becomes is whole, healthy, authentic, and maturing. Becoming vision says, "Grow it!"

All three overflow templates are represented as figure 9.2, with the basic shape in the upper right.

Becoming through Spiritual Formation

Definition

Your church's vision is for a spiritual formation that changes people and takes them along a significant pathway toward spiritual maturity. You might state it as, "We will grow as God's people to reflect individually and corporately the spiritual maturity of Christ in specifically defined ways."

Circle Basic Shape for the Become Templates

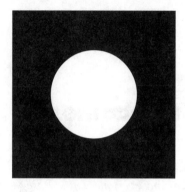

Figure 9.1

Three Become Templates
with Basic Shape

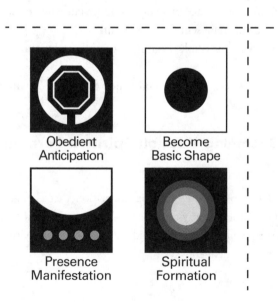

Obedient
Anticipation

Become
Basic Shape

Presence
Manifestation

Spiritual
Formation

Figure 9.2

Spiritual Formation Vision Template

Figure 9.3

Personal Snapshot

Newport Beach in California is one of the most idyllic locations to be in ministry. My first time visiting Saint Andrew's Presbyterian, located almost within visibility of the beach, the flowery aroma of the parking lot caught me by surprise. The nearby beach, the flowers and greenery, and the large yet cozy outdoor campus, made it one of the most pleasant walks from car to worship center I've ever experienced.

When Rich Kannwischer, a young and brilliant communicator, came in 2009 to lead Saint Andrew's, he paid close attention to the local culture, which he described as an intoxication of the good life—that is, the good life defined by the world. Spend one day in Newport and you'll feel the power of that image. For me it started with the Ferrari dealership across from the hotel, the counter of plastic surgery promotional cards at the local Banzai Bowl, the endless healthy eating options, and the countless joggers with their Lululemon-wrapped pristine bodies. Who else has named their local mall Fashion Island?

When it comes to church vision, Saint Andrew's chose to make a dynamic contrast from, while building on, the pursuit of the good life. God has a good life too, not defined by the image of the world but by His image, made crystal clear in the life of Jesus. Saint Andrew's mission is following Jesus Christ to lead lives that reveal *God's* goodness. They chose the spiritual formation vision template, and the church plans to use its strength in education, its intellectual bent, and its leadership influence to found a discipleship institute that will extend its robust and replicable model for growing believers.

Biblical Reflection

Maturity is an important goal for the New Testament church. The oft-quoted passage in Ephesians 4 about God raising up pastors (and other gifted individuals) is actually one long sentence in the Greek from verses 11 to 16. Using several different metaphors, the passage affirms that the goal of the church and its leaders is to grow the body of Christ into spiritual maturity. The visual force of Paul's teaching is conveyed by the contrasting image of silhouettes: a man's versus a young boy's. There's nothing wrong with being a boy, but there's something unnatural about staying a boy and not growing up to a full stature of maturity. See also Colossians 1:28 where Paul wants to "present everyone mature in Christ."

Another relevant passage is Acts 11:19–26 where the believers, after one year of teaching and growth, were called Christians for the first time in the biblical record—a term which means "little Christs." Why did it take a year? It required a season of formation from teaching and from applying and living out those teachings.

Consider as well the warning and exhortation to the seven churches in the book of Revelation. Note that the Spirit at times salutes a church for the *work they have done* but calls them to repent for *who they have become*. The spiritual formation template in this sense is more about *being* than *doing*. The church at Ephesus is commended for "your works, your toil and your patient endurance, and how you cannot bear with those who are evil" (Rev. 2:2). But then they are rebuked in verse 4: "You have abandoned the love you had at first."

What template do you use when your vision is to resurrect a life of love for Jesus across a congregation? The spiritual formation template.

Metaphors for Communication

Figure 9.3 shows a series of circles where, if white represents God across these symbols, the Holy Spirit is transforming people from the inside out. Think of the metamorphosis of a squirming caterpillar frozen in its cocoon only to become a gold and bold monarch butterfly.

Another image that depicts spiritual formation is a majestic tree, reaching not only upward and outward but founded by a strong, healthy root system that has also penetrated the ground deeply. Picture the individual described by Psalm 1:3: "He is like a tree planted by streams of water that yields its fruit in its season, and its leaf does not wither. In all that he does, he prospers."

Still other images that convey this idea are a seed falling on fertile ground or a water purification process. Imagine places that connote development, like a family having devotions around their dining room, a fitness center filled with exercise equipment, or a monastic setting made for silence and solitude.

Historical Examples

One essential component to spiritual formation is a solid understanding of Scripture. In earlier centuries most sermons in the United States were devotional, motivational, and/or topical three-point messages followed by a poem. Lawyer-turned-Bible-teacher C. I. Scofield influenced a large section of the evangelical world to use the Sunday morning sermon not as a motivational pulpit but to teach the Word of God. His *Scofield Reference Bible*, published in 1909 by Oxford University Press, became one of the most influential books of evangelical Christianity in the last century. It was one of the first published Bibles with doctrinal and study notes on which several generations of pastors and lay leaders built their teaching.[1]

Contemporary Examples

Some churches focus on a particular aspect of spiritual formation while others carry a special focus and energy for holistic development. An example of the latter is Robby Gallaty during his time at Brainerd Church and founder of a ministry named Replicate. Robby embodies a total focus on spiritual maturity as reproducing discipleship. Every story, every ministry environment, and every tool are shaped to transition a relatively traditional Baptist church to become a disciple-making force in Chattanooga. Their simple discipleship strategy to "worship, deliver, develop, and deploy" has become the "operating system" of the church.

Another example of a masterfully designed approach to spiritual formation is Randy Frazee's thirty core competencies or big ideas. Designed originally while pastoring Pantego Bible Church, the thirty-point definition of discipleship was initially published as a set of tools called the Christian Life Profile. It was rereleased by Harper Collins under the banner *Believe, Living the Story of the Bible to Become Like Jesus*. The tools for Believe (believethestory.com) are built around a spiritual-growth experience that helps Christians of all ages think, act, and be more like Jesus. The thirty big ideas are made up of ten key beliefs of the Christian faith, ten key practices of a Jesus follower, and ten key virtues of a person who is becoming more like Jesus.

The most impressive aspect of the tools is not the tools themselves but the idea of a church community using them together to grow collectively more like Jesus. When I consulted with Randy Frazee at his current church, Oak Hills in San Antonio, I was impressed by how deeply embedded these ideas are in his personal life. For example, when Randy runs, he prays through the thirty big ideas asking the Lord to direct where he needs to grow. It's amazing to me how many churches do not have a basic defini-tion of a disciple with accompanying ministries designed to produce disciple-making outcomes.

Some churches focus on one aspect of spiritual formation. Grace Fellowship in Katy, Texas, has focused their ultimate contribution as a church to be a "house of prayer for all nations." Being people of prayer is the cornerstone attribute of disciple-ship for them and the "mortar" that holds together everything they do as a church.

Watermark Community Church in greater Dallas believes so strongly in support-ing healthy marriages that they continually sponsor ministries designed to help couples have a winning marriage. They don't just talk about good marriages, but they invest time and resources as well. One of the simpler things they do is to sponsor occasional "Date Nights" for couples.[2] This may seem insignificant, but as one researcher dis-covered,[3] couples who spend two hours together at least once a week (a "date") have expressed a level of satisfaction 3.5 times higher than couples who don't date regularly each week.

Exercise: Should This Vision Be Your Church's Focus?

1. How closely does this template match **your own vision** for your congregation as a gospel-centered, disciple-making church over the next ten years? Use a scale of 1 (low) to 10 (high):

1   2   3   4   5   6   7   8   9   10

2. How would you rate your **key opinion leaders' buy-in** at present for this tem-plate as the focus of their vision? Same 1 (low) to 10 (high) scale:

1   2   3   4   5   6   7   8   9   10

3. How would you rate the **entire congregation's buy-in** at present for this tem-plate as the focus of their vision? Same 1 (low) to 10 (high) scale:

1   2   3   4   5   6   7   8   9   10

4. How would you rate the level of **momentum and progress to date** your church has made on this particular vision template? Same 1 (low) to 10 (high) scale:

1   2   3   4   5   6   7   8   9   10

Now add up these four scores: _____ (You'll compare the tallies after you've reviewed all twelve templates.)

Presence Manifestation Vision Template

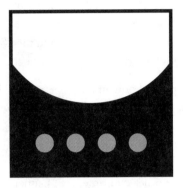

Figure 9.4

Becoming through Presence Manifestation

Definition

Your church's vision is to welcome and experience God's presence anticipating ripple effects far beyond the life of your congregation. You might state it as, "We will seek God's presence to be manifested to do whatever He wants and however He wants through our response, renewal, and revival."

Personal Reflection

When developing this template, I was thinking primarily of charismatic strands of evangelicalism and churches I have worked with in the Assembly of God, Foursquare denominations, and other faith tribes that are "supernaturally sensitive." I think of conversations with Vanguard University's leadership (an Assembly of God school), where the big idea of "opening worlds" represented not just the bodies of knowledge and vocational opportunity for undergraduate students but the Spirit-empowered life in God's supernatural world. Or I think of Visalia, California, First Assembly whose mission is "to help people see that God can do more than they believe," conveying the mind-stretching reality of God's present miraculous power.

But churches that work with the manifest presence template are not necessarily from a charismatic or Pentecostal background. One example is Hope Church in Las Vegas pastored by the founding planter, Vance Pitman. Vance and his team are deeply drawn to a practical expression of "the abiding life." Take note of the language they use to describe what they call the marks of abiding. Here are three from a list of fifteen they have articulated:

- **Intimacy:** Understands that God's primary call on my life is to be with Him, not to do things for Him.
- **Word:** Pursues time in, under, and around the Word, alone and with others.
- **Prayer:** Talks with God consistently, desperately, and expectantly.

To empower these spiritual outcomes, Hope uses a "5 percent time strategy" for how to build a relationship with God. All relationships require time, so Hope's ministry is designed around four kinds of time, including daily individual "God time" (fifteen minutes a day is 1 percent of your life's time) and "Go time" which is the investment of time with people in cross-cultural settings (one week of your year is 2 percent of your time). The other two times are "Gather time" (a weekly worship service) and "Group time" (a home-based small group setting with other believers) that each make up an additional 1 percent.

Not only is God's daily presence and emphasis individual, but it is an important part of sharing the church's history. Every significant event in the church's life can be directly attributed to God's intervention and leadership. For example, the unlikely idea that a pastor like Vance from the deep South should uproot his family and go to a city like Las Vegas. Or the unexpected dynamic of God's leading Hope to become a multiethnic church or rescuing them from a financial crisis that should have closed their doors. Hope does a lot as a church, but its primary template is based on God's speaking and showing up *first*.

Bible Reflections

The Israelites' wilderness journey contains many pictures of the Christian's walk with God today. The pillar of fire taught that when God moves, we move. When God does not move, we stay put as well (Exod. 40:36–38). The children of Israel would respond with awe and worship as God met with Moses: "When all the people saw the pillar of cloud standing at the entrance of the tent, all the people would rise up and worship, each at his tent door" (Exod. 33:10).

Likewise the New Testament, especially in the book of Revelation, forecasts the worship of heaven as a continual experience of God's presence before His throne. People in heaven don't even need the sun to shine "for the glory of God gives it light" (21:23; cf. 22:5) as God dwells among His people: "He will dwell with them, and they will be his people, and God himself will be with them as their God" (21:3).

Starting Point Metaphors

Figure 9.4 shows a big circle coming down upon smaller circles, representing God's coming down from heaven onto His people, descending on various people in church or other holy gatherings.

Another image that depicts manifest presence might be smoke rising from a fire, marked by power, vitality, uniqueness, and mystery. These qualities could symbolize God's pervasive presence in a church.

Still other images that convey this idea are Damascus road (Luke 24:32), worshippers with arms lifted, a crowd watching a countdown clock, raindrops beginning to fall, or a waterfall washing trees and rocks as it cascades.

Historical Examples

The book *A God-Sized Vision: Revival Stories that Stretch and Stir*[4] recounts the fascinating details of world-changing revivals, beginning with biblical events and continuing through awakenings and revivals of recent centuries. It also explores what these revivals have in common and how people prepare for them. A vision of God's manifest presence was often part of that preparation.

One illustration is Timothy Dwight, grandson of Jonathan Edwards (the key figure in North America's First Great Awakening in the 1730s) who became the president of Yale in 1795. At that time only 10 percent of Yale students would claim Christ's name in public, even though the school had been founded to produce great pastoral leaders. But Dwight believed in revival and led with several means of pursuing it: gospel preaching, Bible reading, prayer, talking with Christians, catechism, and self-examination. During his tenure revival broke out three different times. In his own words describing one of them:

> So sudden and great was the change in individuals, and in the general aspect of the college, that those who had been waiting for it were filled with wonder as well as joy, and those who knew not what it meant were awe-struck and amazed. Wherever students were found in their rooms, in the chapel, in the hall, in the college-yard, in their walks about the city, the reigning impression was, "Surely God is in this place." The salvation of the soul was the subject of thought, of conversation, of absorbing interest; the "peace in believing" which succeeded was not less strongly marked.[5]

The revival at Yale, like all revivals, owes its ultimate timing and power to God's sovereign initiative. But men and woman have nonetheless pursued a vision for revival and seen God work in dramatic ways in their lifetime. For Timothy Dwight, that meant a huge surge in the quality and quantity of fervent pastors who left Yale over the decades to influence the world with a similar vision.

Contemporary Examples

Vertical Church is an association of worship-centered churches pioneered by James MacDonald. He begins his book *Vertical Church* by asking, "Is your church experiencing a window-rattling, earth-shattering, life-altering encounter with the living God? That's not a common experience in North America today. But it should be. And it can be."[6] Worship that seeks and welcomes God's presence is a priority for churches like this.

When I navigated Bellevue Baptist Church, in greater Memphis, Tennessee, through a year of visioning, the church changed its one hundred-year template of anointing amplification to a new template of presence manifestation. Their ten-year vision is to be a *catalyst for spiritual awakening in Memphis and beyond*. This led to many new initiatives including a redesign of Sunday evening worship to become an "Awaken" service where pastors from across the city—including the different ethnic churches—preach and where multiple congregations come together to pray for spiritual awakening for the city.

Exercise: Should This Vision Be Your Church's Focus?

1. How closely does this template match **your own vision** for your congregation as a gospel-centered, disciple-making church over the next ten years? Use a scale of 1 (low) to 10 (high):

    1 2 3 4 5 6 7 8 9 10

2. How would you rate your **key opinion leaders' buy-in** at present for this template as the focus of their vision? Same 1 (low) to 10 (high) scale:

    1 2 3 4 5 6 7 8 9 10

3. How would you rate the **entire congregation's buy-in** at present for this template as the focus of their vision? Same 1 (low) to 10 (high) scale:

    1 2 3 4 5 6 7 8 9 10

4. How would you rate the level of **momentum and progress to date** your church has made on this particular vision template? Same 1 (low) to 10 (high) scale:

    1 2 3 4 5 6 7 8 9 10

Now add up these four scores: _____ (You'll compare the tallies after you've reviewed all twelve templates.)

Obedient Anticipation Vision Template

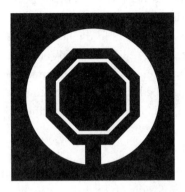

Figure 9.5

Becoming through Obedient Anticipation

Definition

Your church's vision is to live in strategic or obedient anticipation of more clear revelation from God and with the intent to respond as He leads. For now, however, you are waiting only, posturing to hear because God has not yet given direction. You might state it as, "We will posture our lives individually and corporately to hear from God and receive His direction for our congregation."

Personal Snapshot

For predictable reasons this template is not as familiar in my consulting experience because a church that waits doesn't need the kind of collaborative vision journey I guide.

A few years ago I talked at length with a pastor from Mississippi. As far as I could tell from a few hours of conversation over a several week period, he was as thoughtful, smart, and godly as any pastor I have met. He had read *Church Unique* and was a fan of Auxano. He really wanted to go through a visioning process but kept feeling a check in his spirit that was hard to identify.

As I probed and asked questions, I began to talk him out of the process. It became clear to me that God was calling him and his church to a season of strategic waiting. This pastor knew God was not ready to disclose the next stage of the church's ministry and believed some shared experience must come first. I discerned that he had 100 percent clarity and that it was important not to pursue a visioning process at this time.

As I mentioned earlier in the book, I was a spiritual formation pastor before I was a church vision consultant. In some ways I still am. During my seminary days I enjoyed reading the Christian mystics in the library more than my assigned reading. It's this influence of mystery, the reality that God is infinitely unfathomable, that leads me to have a "mystery template" or a "template of unknowing."

This is the heart of the obedient anticipation template: it's okay not to know. It's God's universe not ours. He is in control and sometimes, by faith, we wait.

Biblical Reflections

Throughout Scripture good things happen when people wait on God. As Isaiah 40:31 says, "They who wait for the LORD shall renew their strength; they shall mount up with wings like eagles; they shall run and not be weary; they shall walk and not faint."

God's Word abounds with examples of people taking an intentional pause while they wait on God's direction. Some are prominent like Abraham who waited numerous times on God's guidance. Other stories are told more succinctly, but it's easy to sense their heart, such as the prophet Habakkuk, to whom the Lord said: "Write the vision; make it plain on tablets, so he may run who reads it. For still the vision awaits its appointed time; it hastens to the end—it will not lie. If it seems slow, wait for it; it will surely come; it will not delay" (Hab. 2:2–3).

In Acts 1:4–5, Jesus ordered His disciples to wait in Jerusalem until they were baptized in the Holy Spirit. That happened on the day of Pentecost, but the New Testament church practiced other seasons of fastings and otherwise waiting on God before moving into action. Examples include the fasting of Acts 13:2–3 and 14:23 and the seasons of prayer implied in Acts 4:31; 10:4, 9, 30; 12:5, 12; 16:25; 22:17; and 27:29.

Starting Point Metaphors

Figure 9.5 shows something like a stop sign, perhaps God's voice indicating to wait and pause, instructing, "Don't go into the future yet."

Another image that depicts obedient anticipation is a door just starting to open with brightness pouring in; the wider the door opens, the more light will come through. Images of stillness come to mind like a pond on a quiet morning with a mirror-like unmoved surface.

Other images that convey this idea are kneeling in surrender to God and waiting on Him, sails or kites awaiting the wind, or an airplane on a runway.

Historical Examples

Many books on revival describe a stage where God's people wait on God in prayer, looking for instruction and leading. Leonard Ravenhill, author of *Why Revival Tarries* and other books on the topic, emphasized the season of waiting as essential. "We mistake the scaffolding for the building," he would say. Armin Gesswein, another great preacher and writer on revival, saw seasons of waiting in prayer as foundational to revivals in the book of Acts as well as to historic revivals from Norway to New York City.

Contemporary Examples

Many in the charismatic world know of The Church on the Way, Van Nuys, California, as, for many years, the largest-attendance church in the Foursquare denomination. Few know that early in its story the vision was simply to wait on God through prayer and worship. In 1969 Jack Hayford, age thirty-five, accepted a six-month position to pastor there. At the time the congregation regularly drew fewer than twenty people, and the average age was sixty-five or higher. One day as Hayford was praying, "There descended on me an awareness that I was to stay at the church," he says.[7] In another season of prayer he received the strong mental impression that God would bless the church "here," and even as attendance grew to exceed maximum seating capacity, he didn't want to expand or relocate the small church facility. He led the congregation to pray and wait "here" at that site until God made clear what the next chapter in their vision as a church should be.

Exercise: Should This Vision Be Your Church's Focus?

1. How closely does this template match **your own vision** for your congregation as a gospel-centered, disciple-making church over the next ten years? Use a scale of 1 (low) to 10 (high):

    1   2   3   4   5   6   7   8   9   10

2. How would you rate your **key opinion leaders' buy-in** at present for this template as the focus of their vision? Same 1 (low) to 10 (high) scale:

    1   2   3   4   5   6   7   8   9   10

3. How would you rate the **entire congregation's buy-in** at present for this template as the focus of their vision? Same 1 (low) to 10 (high) scale:

    1   2   3   4   5   6   7   8   9   10

4. How would you rate the level of **momentum and progress to date** your church has made on this particular vision template? Same 1 (low) to 10 (high) scale:

   1   2   3   4   5   6   7   8   9   10

Now add up these four scores: _____ (You'll compare the tallies after you've reviewed all twelve templates.)

How Do You Rate on Vision That Becomes?

The three vision templates in this chapter each explored some aspect of vision that becomes. At the conclusion of each template, you rated how this model applies to your church. You'll do likewise for all twelve templates, and then I'll ask you to look back and see which one or two you scored as highest.

Chapter 10
Vision That Overflows

Brothers and sisters, choose seven men from among you who are known to be full of the Spirit and wisdom. We will turn this responsibility over to them.

—Acts 6:3 NIV

The previous chapter looked at vision that becomes. Now this chapter will look at three templates all characterized by vision that overflows. The dominant symbol for overflow is the image of a wave. See figure 10.1. The white coloring, here and in all of the templates, represents the work of God. Vision that overflows is good, bountiful, extending, and blessing. Overflowing vision says, "Let it go!"

All three overflow templates are represented as figure 10.2, with the basic shape in the lower right.

Overflowing through Leadership Multiplication

Quick Definition

Your church's vision is to develop more leaders so as to take the church to where God wants you to go. You might state it as, "We will raise up and release leaders to accomplish whatever God calls them to do."

Wave Basic Shape for the Overflow Templates

Figure 10.1

Three Overflow Templates with Basic Shape

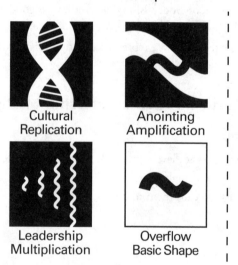

Cultural
Replication

Anointing
Amplification

Leadership
Multiplication

Overflow
Basic Shape

Figure 10.2

Leadership Multiplication Vision Template

Figure 10.3

Personal Snapshot

The day started at the "yellow box," the term for Community Christian Church's largest campus in Naperville, Illinois. I was grateful for another opportunity to learn from founding pastors Dave and Jon Ferguson and their team. From the onset as Dave shared the story of the church, it was clear that two things were important: reaching the city of Chicago and reproducing leaders. One of the first drawings Dave made was a general map of the city broken down into quadrants reflecting their desire to multiply and not just have one campus. You could see both values at play in the drawing. At the break I asked him what the bigger idea in his heart was: reaching the city or releasing leaders. (As you read through these templates, I want to encourage you to wrestle with this question. It's easy to like many of the templates, so keep forcing yourself to consider the *most* important one for your church.)

I remember watching Dave process my question. I had a hunch that reproducing leaders was the bigger idea. And indeed it was. Not only does Community Christian strive to develop leaders by multiplying at every level, but they have started a church-planting network called NewThing, a relational network designed to be a catalyst for movements of reproducing churches. If you listen to their introduction video, you will hear the word *reproduce* more than any other word (Newthing.org/about).

The heartbeat to model "we're always multiplying" is captured in their book titled *Exponential* with the subtitle *How You and Your Friends Can Start a Missional*

Church Movement.[1] Churches like this are comfortable with a lot of expressions of what those leaders do—some lead small groups, others start new campuses of this multisite church, others start entirely new churches through their NewThing network. Hybrid models are also welcome; what matters most is that leadership bubbles up and goes anywhere. As Bill Easum comments, "The only way they can achieve such multiplication is because they have a culture of developing leaders. They develop leaders whether or not they need them because they want to see people grow in their faith, not because they want people to run their programs."[2]

Biblical Reflections

Exodus 18 is one of the quintessential leadership texts in the Bible. Before Israel could accomplish anything of significance after the exodus, it needed a full-scale leadership pipeline. Moses, with the prompting of his father-in-law, Jethro, was awakened to a massive leadership deficit and got to work to deploy leaders of tens, fifties, hundreds, and thousands, in the mobile community of over one million people. In the end God provided one leader for every eight Israelites. The problem was not a lack of leadership supply, for God had provided the leaders; it was the missing vision and strategy to discover and develop them.

Jesus' entire ministry was built around His training of the twelve apostles and of many other leaders as well, such as the women that traveled with the apostles and of the seventy. One poignant passage is Mark 3:14–15 where He called the twelve "that they might be with him," learning from His modeling, mentoring, and presence, and also that they might "have authority" as He trained them through empowering them. Jesus spent disproportionately greater time with three among the twelve—Peter, James, and John. These were not His favorites but a functional leadership core that received additional modeling and shared experiences with Jesus. Paul describes Peter, James, and John in Galatians 2:9 as those who are "reputed to be pillars" (NASB) in the church. Additionally we see the twelve multiplying sixfold in Luke 10:1 when the young movement multiplies.

Metaphors for Communication

Figure 10.3 shows wavy lines going out and increasing in size and number. These symbolize the multiplication of leaders rather than merely the addition of leaders. In this image picture a movement of people ever expanding, moving from left to right, or what my friend Alan Hirsch calls "the sneeze" of movement. (Imagine the wet particles of a sneeze spreading rapidly through the air at the moment of achoo.) Leadership multiplication is also pictured by boot-camp ideas of military training and the language of rounds and residencies of medical training. Other ideas include:

- **Launching and mobilizing:** Think rockets and aircraft carriers.
- **Reproducing and spreading:** Think greenhouses and unending rows of corn.
- **Releasing and sending:** Think commissioning and kicking someone out of the proverbial "nest."

Another image that depicts leadership multiplication is the mathematics of expanding exponentially, for example when a group of leaders keeps multiplying by two: 1, 2, 4, 8, 16, 32, 64, 128, 256, 512, etc. A church that doubled its leadership every year starting with one leader would have more than thirty million leaders in twenty-five years. An image like that could show the beginning of a network of multiplication, moving from a few to a potentially unlimited outcome.

Still other images that convey this idea are healthy antibodies spreading, a viral video, an image of an acorn with a forest inside, or kudzu vines that take over a field or mountain.

> A church that doubled its leadership every year starting with one leader would have more than thirty million leaders in twenty-five years.

Historical Examples

The Protestant Reformation, with its emphasis on faith alone and Scripture alone, laid the foundation for the liberation of the laity to exercise new levels of leadership. Teachings on the priesthood of the believer (see 1 Pet. 2:5, 8) and on equipping the saints to do the work of ministry (see Eph. 4:11–12) are at the heart of recent movements about body life, spiritual gifts, and lay mobilization.

In 1951, a student at Fuller Theological Seminary named Bill Bright received a unique impression from God, while studying Greek, to invest his life to help reach the entire world starting with college students.[3] Within the first year 250 students would receive Christ through the ministry, and six staff would join. For the next six decades, what's known today as Cru would grow to be one of the largest Christian ministries in the world with more than twenty-seven thousand staff and 225,000 volunteers in 190 countries.

How did this ministry expand so rapidly over the decades? Cru is known for its world revolutionary leadership training in evangelism and discipleship. While I was never on staff, my role in student leadership in the late 1980s changed my life. I can still remember the tools and training I received, and I can still recite the Four Spiritual Laws by memory! Bill Bright could have never created that impact without the core conviction that one person could change the world through the power of multiplication. And while I never personally met Bill, he, indirectly through leadership multiplication, passed that belief on to me.

Contemporary Examples

In recent meetings with the leaders of Kensington Community Church in Troy, Michigan, I've been blown away by their commitment to multiply leaders. Kensington has been noted as one of America's top twenty-five multiplying churches.[4] Steve Andrews, Dave Wilson, and Mark Nelson are cofounders of the church and display a rare blend of apostolic, evangelistic, and prophetic functions (respectively) that keep their scorecard focused on mobilizing the next person and group. Whether it's a new church, campus (local or translocal), or ministry, the biggest idea of the church is mobilization. They have planted scores of churches (giving an impressive portion of their budget toward multiplication) while growing their own attendance to fifteen thousand in worship across seven campuses and spinning off countless ministries like Portable Church Industries.

Another church noted for multiplication is Larry Walkemeyer, pastor of Light & Life Christian Fellowship in Long Beach, California. Light & Life is highlighted in Todd Wilson's book on multiplication entitled *Spark*. Larry recounts his "conversion" from a mind-set of addition growth to multiplication growth: "The vision was to stop becoming a lake church and instead become a river church. In a lake church, people flow in and stay. It seeks to get more and more people around one pastor in one place. In a river church, the people flow in but keep moving downstream. God takes them to other places to minister. The measurement becomes about 'flow rate' instead of 'volumes contained'; about 'gallons per minute' instead of 'gallons retained.'"[5]

Exercise: Should This Vision Be Your Church's Focus?

1. How closely does this template match **your own vision** for your congregation as a gospel-centered, disciple-making church over the next ten years? Use a scale of 1 (low) to 10 (high):

    1   2   3   4   5   6   7   8   9   10

2. How would you rate your **key opinion leaders' buy-in** at present for this template as the focus of their vision? Same 1 (low) to 10 (high) scale:

    1   2   3   4   5   6   7   8   9   10

3. How would you rate the **entire congregation's buy-in** at present for this template as the focus of their vision? Same 1 (low) to 10 (high) scale:

    1 2 3 4 5 6 7 8 9 10

4. How would you rate the level of **momentum and progress to date** your church has made on this particular vision template? Same 1 (low) to 10 (high) scale:

    1 2 3 4 5 6 7 8 9 10

Now add up these four scores: ____ (You'll compare the tallies after you've reviewed all twelve templates.)

Cultural Replication Vision Template

Figure 10.4

Overflowing through Cultural Replication

Quick Definition

Your church's vision is to replicate its model, whether via multisite or other forms, spilling over to many places, new franchises, and new brands of "our" kind of ministry. You might state it as, "We will expand our influence by starting more campuses or church expressions that carry our ministry philosophy, unified vision, and brand."

Personal Snapshot

What does it feel like to be a church with the ability to do cultural replication? Unique! Let me introduce you to Ken Werlein, pastor of Faithbridge Church in Houston, who pastors what is currently the fastest-growing church in the United Methodist denomination.[6] Ken doesn't just empower others, but he does so with as a cultural-savvy style. You might describe the Faithbridge fusion as a blend of Wesleyan spirituality that brings fervent prayer together with an amazingly transparent leadership style and disciple-making zeal. Faithbridge is truly one of a kind. While they are involved in church planting efforts in their city, their greatest contribution is to expand by replicating the Faithbridge DNA. Ken is a cultural architect in the truest sense. He doesn't build with wood and steel but with values, leadership philosophy, and brand reputation. Some of the skills Ken embodies include a big-picture perspective but also attention to detail, a bias for action but a sensitivity to people. Most importantly Ken releases other leaders to represent the Faithbridge culture to keep it "overflowing" to others.

How does Ken champion and protect the culture? Like all the churches I serve through Auxano, Ken has developed a Vision Frame that captures the unique mission, values, strategy, and mission measures of the church. But Ken is particularly adept at continuing to emphasize the culture itself, allowing the time for each new wave of staff to deeply process and rehearse how Faithbridge has become who it is.

People in the city love Faithbridge. One public school, aware of the interest for church plants to rent their space, actually invited Faithbridge to apply as a rentor. While Faithbridge is not in a hurry to franchise (true cultural architects rarely are), there is no question that cultural replication will be their long-range template.

Biblical Reflections

The New Testament offers many healthy examples of imitation and modeling, such as the church in Thessalonica: "And you became *imitators* of us and of the Lord, for you received the word in much affliction, with the joy of the Holy Spirit, so that you became an *example* to all the believers in Macedonia and in Achaia" (1 Thess. 1:6–7, emphasis added). In the next chapter Paul commends them as "imitators of the churches of God in Christ Jesus that are in Judea" (1 Thess. 2:14).

In like manner Paul established consistent teaching among the churches he planted. "This is my rule in all the churches," he said at one point (1 Cor. 7:17). He likewise also established similar structures among all church plants, such as appointing elders "in every church" (Acts 14:23). Paul also directed his followers like Titus to follow suit: "Appoint elders in every town as I directed you" (Titus 1:5).

The Jerusalem Council (Acts 15:1–35) was a watershed event in the life of the early church as leaders prayerfully wrestled with whether the requirements to follow Jesus should be the same for both Jews and Gentiles. One major question was which Jewish practices Gentile believers would need to follow. The decision was to define a set of universal qualifications, which were then to be replicated across all new congregations. These issues were difficult ones as many New Testament chapters, such as in

Galatians and Romans, had to keep showing believers how to walk in the freedom of grace without abusing it.

Starting Point Metaphors

Figure 10.4 shows a DNA strand, which carries the components of life, containing everything necessary to replicate a culture an infinite number of times.

Another way to depict cultural replication is the idea of an apple full of seeds, each of which leads to an entire orchard and a similar-looking orchard at that.

Still other images that convey this idea are a restaurant franchise system, a chain of department stores, seashell fractals in nature, a message being retweeted on Twitter, or a fish or other animal that can birth dozens if not hundreds of near-identical babies.

Historical Examples

Calvary Chapel Costa Mesa, started in 1965 in Southern California, has birthed an association of more than sixteen hundred churches, all recognizable as examples of cultural replication. Whichever Calvary Chapel you visit, you're likely to find the same characteristics: an emphasis on the teaching of the Word of God, typically using an expositional approach, accompanied by a strong emphasis on worship. See Donald E. Miller's *Reinventing American Protestantism*[7] for more on the Calvary Chapel approach to training prospective pastors and raising up new churches.

Contemporary Examples

Some of the more well-known and codified church cultures that have turned into franchise models include Northpoint Ministries pastored by Andy Stanley, LifeChurch. tv pastored by Craig Groschel, and Hillsong Australia led by Brian Houston. At the time of this writing, Hillsong has thirty-six sites in ten countries. Northpoint Church has its "Northpoint Partners" which includes thirty-two churches, most of which are in North America, and LifeChurch.tv shows forty-eight churches, mostly in North America.

The advantage of being a NorthPoint Partner illustrates the value of being a franchise. The leader doesn't need to articulate the ministry philosophy or strategy from scratch but can utilize, for example, the language of strategic environments (foyer, living room, kitchen), the five faith catalysts, and a host of other curricula (Starting Point, Orange) as well as frequently beaming in Andy Stanley himself for the Sunday morning teaching event.

Exercise: Should This Vision Be Your Church's Focus?

1. How closely does this template match **your own vision** for your congregation as a gospel-centered, disciple-making church over the next ten years? Use a scale of 1 (low) to 10 (high):

    1 2 3 4 5 6 7 8 9 10

2. How would you rate your **key opinion leaders' buy-in** at present for this template as the focus of their vision? Same 1 (low) to 10 (high) scale:

    1 2 3 4 5 6 7 8 9 10

3. How would you rate the **entire congregation's buy-in** at present for this template as the focus of their vision? Same 1 (low) to 10 (high) scale:

    1 2 3 4 5 6 7 8 9 10

4. How would you rate the level of **momentum and progress to date** your church has made on this particular vision template? Same 1 (low) to 10 (high) scale:

    1 2 3 4 5 6 7 8 9 10

Now add up these four scores: _____ (You'll compare the tallies after you've reviewed all twelve templates.)

Anointing Amplification Vision Template

Figure 10.5

Overflowing through Anointing Amplification

Quick Definition

Your church's vision is to do all you can to leverage and amplify the impact of a particular leader, often someone who is a stellar teacher. You might state it as, "We will promote the special gifting and anointing of a person whom God chose to make a unique contribution to our society or world."

Personal Snapshot

Like many I was a bit skeptical when First Baptist Dallas announced what would become a $135 million building project to recreate the presence of the church in downtown. *What else could you do with that money?* many wondered. But when I learned more about their history, context, and culture, my perspective changed to imagine God's smile on the massive project.

First, it's important to consider the legacy of First Dallas. Pastors like George Truett and W. A. Criswell were nationally known and politically active over a century. In 2006 the church's pastoral search committee carefully considered more than 150 candidates to stem the tide of attendance decline and restore First Dallas's national platform. Robert Jeffress was selected in 2007 to be the next pastor. The church's vision is to be a national voice for biblical truth, guided by the mission to transform our world with the power of God's Word, one life at a time.

Behind that vision is an anointing amplification template. Truett and Criswell were anointed leaders, not just preachers but champions for biblical truth. Robert Jeffress is a relatively short person, but when he steps into the pulpit, he is a gladiator. The world-class investment into a facility and extensive search for the right leader reflect a 150-year-old strength to amplify God's Word and the practical forcefulness of it.

How many pastors give dozens of interviews on Fox News each year for political and cultural commentary? How many pastors have been aired on HBO's brashly liberal *Real Time with Bill Maher*? Robert Jeffress has and continues to baffle his would-be detractors with an endearing kindness as he boldly proclaims the power and practicality of God's Word. He leads with humble genius and represents God's Word with simple clarity, unwavering confidence, and honest kindness. And that's what makes Jeffress so meaningful to the people of First Dallas.

The credibility of the congregationally owned vision was validated through a congregational survey Auxano conducted just before the opening of their facility. It revealed that over 90 percent of the congregation is motivated to have a public voice for God's Word with the primary result of cultivating everyday boldness for representing Jesus and sharing the Bible with others.

Biblical Reflections

Throughout the Bible, God raises up people for a certain time, anointing them in the sense of choosing them, from judges to kings, from artists to prophets. Each was raised up with the sense, as Esther, "for such a time as this" (Esther 4:14).

As just one example, Exodus 17 shows how people sought to magnify the gifts of Moses. The Israelites were encountering their first opposition while wandering in the desert. While Joshua led the troops into battle against the Amalekites, Moses, along with Aaron and Hur, watched from a nearby hill. Exodus 17:11 reads, "Whenever Moses held up his hand, Israel prevailed, and whenever he lowered his hand, Amalek prevailed." Eventually, Moses became weary, so Aaron and Hur held up his arms until the Israelites were finally able to repel the Amalekites.

In the New Testament the story of choosing seven new leaders in Acts 6, often interpreted as the first deacons being named, is in part motivated by needing to free the apostles to use their gifts to reach as many people as possible. "It is not right that we should give up preaching the word of God to serve tables," the apostles said, so the new role was created so the apostles could devote themselves "to prayer and to the ministry of the word" (Acts 6:2, 4).

Similarly, Ephesians 4 speaks of exercising whatever gifts you've been given, so that those gifts can be amplified. For example: "If your gift is serving others, serve them well. If you are a teacher, teach well" (Rom. 12:7 NLT).

As church consultant Bill Easum comments: "All people are equal in the sight of God, but not all leaders are equal, not even in God's sight. In fact, treating all leaders as if they're equal, even for fairness' sake, is not only unrealistic, it's not biblical. Jesus chose twelve from the crowd to be his apostles. Then he selected Peter, James and John to be in his inner circle. Ultimately, he charged only Peter to be the keeper of the flock."[8]

Another example of gift amplification is how the church in Philippi had a special "partnership in the gospel" with Paul (Phil. 1:4–5; 4:14–16). They supported him, cared for him, and resourced him in his missionary journeys. Apparently they saw one of their roles in amplifying his gifts.

Metaphors for Communication

Figure 10.5 shows a small wave within the big wave, indicating that the smaller wave is being amplified.

Another way to depict anointing amplification might be the way people rally behind a personally impacted figure to elevate to public awareness a particular cause that may otherwise never have been recognized apart from that figure's circumstance.

Still other images that convey this idea are a magnifying glass, a megaphone, and a ship's wheel or rudder.

Historical Examples

At age twenty Charles Spurgeon's anointing as a gifted preacher was so evident that he was invited to become pastor of one of London's largest-attendance churches. He pastored there from 1854 to 1892. In his early years the crowds grew so large the twelve-hundred-seat facility filled quickly. The church relocated to a larger setting, and during Spurgeon's heyday its five thousand seats were filled many times a week, with the remainder of the crowd standing in the yard outside, listening from as far away as Spurgeon's voice could be heard.

Contemporary Examples

It's easy to think of dozens of nationally known preachers and teachers whose churches or ministries amplify their gifts with radio, television, and/or the Internet. But what makes this vision template useful for a church is when the congregation's vision is wed to the platform. To validate the connection, usually look for some continuity between the gifting of the individual leader and the culture of the church. In other words, if you lose the leader, some special ability the leader possessed is resident in the body.

For example, when I worked with Max Lucado at Oak Hills, while he was the senior minister, a storytelling identity was built into the fabric of discipleship, distinct from but related to Max's special gift of storytelling and writing. Or when Chuck Swindoll planted Stonebriar Community Church in Frisco, Texas, a congregation was formed around his gift for expository preaching and his emphasis on a lifestyle marked with joy. They articulated their mission around the idea of a joy-filled relationship with Christ, and they plan services around a preaching time that enables for two, twenty-two-minute radio messages. When I visited both churches, Oak Hills in San Antonio and Stonebriar in Frisco, tour buses of people from other churches were visiting these well-known communicators.

Another example is Bellevue Baptist Church in greater Memphis, Tennessee. Bellevue has had only a handful of senior pastors since its founding in 1903. Most recently Adrian Rogers was pastor from 1972 to 2005, followed by Steve Gaines through the present. The church has a long heritage of world-renowned Bible teachers, whose teaching ministry has overflowed from the church across the globe. From the church's television, radio, and Internet broadcasts to its large seating-capacity auditoriums—a three-thousand-seater built in 1952, a seven-thousand-seater built in 1989—everything you see in that culture was meant to magnify gifts and anointing of their teaching ministry.

Exercise: Should This Vision Be Your Church's Focus?

1. How closely does this template match **your own vision** for your congregation as a gospel-centered, disciple-making church over the next ten years? Use a scale of 1 (low) to 10 (high):

    1 2 3 4 5 6 7 8 9 10

2. How would you rate your **key opinion leaders' buy-in** at present for this template as the focus of their vision? Same 1 (low) to 10 (high) scale:

    1 2 3 4 5 6 7 8 9 10

3. How would you rate the **entire congregation's buy-in** at present for this template as the focus of their vision? Same 1 (low) to 10 (high) scale:

    1 2 3 4 5 6 7 8 9 10

4. How would you rate the level of **momentum and progress to date** your church has made on this particular vision template? Same 1 (low) to 10 (high) scale:

    1 2 3 4 5 6 7 8 9 10

Now add up these four scores: _____ (You'll compare the tallies after you've reviewed all twelve templates.)

How Do You Rate on Vision That Overflows? How Does That Template Compare to Others?

The three vision templates in this chapter each explored some aspect of vision that overflows. At the conclusion of each template, you rated how this model applies to your church.

Now it's time to compare your scores on all twelve templates from chapters 7 to 10. Please write them below. Note especially the one or two you scored as highest. Then before reading further, discuss the suitability of these templates as an expression of your church's disciple-making vision.

Write the scores from the exercises, in order from highest to lowest and the corresponding name of each vision template:

Which Vision Templates Seem Closest to Your God Dream?		
Write your scores from the previous exerecises in order from highest to lowest. Also write the corresponding name of each vision template.		
	Score	Name of Vision Template
1.		
2.		
3.		
4.		
5.		
6.		
7.		
8.		
9.		
10.		
11.		
12.		

Figure 10.6

Where Do These Templates Lead?

I hope you will pause now to experience meaningful dialogue as a team around these twelve vision templates. I've observed many times, as I've watched these conversations begin in various churches, that a moment of God's revelation often occurs, an "aha!" discovery that proves to be meaningful. Typically it happens as you're looking at one of these vision templates and someone notices, "Wow, we're a such-and-such model, and I never realized it before." Or "historically our church was this model, but in recent years we've been moving to that model."

The twelve vision templates are not meant to limit you but to offer a meaningful sense of trajectory for your beyond-the-horizon vision. The next chapter will help you do just that, leading your team to select two top vision templates that you'll combine into one idea and direction.

Take a peek at figure 10.7 on the next page for how the twelve templates all fit together, and then let's jump into finding and focusing the Horizon Storyline for your own church.

Twelve Vision Templates Overview
Surrounding the Four Basic Shapes

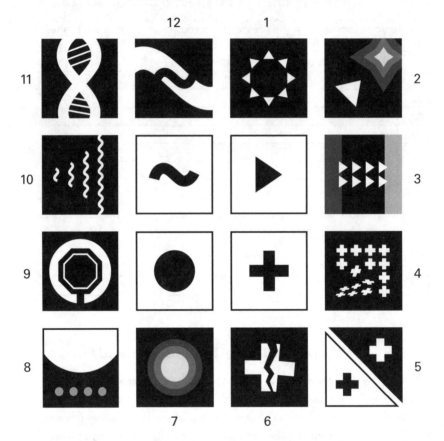

Advance Templates
1. Geographic Saturation
2. Targeted Transformation
3. People-Group Penetration

Become Templates
7. Spiritual Formation
8. Presence Manifestation
9. Obedient Anticipation

Rescue Templates
4. Institutional Renovation
5. Need Adoption
6. Crisis Mobilization

Overflow Templates
10. Leadership Multiplication
11. Cultural Replication
12. Anointing Amplification

Figure 10.7

Chapter 11
Creating a Picture Idea of Your Vision

The most valuable of all talents is that of never using two words when one will do.

—Thomas Jefferson

Now that you have taken a whirlwind trip looking over the twelve templates, it's time to land the plane on an image unique to your church. In order to paint the picture of your church's future, you will select and relate *two* of the twelve templates you just read about and create a *single* picture idea. The next chapters will help you develop a vivid description of that picture.

Your beyond-the-horizon vision is the context for framing your ministry's future. In Bible study you probably learned the little phrase that "context is everything." If you take a verse out of context, it can easily lose its intended meaning. This is likewise true with your visionary planning.

This chapter will provide a how-to debrief for you and your team after everyone has toured the templates in the previous chapters. Specifically I'll address three practical questions:

- How long should your long-range thinking be? I will provide six guidelines to help you tailor this question for your church.
- How do you make a final decision on which templates best represent your church's future? To answer this question I will walk you step-by-step through the primary exercises I use.

- How do you take your top two templates and create one picture idea from them? The compelling nature of your long-range vision comes from being rooted in one big dream.

As we work through this chapter, let's go back to our earlier definition: Your beyond-the-horizon vision is a narrative (up to twenty sentences) that vividly describes your church's future for the purpose of inspiring people and providing a context for more specific planning. Think of a beyond-the-horizon vision as the future picture of your church and a declaration of your congregation's ultimate contribution. It is a destination in time that you choose somewhere between five and twenty years.

Initial Exercise: Narrowing to the Top Two

Part 3 of *God Dreams* has been serving as a virtual tour guide. Now that you've visited twelve dreamy destinations, it's time to discern where God wants your church to go!

This baseline exercise involves a team debrief of the initial assessment questions for each of the twelve vision templates (chapters 7–10). With four questions per template, each person on your team has potentially assessed forty-eight questions. For many teams, this is all you will need. Next use the recommended steps below to select and relate your top *two* templates.

Overall Goal: In an initial two-hour session, review individual feedback from the assessments in chapters 7–10 with the right size group (see Step 1 below) in order to *select* your top *two* templates. The next exercise will be to *relate* them to each other.

Step 1. Choose the right team.

The team should have no more that twelve people in the room with five to nine being ideal. If you need to get feedback from a larger group of people, be sure to clarify that it is "input only" and not a final decision-making group. Take as much time to listen to broader groups for input as you need, but have a "right-sized," empowered leadership team in the room when you make the final decision.

Step 2. Don't start the collaborative session without serious prayer.

Let me recommend some of the prayers that our Auxano team regularly uses in consulting for you to adapt for your own prayer time. See GodDrea.ms/prayer.

Step 3. Ask each individual to share.

Using the quick assessments across chapters 7–10, engage a collaborative conversation with your leadership team. Ask all team members to review their responses for each template (using the averages of all four questions) in order to identify the two highest-ranking templates. Then let all team members share their top two templates and how strongly they feel about them. When I facilitate, I like to have a visual representation on a white pad. I then record the team members' top two votes on the pad, drawing check marks for each vote. For example, the team has nine members, I will record the eighteen votes as follows (see figure 11.1).

Example of How to Record Your Team's Voting

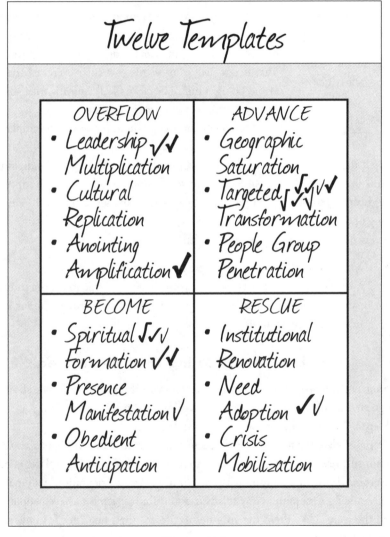

Figure 11.1

The team prays and votes, and the visual representation by itself will produce the top two templates based on team discussion.

If the top two templates are not abundantly clear from the tally of the team's impressions, I encourage dialogue around this question until the team decides. I encourage the following question as the final litmus test: What template represents both our deepest longing as leaders and the future toward which our people will respond most heroically?

As you finalize your selection, be aware of one important principle: There is no right answer. Sometimes a team gets stuck because they are paralyzed by the need to be precise or accurate in attempting to understand the future. That is not the point of this particular exercise. The goal is not to be right but to be clear. God's Spirit is with you. Trust His leadership in your group dialogue.

> The goal is not to be right but to be clear.

Step 4: Acknowledge the top *two* vision templates and reflect briefly as a team.

With the top two templates clearly identified, give a moment for individuals on the team to respond. Your goal is to increase the understanding *of* and appreciation *for* the top two templates. You are creating a shared experience that will increase the meaning of the exercise.

A few questions you might ask include:

- What do you like best about these two templates?
- What do these templates mean to you when you think about the future?
- Can you imagine our entire congregation becoming excited about a future defined by these templates? How so?

Next Exercise: Creating One Single Idea

Step 1. Before beginning your next session with this group, everyone should read through the rest of this chapter. Plan for an additional two-hour session.

Step 2. As you gather, again pray for God's leading.

Step 3. Relate the top two templates in some way in order to create a *single* idea.

I am surprised how many times the step of relating the two templates is obvious to the group. Those in the group with the gift of "strategic orientation" will make con-nections quickly. One simple way to advance this fourth step is to have people pair up around the team. Give them five minutes to present their best idea for how to relate the top two templates. Use the first five ways covered below as illustrations: *cause and effect, cyclical, combined (in some manner), staging, or by means of.* Do not limit ideas of relating templates to these initial illustrations. They are simply here to spark your own thoughts.

Invite each pair to share their ideas. As you do, look for patterns from the different pairs and keep an eye out for the ideas that create the most energy from the team. Take as much time as needed to make a final decision.

How Long Should You Be Thinking?

Which time frame should you choose: five years or twenty? Generally speaking, the longer your church has been around and has continued to grow, the longer your time frame can be. The answer is not an exact science, but you can follow these six general guidelines based on your church's age and life stage.

Guideline 1. If your church is new or less than five years old, the beyond-the-horizon time frame shouldn't be longer than five years. Why? Because your credibility for a longer vision time frame is still being established.

Guideline 2. If your church is five to twenty years old and is still growing, you may consider a time frame in the future that matches but is not longer than the age of the church. It is always fine to choose less. For example, if you are having a ten-year anniversary, you might imagine your beyond-the-horizon for the next ten years. (It has nice symmetry when vision casting.) But if for any reason five years feels more natural, then five years is okay.

Guideline 3. If the church is five to twenty years old and is plateaued or declining, I recommend using five years. Why? Because your credibility for longer term vision is contingent on demonstrating organization renewal or turnaround.

Guideline 4. If the church has a history of more than twenty years and is coming from a position of strength, then you can set a longer time frame of ten, fifteen, or twenty years. A position of strength might include a positive numerical growth trajectory, strong financial growth despite attendance plateau, or a new and highly trusted and/or demonstrated leader takes the helm of a stable church.

Guideline 5. If your church has a history of more than twenty years and is plateaued or declining, set the time frame for five or ten years. The more the decline, the shorter the horizon should be.

Guideline 6. Use both the church's anniversary years and even calendar years to set a date that best corresponds to an approximate five-, ten-, fifteen-, or twenty-year time frame, based on the general rules. For example, if your church celebrates a ten-year anniversary in 2016, consider either a nine-year vision that rounds out to the quarter-century marker of 2025, or an even-year ten-year vision that goes until 2026.

At this point the difference is subjective and artistic and should be chosen based on what makes the most sense for motivational purposes.

How Do I Know Which Templates to Use?

Let's answer this question by providing several exercises to use for discernment and clarification. As you review each exercise, keep in mind that you are trying to *select* and *relate* the top two templates for your church.

First, you will *select* your top two templates.

Remind your planning team that the purpose of the templates is to create a starting point for painting a picture with words. You are choosing a doorway, if you will, that will lead to a more fully described vision. And the doorway is best defined as the interrelationship between the top two templates. The primary value for the templates, whether, for example, it is "leadership multiplication" or "need adoption," is how they assist you in the picture-making process. Therefore the next step will be assigning a smaller team (three people maximum) to actually develop a vivid description. The templates themselves are not the vision but rather a stepping-stone for further development of the vision. *Keep in mind that the ownership of the vision is transferred strongly through the decision-making around the template itself more than the final development of the picture.*

Second, you will *relate* your top two templates.

Not only will you choose the top two templates, but you will connect them in a meaningful way. Try to show a relationship between the top two templates. Here are several examples of kinds of relationships between templates.

- *Cause and effect:* "Spiritual Formation *that leads to* Geographic Saturation"

    For example, The Heights Baptist Church in metro Dallas, Texas, wants to see everyday missionaries "take personal risks" through six personal crossroads of missional engagement, unique to the 750,000 people within the reach of their crossroads of US-75 and the George Bush Turnpike.

- *Cyclical:* "Leadership Multiplication *that results in* Targeted Transformation *that produces more* Leadership Multiplication"

    For example, Newbreak Church in San Diego, California, wants to multiply and send leaders into the many unique community identities of San Diego. Through the transformation of these neighborhoods, leaders will continually be multiplied and sent into new neighborhood pockets to establish "campus causes."

- *Combined:* "Leadership Multiplication *integrated with* Need Adoption"

For example, by the end of 2015, Stadia (a church-planting organization) will have planted more than 235 churches in the US and more than ninety in Latin America catalyzed by meeting the physical, emotional, and spiritual needs of children. The churches planted will correspond with more than seventeen thousand children sponsored in collaboration with Compassion International.

- *Staging:* "Institutional Renovation *in order to pursue* Geographic Saturation"

  For example, in 2016, Calvary Church in Clearwater, Florida, will celebrate its 150th anniversary. The year prior, Pastor Willy Rice celebrated a ten-year run characterized by institutional renovation—an amazing success story of relocation, successive building projects, and a renewed culture mission—"building relationships that bring people to dynamic life in Christ." As a vibrant and growing congregation, they are prepared to launch campusing and planting initiatives guided primarily by geographic gospel saturation for the next ten years.

- *By means of:* "People Group Penetration *by means of* Institutional Renovation"

  For example, Antioch Church of the Y, in Lebanon, Ohio, is led by David Newman who has started a network for churches that meet in YMCAs. His vision is to see this long-established evangelical organization (which has drifted in practice from its original up-front evangelical intent) revitalized as a platform for church planting all over the world. He hopes to see a church in every one of the YMCAs fourteen thousand global locations.

The power of the idea will come from its singularity. That is, you are using two templates to articulate one idea.

It is fine, by the way, to use a single template if the team does not need two. But most teams will naturally find two they want to connect or relate in some way.

Now let me show you some additional exercises your team can use.

Additional Exercises

Depending on the clarity gained from the baseline exercise, you may want to engage further exercises. In some cases these exercises bring further perspective and clarity if your team gets stuck. In addition, these exercises always bring additional meaning to the group and will help for the next step of creating a vivid description. In other words, while you many not need these additional exercises, you can't lose by taking the time to do them.

The step-by-step guide for each of these exercises is available at the URL GodDrea. ms/exercises.

Visionary Style Exercise

The basic template categories defined by the four shapes—advances, rescues, becomes, and overflows—each reflect an underlying leadership style.

I use a basic matrix to describe the leader's "spark," or the point of origination of the vision, and the leader's "posture," which speaks to how a leader engages the future. The "spark" or initial idea of the vision can come from one of two places, either outside the leader (external) or inside of the leader (internal). For example, when Nehemiah heard the report of the broken walls of Jerusalem (Neh. 1:3), his vision came from an external spark. By contrast, Abraham's being called by God (Gen. 12:1–4) represents an internal spark. The posture is defined as either initiating or responding. An initiating leading tends to act first and then observe, and a responding leader tends to observe first and then act.

You can use the visionary style exercise as an added dimension for collaboration with the twelve templates or if your church's polity empowers one person to provide direction for the future. For example, if I am working with the strong visionary senior pastor and the church is ready for direction, the visionary style of the senior leader can play a disproportionately greater weightiness in decision making (see figure 11.2).

Church Achievements Exercise

Another exercise you can do with your team that will enrich your understanding of the templates is a short historical review of the church's greatest achievements. I typically take about forty-five minutes and walk through a list of top achievements, telling stories along the way. Depending on the age of the church, I will have a list of five to fifteen high points. Then for each one I ask the church what template the achievement represents.

This simple exercise helps your team gain perspective of the longer trajectory of accomplishment and impact many churches experience. In some cases this helps crystallize quickly what the next five, ten, or fifteen years should look like.

Team Member Ultimate Contribution Exercise

As you move toward developing one idea for the beyond-the-horizon, it will become evident that not every person sees and feels the vision in the same way. I like to have an exercise for the key leadership team members to share how they feel about their individual contribution to the vision. I recommend taking a moment to have each team member answer the question: *As we move toward the vision that God has for us, what do you want your ultimate contribution to be; that is, in what way has God used*

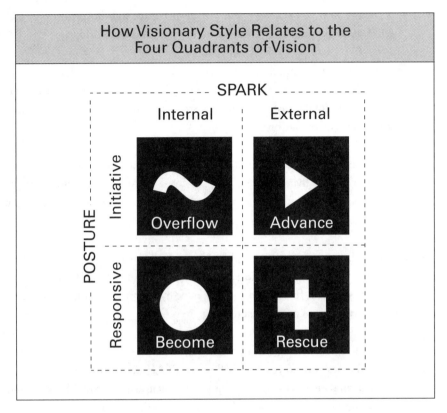

Figure 11.2

you to contribute to the advance of the vision that may have been different without your contribution?

This will most likely become a special shared experience for your team. I like to do this after some clarity has been gained.

Always record these responses as they will be useful to the smaller team that will build the vivid description.

Articulating Your One Picture Idea

Using the twelve templates to select your top two as a church gives you 132 different possible combinations (12 x 11). Which ones will you prayerfully choose? Your one picture idea will be one or two templates related in a meaningful way. Be sure to include the time frame you have chosen. Here are six actual examples:

- Hope Church, Las Vegas, Nevada

In the next ten years we will pursue **presence manifestation** *that will open doors to* **geographic saturation** to the west and the world.

- Kingsland Baptist Church, Katy, Texas
  In the next ten years we will see the training of parents (**spiritual formation**) *lead to* a total transformation by restoring the image of God in the home (**targeted transformation**).

- Good Shepherd United Methodist Church, Charlotte, North Carolina
  In the next five years we will see local **institutional renovation** of Methodism *through* **cultural replication** of Good Shepherd by opening new campuses.

- Bellevue Baptist Church, Memphis (Cordova), Tennessee
  After decades of **anointing amplification**: In the next ten years we will focus on **spiritual formation** *in order to* be a catalyst of spiritual awakening in our city (**presence manifestation**).

- Harvest Church, Billings, Montana
  In the next fifteen years we will renew the reputation of the local church (**institutional renovation**) to bring **gospel saturation** across Montana and surrounding states within a five-hundred-mile radius of Billings.

- Gateway Community Church, Houston, Texas
  In the next five years we will leverage our strengths for **crisis mobilization** that were developed through our response to Hurricane Katrina.

Final Exercise: Summarize

Now it's your turn. Pray once again and then dream on paper:

Our church in the next _____ years will . . .

_____

_____

_____

_____

_____

_____

_____

Figure 11.3

PART FOUR

Focus Your *Long-Range* Vision

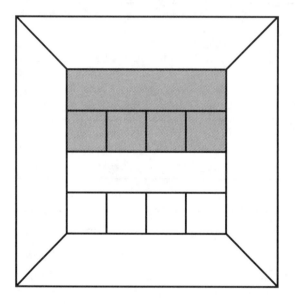

Chapter 12
Making Vision Move

Goals can be energizing—when you win. But a vision is more powerful than a goal. A vision is enlivening, it's spirit giving, it's the guiding force behind all great human endeavors. Vision is about a shared energy, a sense of awe, a sense of possibility.

—Boston Philharmonic Orchestra conductor, Benjamin Zander

In writing this chapter, I was tempted to resign the job I love, leaving Auxano, the nonprofit I founded in 2004. The vision of a company named Banjo had captured my heart after I read a public-debut article in *Inc.* magazine, which reported Banjo as "the most important social media company you have never heard of."

Why did Banjo's vision move me so profoundly? Its founder has created a tool that made my brain explode as I thought of the future possibilities. Imagine a giant computer that automatically follows everyone on all the major social media sites like Facebook, Twitter, and Instagram. Most people who use these tools allow their posts, pictures, and videos to be geotagged. So for the last four years, Banjo has been mapping this world feed of posts coming in at hundreds of thousands per minute.

What are the implications? Banjo turns this feed into an "event detection engine" with potential to disrupt all of the industries of the world. For example, Banjo saw all of the social media feeds before, during, and after the 2013 Boston marathon bombing, and they played a role in finding the bad guy. At one point it detected a diesel pipeline fire almost two hours before the news media reported the story. They calculated that their team gained a fifty-three-minute lead time over the fastest technology Wall Street brokers have when an event like this changes stock prices.[1]

Your Storyline Can Wield Influence of Epic Proportions

Could your church's vision likewise be so compelling that people want to invest their talents, time, and treasures to make it happen? Would you like to learn how God's calling can move people as never before at your church?

Welcome to part 4 of *God Dreams*. Now it's time to roll up your sleeves and build out your visionary plan with your church's Horizon Storyline. In these chapters we will develop your two long-range horizons—your beyond-the-horizon vision and your background vision—and take them to a level of clarity you can go public with.

The purpose of this chapter is to run you through a mini boot camp for vision writing. Now that you have been praying, thinking long, and listening to your team's feedback on the vision templates, I want you to practice communicating with some specific visionary skills in order to accomplish a top goal of this book: *creating the vivid description of your church's beyond-the-horizon vision.* This is the most neglected horizon and yet the most important and logical starting point for all other planning. This is the one place in all of your visionary ideas that you wield an influence of epic proportions, like the resigning moment.

Don't think old-school vision statement.

Even though the outcome is a written statement, this vivid description is not a vision statement in the old-school sense. You will not walk around parroting this statement like a robot or hanging it nicely framed in your church hallways. Rather it is a mental charging station for your team. Remember how we opened chapter 3: You don't need a vision statement; you need a visionary state of mind. You need a vision storyline.

The written description will eventually be the tool for you and your team to deliver vision daily. Even though you will start with writing, *putting your vision on paper is only a drill.* Like layups before the big game, you practice with written form. Game time is when you communicate verbally, eyeball to eyeball. Ultimately vision transfers through people not paper. We will discuss the moment of vision casting after we finish this step. For now, when I refer to the vivid description, I want you to think of it as your team's mental charging station.

> Ultimately vision transfers through people not paper.

The starting point for your vivid description is the one picture idea from chapter 11 and your selected time frame between five and twenty years. Now I will show you the key ingredients for turning that idea into a full-blown picture. I want to equip you to take a simple template and transform it into a unique masterpiece. Imagine the power of a mental charging station for your team. Every week dozens of leaders connect to it and then share frequently and skillfully the faith-stretching, mountain-moving vision of your church.

Specifically I will give you four imperatives to make vision move. What needs to move? Everything. Attenders need to be moved emotionally and volitionally. Leaders must move intentionally and passionately. Resources must be channeled, conversations initiated, and decisions calibrated. Vision must move all the stuff of ministry.

So how do you go from the single picture idea to a moving and vivid description? Let's start by scanning some biblical and cultural examples of inspirational long-range vision.

Vivid Vision Paragraphs from Scripture

From Genesis to Revelation God speaks and reveals. And when He does, He is often painting a picture, solving a problem, stirring the heart, and showing off how big He really is. Consider this vision excerpt from Revelation 21:1–4 as the apostle John dramatically opens the curtains of time's final scene:

> Then I saw a new heaven and a new earth, for the first heaven and the first earth had passed away, and the sea was no more. And I saw the holy city, new Jerusalem, coming down out of heaven from God, prepared as a bride adorned for her husband. And I heard a loud voice from the throne saying, "Behold, the dwelling place of God is with man. He will dwell with them, and they will be his people, and God himself will be with them as their God. He will wipe away every tear from their eyes, and death shall be no more, neither shall there be mourning, nor crying, nor pain anymore, for the former things have passed away."

How's that for solving a problem and stirring the heart?

One common pushback that comes from the work we do: "Is this vision stuff even biblical?" Much of what was covered in the first part of this book I hope addresses this concern. We have rooted vision in the nature of faith itself. Nevertheless, I wanted to provide a few specific biblical examples of vivid description paragraphs of a long-range future. Revelation 21 happens to be my favorite.

Let's zoom out from the book of Revelation and rewind all the way back to Genesis and the call of Abraham, at this point still called Abram. God has big plans for Abram, and He speaks as a compelling God. Between chapters 12 and 15, God speaks four different times. I have edited out everything but God's direct words to capture the vivid communication to Abram (see Genesis 12:1–3, 7; 13:14–17; 15:1, 4–5).

> Go from your country and your kindred and your father's house to the land that I will show you. And I will make of you a great nation, and I will bless you and make your name great, so that you will be a blessing. I will bless those who bless you, and him who dishonors you I will curse, and in you all the families of the earth shall be blessed. . . .

> To your offspring I will give this land. . . .

> Lift up your eyes and look from the place where you are, northward and southward and eastward and westward, for all the land that you see I will give to you and to your offspring forever. I will make your offspring as the dust of the earth, so that if one can count the dust of the earth, your offspring also can be counted. Arise, walk through the length and the breadth of the land, for I will give it to you.

> Fear not, Abram, I am your shield; your reward shall be very great.

> This man shall not be your heir; your very own son shall be your heir. . . . Look toward heaven, and number the stars, if you are able to number them. . . . So shall your offspring be.

I like to call this vivid description, "Countless Blessing." Let's run this vision through the four imperatives that make a vision move.

Paint a Picture

God references "counting dust" and "numbering stars" to anchor the image of the future in Abram's mind. Genesis 15:5 reports that God told Abram to go outside in order to see the stars. God didn't need a PowerPoint or video to cast His vision. He simply used the galaxy-lit sky.

Solve a Problem

God is solving two problems with this vision. One is on the scale of worldwide redemption, and the other is a deeply personal fertility issue.

On the grand side of things, Abram represents a new kind of multiplication. With people spread across the globe, God sets up Abram to spiritually bless the physically populated earth.

On the personal side Abram and Sarah can't have children. Anyone experiencing fertility challenges knows firsthand how gut-wrenching the journey can be. So God tenderly reaches down and reminds Abram that a son is coming, his very own son.

Stir the Heart

Can you imagine for a moment how Abram must have been thinking? The vision is massive in scope, ridiculous in size. From a wanderer going to an unknown place to the father of a great nation, with a great reputation, that will be known and protected throughout the world. How inspiring it must have been to look at the sky and imagine his children's children's children, coming from *his very own son*.

God-Size It

Since this is God's vision, I think this imperative is pretty much covered. The notion of one man becoming a nation that would be a conduit of raw happiness for the rest of the world is downright epic.

Vivid Description Paragraphs from Culture

A hundred years ago the automobile was not a tool for the everyday Ben or Beatrice. But Henry Ford thought it should be. Ford could see what others—maybe no one else—could not. He once mentioned that if he gave people what they wanted, it would have been a faster horse.

As Henry Ford peered into the long-range future, he inspired others to come along by using his words to create worlds. One such inspiring statement appeared in 1913 in the company magazine, *Ford Times*:

> I will build a motor car for the great multitude. It will be large enough for the family but small enough for the individual to run and care for. It will be constructed of the best materials, by the best men to be hired, after the simplest designs that modern engineering can devise. But it will be so low in price that no man making a good salary will be unable to own one—and enjoy with his family the blessings of hours of pleasure in God's great open spaces.

In these few heavyweight sentences, known as the "democratize the automobile" vision, you can glean the four imperatives of a *moving* vision.

First, Henry Ford was *painting a picture.* As you read it, you can imagine a family driving out in the country—in the "wide-open spaces" as he says. Second, he was *solving a problem.* The motorcar was simply too expensive for the common man to afford and too complicated for a nonexpert to maintain. Third was *stirring the heart.* He spoke to pride of ownership. He appealed to freedom, both for the enjoyment of family adventure and for an individual to escape. Finally he was *"God-sizing" it.* The vision was for the great multitude—for the blessing of hours of pleasure enjoying God's creation. He was thinking grand and helped his listeners see into another world. No one at that time could see highways without horses.

Let's review these imperatives and continue to look for them in other vivid description examples.

Imperative 1. Paint a picture.

You must enlist metaphor and imagery to deeply root the future picture in the minds of those listening. Your words create a film reel of the future for their mind's eye. People must see with their ears.

Imperative 2. Solve a problem.

You must show that tomorrow will be significantly better in a specific, tangible way. A vision at the end of the day is only a solution to a prior problem. If people are not emotionally connected to the prior problem, they couldn't care less about the vision.

Imperative 3. Stir the heart.

You must appeal to the desire for beauty and wonder, even urgently so. Why is the vision a better world in which people will want to live? Why this vision now?

Imperative 4. God-size it.

You must stretch the mind with an absurd idea, bold outcome, or a daring destination, centered in God's pleasure. Remember that your ability to be audacious is connected to God, not to a sense of overconfidence. Does the idea immediately foster a spirit of God dependence?

Another ever-inspiring moment of vivid vision is President John F. Kennedy's 1962 "Man on the Moon Speech." Again, this address was delivered for the same reasons a church vision will be created: to inspire people, secure commitment, and focus resources. Also keep in mind that JFK was thinking on a ten-year time frame:

> Those who came before us made certain that this country rode the first waves of the industrial revolution, the first waves of modern invention, and the first wave of nuclear power, and this generation does not intend to flounder in the backwash of the coming age of space. We mean to be a part of it—we mean to lead it. For the eyes of the world now look into space, to the moon and to the planets beyond, and we have vowed that we shall not see it governed by a hostile flag of conquest, but by a banner of freedom and peace. We have vowed that we shall not see space filled with weapons of mass destruction, but with instruments of knowledge and understanding.
>
> Yet the vows of this nation can only be fulfilled if we in this nation are first, and, therefore, we intend to be first. In short, our leadership in science and in industry, our hopes for peace and security, our obligations to ourselves as well as others, all require us to make this effort, to solve these mysteries, to solve them for the good of all men, and to become the world's leading space-faring nation.[2]

Notice again the use of visual imagery: innovation is a wave, failure is backwash, the world has eyes, and freedom is a banner. JFK is *painting a picture*. But he is also *solving a problem*. If America doesn't get to space first, the advantages of space may fall into the hands of a freedom-hostile country and threaten us. Along the way the speech *stirs the heart*—there is excitement for being "the leader," the pride of not floundering in our generation's moment, and the selfless responsibility to others. Finally, the vision *is God sized*. The competition of nations makes this vision grand. The declaration though not stated in the excerpt, was, "We choose to go to the moon." The vision would stretch the imagination of a nation, who would respond with dramatic achievement—"one small step for man, one giant leap for mankind."

Before moving on, let's unpack the pull Banjo had on me:

Paint a picture. Banjo skillfully uses visual language like "keeping the pulse of the planet," comparing the size of their global grid to a series of football fields, and describing event detection as an "engine."[3]

Solve a problem. Banjo is designed to generate a range of potential solutions yet to be dreamed up. At a minimum it can save lives, solve crimes, and connect people to global opportunities like never before.

Stir the heart. In my first few moments of understanding and using Banjo, it was hard to escape the Godlikeness of the whole thing. From immediate access to heartbreaking tragedy to unbelievable visibility of global entertainment, the idea created wonder. It spurred me to prayer.

God-size it. While not a Christian entity, this company oozes with big thinking. The creators want to disrupt every industry on the planet but only for the end goal of helping everyone gain more meaningful insight from every social media user on the planet.

Now It's Your Turn

In the next chapter we will provide some specific tools and examples for writing your vivid description. The purpose of this chapter is to drive deep the four imperatives for making vision move.

Before starting the next step, I encourage you to write down any initial ideas this chapter has sparked. Doing so will help you clarify and organize your prayerful imaginations to date. Use figure 12.1 to jot your initial thoughts.

Compare with Others, Take Another Step

If you're curious what other churches came up with, take a look at appendix A. Then turn the page to take the next step toward transforming the picture idea from your work in this chapter into a vivid description.

Creating a First Draft from Your "One Picture" Idea

How might you paint a picture? What images and metaphors come to mind? Write down a few ideas.

- _____ ,
- _____ ,
- _____ ,
- _____ .

How might you solve a problem? What inherent dilemmas does your vision address? Write down a few ideas.

- _____ ,
- _____ ,
- _____ ,
- _____ .

How might you stir the heart? What makes the vision attractive, beautiful, desirable, and wonderful? Think about your typical church attender. Write down a few ideas.

- _____ ,
- _____ ,
- _____ ,
- _____ .

How might you God-size it? What kind of stretch-thinking would be a step of faith for your people? Write down a few ideas.

- _____ ,
- _____ ,
- _____ ,
- _____ .

Figure 12.1

Chapter 13
Transforming Your Picture Idea into a Vivid Description

Words create worlds.

—Philosopher and rabbi Abraham Joshua Heschel

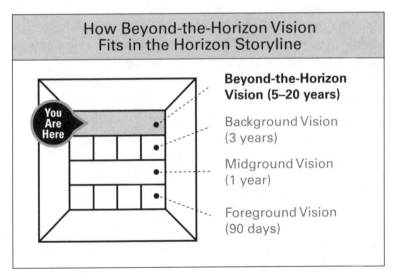

Figure 13.1

Having introduced the four imperatives for vivid vision in the last chapter, it's now time to give you some practical tools to describe your own unique picture of the future. Remember, don't retreat to vision statement "old school." You are simply writing down your beyond-the-horizon vision so it can serve as base camp for all of your day-in and day-out vision-casting efforts. Or as chapter 12 said, it's your team's charging station.

Here again is what you will be writing: *The beyond-the-horizon vision is a narrative of up to twenty sentences in length that vividly describes your church's future for the purpose of inspiring people and providing a context for shorter-term planning. Think of the beyond-the-horizon vision as the future picture of your church and a declaration of your congregation's ultimate contribution. It is a destination in time that you choose somewhere between five and twenty years.*

Three steps of practical advice for each imperative follow along with some examples of beyond-the-horizon vivid descriptions to use in benchmarking.

1. How to Paint a Picture with Vision

The first imperative is a cornerstone: you must become an artist with words.

Do this by mining and refining the gold nuggets of metaphor. By working with a few crown-jewel phrases, you'll have a twenty-four-karat paragraph that will wow people. Don't settle even for sterling sentences. Bronze is boring. Who wants a vivid vision that gets no bids on eBay?

If you don't use images and metaphors, your vision will likely come across as generic (see all the downsides in chapter 2). You don't want it to feel pedestrian and peanut butter and jelly, like it came from a discount store.

If you fail to use picturesque language, you will leave your followers blind. You don't want unintentionally to close the shades of your congregation's imagination.

> You don't want unintentionally to close the shades of your congregation's imagination.

The cool thing is that it's not that hard to become an artist with words. I'll give you a few reminders and a few tools. Before long you'll become a Picasso.

The first step is simply to use more metaphors. The second step is to grab a basic palette for verbal color. At the risk of going all the way back to Mrs. Huskin's fifth-grade English class, your verbal color palette contains things like metaphor and simile, alliteration and consonance. Remember that not all words are created equal. Only some open the eyes. (By the way, I used twenty figures of speech, primarily metaphors in the last sixteen sentences.)

Let's make sure you appreciate the power of metaphor. Remember that Jesus laced His communication with vivid images. He preached about a different kind of kingdom, which is a little hard to get your mental arms around at first. So Jesus explains the kingdom using concrete terms; He didn't abandon us in the abstract:

- In seven parables the kingdom is compared to a house.

- In six parables it is a great and festive feast.
- The kingdom can be entered or not.
- You can sit down in it.
- You can eat and drink in it.
- It has a gate at which you can knock.
- It is like a walled city.
- Men can take it by force.[1]

Martin Luther King Jr. did the same thing when he voiced his "I Have a Dream" speech in 1963. He helped people not just understand justice but see it. Justice is not just an abstract concept in this famous message; justice is—all terms he used within one sixteen-minute speech—a bank vault that's not bankrupt, a promissory note, a solid rock, a frequented palace that some can't enter, a mighty flowing stream, and an oasis in sweltering desert heat.

I've always believed in the importance of metaphors, having written about them in two previous books (*Building Leaders*, chapter 5, and *Church Unique*, chapters 16 and 17). More than repeated teaching, I believe most leaders just need helpful tools to use metaphors in more intentional ways. Scripture as a figure-of-speech treasure chest is always the best tool. And keep in mind that many of you are teaching and preaching on a regular basis so you have a great ongoing context to practice.

Carve out some time to apply stronger, more vivid, and more precise metaphors. Don't quit until your beyond-the-horizon vivid description is jaw-dropping and heart-stopping. The most important question to ask after you have initially drafted your vivid description is: Where else can I replace an abstract, generic, or common term with a vivid one that is more concrete, specific, or original?

For example, I was working with a church that was casting a vision for a leadership development process. Think about those words: *leadership development process*. The leader part of me loves these words and what they mean. But to the artist in me, those nines syllables taste like biting a stick.

Here's a little trick: You might have to say "leadership development process" to be clear, but first walk up a ladder of abstraction to get there. The ladder of abstraction means to build up to a more abstract idea, like justice, or kingdom, or leadership process by having more concrete rungs to climb on in the beginning. In other words, introduce the main idea with metaphors.

> The most important question to ask is: Where else can I replace an abstract, generic, or common term with a vivid one that is more concrete, specific, or original?

Here is a brainstorm of alternative terms for leadership development *process*. You are trying to make the abstract term *process* more concrete and therefore visual.

- Pipeline
- Steps, escalator, incline
- Journey, itinerary, trek, trip
- Course, route, road

Here is a rough-draft vivid description before the application of your "paint a picture" imperative:

> Over the next ten years we will refine and implement a biblical, balanced, and Christ-centered journey of leadership development. . . . This leadership development journey will revolve around our marks of discipleship. . . . We envision a leadership environment where peoples' lives and families are truly changed through the experience of loving God with all their hearts and loving their neighbors as themselves. The communities we serve will be our families, church, neighborhoods, workplaces, cities, and world.

Next, don't tell about it but instead *show* it. What follows is a rewrite of the previous vivid description:

> In the next decade we will raise up hundreds of guides who will in turn take thousands of people on the journey of a lifetime. Not a vacation but a transforming trip: a biblically fueled, relationally charged leadership development process. The adventure will focus on Jesus and on our twelve marks of following Him. Therefore our leadership development itinerary will not stop until thousands of people become agents of bold change, serving their concentric-circle communities with authentic love. We see dads enjoying their children, marriages welded together, and coworkers radically concerned for one another. We see neighborhoods turned upside down by the unexplainable kindness of our members. We envision more than five hundred small-group life rafts pulling people from the ocean of crowded loneliness. We see dozens of beachheads in our city's niche neighborhoods, with platoons of our people moving to start new campuses and power new causes.

Most of these metaphors are self-evident additions: the use of *journey, trip,* and *itinerary* in place of the term *process* and referring to small groups as lifeboats, to name a few.

Your Turn, More Tools

Ready to take a turn? Practice with the initial ideas you wrote down in the last chapter.

Use this list of metaphor tools that are all free online: they're all in one place at GodDrea.ms/metaphortools.

- For quick reminders and examples on figurative language, go to http://literarydevices.net/figurative-language. This site has great blog posts on kinds of metaphors.
- The Phrase Finder is a fun place to explore: http://www.phrases.org.uk.
- Free audiobook, *Writing Tools* by Roy Peter Clark. This classic book teaches fifty writing tools. I recommended focusing on the following tools for your vivid description: 1, 9, 10, 11, 14, 16, 17, and 22. Go to https://itunes.apple.com/us/itunes-u/roys-writing-tools.
- Google search for lyrics of your favorite songs. You will be blown away. Show your vivid vision description to your kids and ask them for songs you can use.
- Definition.com and Thesaurus.com are basics but are constant go-to sites for me.

2. How to Solve a Problem with Vision

It's time now to put on your solutioneer's hat: If your vision doesn't solve a problem, it will die on arrival.

The good news is that this step is easy, but don't skip it because it's extremely important. The best way to make my point is to be a bit crass about it. The truth is most church attenders could not care less about their church's vision.

That reality hit me one Thanksgiving weekend. While chomping on next-day turkey sandwiches at a party with friends of my extended family, I overheard an extended conversation about church. Most of the people would be considered mature believers and active churchgoers. While present and participating, no one knew my vocation so I listened with great interest. I was saddened by the conversations about pastoral personalities and programs. I felt the visionless reality—there was no significant emotional connection between these people and their church families. Like fitness center members, they pay their dues and received certain services. And if a fancier club moved to town, it would be easy to walk away.

If your vision doesn't solve a problem, it will die on arrival.

My point is not to depress you or throw these people under the bus. Rather I want to convince you that the failure to solve a problem is the number one reason people do not wake up to the vision. It's the primary factor that keeps vision powerless. Here is the single best-kept secret of vision casting: *People connect to the vision only to the degree that they are emotionally connected to the prior problem your vision solves.*

The failure to solve a problem is the primary factor that keeps vision powerless.

It's tempting to forget this principle, but don't—especially since it's not hard to apply it.

Problem Cast While You Vision Cast

Let's have fun with a nonchurch example. While playing on the Internet, I ran across a vision for the Upper Illinois River Watershed:

> The Upper Illinois River Watershed is a special place where the threads of private, public and non-profit partnerships are woven into the regional fabric of economic vitality, environmental stability, and social responsibility. Through its cultural heritage, the legacy of land stewardship, integrated with respect for personal property rights, continues. Natural resources are restored and sustained within a healthy mosaic of fields, forests, farms, woodlands, wetland prairies, pastures, cities, and naturally flowing streams. It is an incubator for green energy, entrepreneurial, educational, and environmental initiatives.[2]

I noticed two things about this statement: First, someone did intentionally try to paint a picture with terms like *threads, mosaic,* and *incubator.* Second, I could not care less about this vision. (Don't hate me for being honest.) Why? Even though someone tried to describe the beauty of the watershed, I am not connected to the prior problem the watershed organization solves.

I use the idea of a "burning platform" to anchor this principle. You must speak not only to the promise of gain but the fear of loss. This is not manipulation but vital spiritual leadership. What sets the platform on fire that makes everyone have to jump off?

The litmus test question for the burning platform is: *What's at stake if we don't engage this vision?* What will we lose? What will we miss out on? What will we regret? Applied to the watershed, we must answer: *What is at stake if the watershed vision doesn't exist?*

This opens up a simple principle I think of as "world reversing." Remember film-based processing that most of us don't do anymore thanks to digital photography? Remember what it was like to pull out the film and look at the negative image? Everything that is black in the fun family photo is white on the film negative. It takes just a moment for your eyes to adjust to what you're looking at. World-reversing is the process of developing the negative image of ideal future. That's right: you want to become as eloquent about your antivision as you are the vision itself. Problem casting precedes vision casting.

Problem casting precedes vision casting.

So let's practice together and build a burning platform for the watershed vision. How might we paint a picture of what's at stake if there is no watershed vision? What is the "world-reversing" negative image? Here is how I might start brainstorming answers to that question:

- Have you ever seen tainted water come out of a water fountain or household sink? How did you respond?
- Have you ever tasted sour water and had to spit it out? For a moment can you remember that tiny moment of terror?
- Have you ever been sick as a dog after drinking bad water on a mission trip?
- Can you imagine a world in which swimming was not allowed—ever?
- What if every year another local species became extinct? What if some day that affected your favorite annual fishing trip?
- Have you ever watched a postapocalyptic movie where a devastated, lifeless world is portrayed?
- What if there is an invisible foundation for all of life that you walk on each day without even noticing?
- What if, when it comes to a watershed, you have taken for granted for your entire life the unseen science of responsibility?

I could easily keep listing ideas and questions. And, again, it will be relatively easy for you to do the same once you know what to look for.

Now look at how I totally recast the vivid description paragraph of the Watershed:

The Upper Illinois River Watershed is a special place because we want you and the tens of thousands living in our land to thrive. Water is a building block for life. And if anything robs us of that foundation, the loss would be devastating. You realize this reality in the tiny moment of terror after you gulp, unaware, a sour glass of water. But most of the time you walk on an invisible foundation of land stewardship governed by the unseen sciences of responsibility. Will you consider, for just a moment, the beauty of our watershed and your role in protecting it?

Did you experience the difference? That's what solving a problem is all about. Remember the scene of those church attenders at Thanksgiving. How will they ever wake up to a vision if a pastor decides to bring one? Problem casting is the key.

Take a moment to think about the problem your one-picture idea solves. Get your team together and brainstorm your burning platform. Juice it like an orange and then choose your best stuff to include in your vivid description.

Take a few moments and consider the problems and solutions you wrote down in the last chapter.

3. How to Stir the Heart with Vision

Now let's talk about making the future more desirable and more attractive. In some ways this is happening automatically by painting a picture and solving a problem. But I want you to tune in to two things as you write your vivid description. The first is making sure it stirs *their* heart and not just *yours*. The second is to stir the heart by creating urgency.

Watch Out for Churchiness

Sometimes I read a vivid description that's written by the pastor and *for* the pastor. Don't get me wrong, I want you to jump out of your skin when you read your beyond-the-horizon vision. But it should be written primarily for your people. You are serving them by giving them something to look forward to. Remember? Here is the key question: *Does your vivid description practically describe a better world in which I—the church attender—want to live?*

The easiest illustration of this principle is that every pastor loves preaching to a full house. But your people don't like sitting in a crowded pew. They want elbowroom. You must give your vivid description some elbow room. It must work for six-pack Bob who walked into your worship service six weeks ago and doesn't have a clue about this whole church deal yet.

Ryan Rush is the senior pastor of Kingsland Baptist Church in Katy, Texas. They recently completed their one picture idea as spiritual formation leading to targeted transformation of homes. Specifically they want to transform ten thousand homes in the next ten years and start by encouraging families to have five catalytic meals a week together. They talk about equipping each parent to be the primary faith trainer in their children's life. They use phrases like, "The parent is the A-team, the church is the B-team."

For the vision to work, it must stir the heart of the parent. Ryan and his team must ask, *"How does being the primary faith trainer of my child create a better world, one in which they will want to live."* Many in full-time ministry think, *Duh, do I really have to spell that out?* The answer is yes, you do.

The challenge here is not just to think like a parent. The challenge is to think like the parent *you are not,* as a fully functioning church leader. You are far more motivated than the average parent coming to your church. And you probably approach this vision of "parent equipping" from a sense of strength and confidence. But what about the average parent in your church? Are most parents overwhelmed already with their existing responsibilities in life? How many parents live with a lingering guilt because they have not done more spiritually for their children already? How will divorced parents respond who only see their children half of the time? These questions will be helpful to think about as you articulate your vision description. How is your vision really good news?

Inducing Urgency

The second part of stirring the heart is creating a sense of urgency. The burning platform brings to the surface the deeper *why* of the long-range vision? Stirring the heart answers the question *why now?*

As you make the vision moving, you must give people a little shot in the arm and kick in the rear end. The immediate action step will be determined by goals further "down" your Horizon Storyline, but even the beyond-the-horizon vision can bring criticality to the present. So ask the question, "Why is it important to bring this vision now?" I don't think you need to say much about this in your vivid description, but try to state at least one thing that signals the timing.

For example in Katy, Texas, the fastest growing demographic is the eighteen- to thirty-year-olds. They and their families have flocked to that area of Houston to experience an idyllic suburb with the best schools on the planet. One reason for *why now* can be to leverage the massive influx of kid-fanatic parents and redefine their definition of success.

It's your turn now. Take a moment and think about your one picture idea. Why is it important now?

How to God-Size Your Vision

The examples employed in the previous chapter all have a largeness and ubiquity to them (cars, space, global social media, new Jerusalem, and Abraham). But don't let the size of those visions distract you from the need to *set the scope* of the vision for your ministry. Whether you're long-range planning for a small missional barbecue ministry, a rapid-growth gigachurch, or a mainline turnaround, you will need to God-size your vision.

The skill to "right-size" your vision is critically important. The idea of "God-sizing it" doesn't mean making it ridiculously large in scope; it means enlarging the faith of your people in your time and place based on your resources. God-honoring vision comes in all shapes and sizes.

Go back for a minute to the story I shared earlier in the book about reaching my dorm floor at Penn State. Was reaching forty people a God-size vision for me? You bet. Within two years I would set my sights on an area of campus that was forty times bigger. My God size got bigger with more experience and a team linking arms with me.

Today I am a part of the church that is reaching 500,000 people. And even that vision would take over ten years of God's favor and growth on a local church before it would emerge in the eyes of leaders. When I came on staff, the senior pastor advised me not to buy a house on the "other side of I-45" as it was fifteen minutes away and a natural community "barrier." Yet a decade later we would have a campus on "the other side." The meaning of God size will flex as you go and grow as a leader.

> The meaning of God size will flex as you go and grow as a leader.

Yet "bigness" is still a slippery idea. No one wants to think small. But no one wants to think too highly of himself either. We want to think big enough but not too big. Most of us are stuck between the cultural rants of "Go big or go home!" and "Small is the new big!"

Calculating Your Vision Factor

For years I have wanted to create some tool to help church leaders understand how to God-size their vision. How do you take some of the "slippery" out of it? Some leaders do it intuitively, but most appreciate some guidance. Because of my engineering background, I tend to think in terms of quotients and factors, which I know risks being a little hokey. But I'm giving it a shot, and I think it will help you. Here is how it developed.

How do you "God-size" a vision in such a way that accounts for both the church planter with barely enough money to put food on the table, and for Rick Warren releasing a global P.E.A.C.E. plan?

The answer: create a simple scale that allows different levels of magnitude for the scope of the vision. *Scope* means "the extent of the subject matter with which something deals or to which it is relevant." What is your extent, range, breadth, reach, sweep, and span? I decided to make a range between one and one thousand to account for the smallest vision as one and for the largest vision as one thousand. Please keep in mind that a vision factor of eight hundred is no more godly or better than a vision factor of eighty. It's simply broader in scope. It's about right-sizing the God Dream based on where you are today.

The next question is, What considerations go into a church's factor? The obvious one is resources—in the largest sense. What is the cumulative total of the talent, volunteer time, money, and the asset base of the church community? Is there incredible cash flow or overwhelming debt?

But some of the external factors can be deceptive. I was recently with twenty-five church planters called the Creo Collective sponsored by the Evangelical Free Church of America. While training on Auxano's leadership pipeline process with Mac Lake, I made an offhand comment that generated conversations afterward. I stated that I would rather have 150 people in my church with complete alignment and passion for the same vision than a typical growing church of a thousand in attendance with generic vision. Several of the planters deeply resonated with this idea. It was freeing for them to embrace.

So what are the most reliable factors to get a handle on the vision factor beyond the obvious variable of resources? I believe there are four: the culture of mission (M), the dynamic of trust (Tr), the history of progress (P), and the tenure of senior leadership, that is the senior or lead pastor (Tn). Let's put these together in a simple formula:

$$\text{Vision Factor} = \frac{M \ \times \ Tr \ \times \ P}{Tn}$$

By using this simple formula, you can take a few steps toward objectifying your vision factor somewhere between one and one thousand. One last caveat: my greatest fear is that anything I would write might limit your imagination and dreaming. So see this as a conversation tool with your team. Bathe every part of that dialogue with God-dependent and bold prayer.

Let's describe each part of the formula. Then you can scope what your God size looks like.

Culture of mission: Does the team have a clear sense of mission in their mind and heart? If so, for how long? Do people in the church know the mission of the church? Are people outside the church valuable to people inside the church? Are apostolic and evangelistic functions working well in your church? If so, score your church a number from one to ten, for the number of years your church has lived with a strong culture of mission. Ten is the maximum. If you've never had culture of mission, score a one. If you are a church plant three years old, score a three.

Dynamic of trust: Does the congregation as a whole trust the empowered leadership as a whole? If so, for how long? Is there a sweet spirit when leaders gather? Are their moments of deep pain, loss, or betrayal that caused a lapse of trust with leaders in the last ten years? Again, score your church based on the number of years you have experienced a strong dynamic of trust. Ten is maximum. If you have had five years of accumulated trust building, score a five. If you have little trust and a recent crisis, score a one.

History of progress: Does the congregation have a visceral sense of momentum? If so, for how long? Can we point to any variable or measure to show sustained progress however we define it (attendance, giving, church planting, etc.)? Do the same thing you did with culture and trust: score on a scale of one to ten with ten being the maximum. Ten years of progress scores a ten. If you are declining as a church, score a one.

Tenure: I define *tenure* as "average number of senior pastors of your church per twenty years of history." To calculate this number, count how many senior pastors your church has ever had. That's your pastor count. Now divide the total age of your church by 20. That's your "per 20" number. (If your church is less than 20 years old, your "per 20" number would be a faction less than one and that's okay.) Next, to calculate your tenure number as I am defining it, divide your pastor count by your "per 20" number. If you have four senior pastors in the last twenty years and your church is twenty years old, your tenure number would be four. If you have three senior pastors for the last sixty years, the number would be one. If your church is ten years old with the same pastor, the number is one. You don't have to go lower than one.

Let's play this with two church scenarios.

Journey Church was planted eight years ago. Three years ago the planting pastor left, and his successor has done a great job. The transition was seamless, and leadership trust was not breached. They have seen steady growth since they started and a strong culture of mission. The church now runs 350 in attendance.

Here are my numbers for this equation: $M=8$, $Tr=8$, $P=8$, and $T=5$. The vision factor is 102, on a scale of 1–1000.

Now the usefulness of this tool is to see how changes in the formula change the scope of the factor.

Let's say the Journey Church pastor never left. Then, $T=2.5$. And the factor doubles to 205.

Let's say the same pastor stays for twenty years. If the church were to score a ten on culture of mission, trust, and progress, and the tenure is now one, the factor maxes out at a thousand.

Suppose the founding pastor significantly breached the trust of the congregation when he left, but the church maintained some momentum. We might keep the culture of mission at eight and progress at eight. But we would reduce the dynamic of trust to three because it had to start over again with a new pastor. This breach of trust would change the vision factor from 128 in our original scenario to 48, reducing by one third.

What does all of this mean? From my perspective—after fifteen years and well over ten thousand hours of facilitation times with church teams—these are the four variables in the life of the church that most impact the scope of the vision. It's not a perfect formula by any means, but it does help teams dream better together.

Obviously tenure is big. A quick glance at any churches history demonstrates this. As Charles Arn reports: "There is an undeniable relationship between pastoral tenure and church growth. While most growing churches have long-term pastorates, and some non-growing churches have long-term pastorates, it is almost unheard of to find a growing church with many short-term pastorates. Frequent change of pastors seems to negate all the other complicated ingredients that go into a church's growth mix."[3]

The other factors are all multiples that significantly reduce the vision factor when the church "starts over."

How do I use the vision quotient? Primarily for encouragement and caution. For encouragement I love to show the increased potential of a positive decade of ministry with one pastor. It really poises the church to dream big. On the other hand, when a vision factor is lower, I encourage the church to focus on some God-sized dreams that fit their situation.

The great news is that God-sizing is usually self-evident within your team. Use the vision factor as a conversation starter.

Getting to the Numbers

While your vivid description does not *need* to have a quantifiable aspect because of its long-range nature, you should strongly consider using numbers to create a sense of magnitude even if you don't set a numerical goal. In other words, is the vision about three, dozens, scores, hundreds, thousands, tens of thousands, millions, or billions?

Use numbers to "surprise with scope"; that is, show off what is possible if God's people focus for a long time. There is something stunning about the thought of transforming ten thousand homes in ten years or completing the renovation of one city block in five years or taking fifteen years to see everyone in a half-million population area invited into gospel community. Einstein once said, "If the idea at first is not absurd, there is no hope for it." Go back to our consistent reliance on Ephesians 3:20. If God wants to do immeasurably more than we can think, is our response to shoot for the stars or to clear the fence? When you surprise with the scope, you are using numbers to create the order or magnitude of the vision.

Again I rely on the team when developing the scope. Perhaps your greatest resource is using the collaborative genius of the team to "zero in" on the God size. I want to hear from the different gifts and perspectives of the team. For example, using APEST (apostles, prophets, evangelists, shepherds, teachers) from Ephesians 4:11–15, I want to know how the apostles are thinking differently from the prophets and the teachers. I want to let the experience of the group speak. Usually emerging leaders are idealistic, and the experienced leaders are realistic. I pay attention to when the experienced leader is thinking bigger than anyone else. I always look for individuals who may have had recent God experiences that speak into the scope or maybe a verse of Scripture God is using to help the team decision. Let the Holy Spirit speak through the group!

As always your greatest tool in the collaborative moment is questions. Take the team on a journey of "high and low." What scope is clearly not big enough? What scope goes beyond being God sized and is just flat out ludicrous? I ask the team constantly, "Are we thinking big enough?" I often put individuals on the spot (they know that's what I am there to do) to make them wrestle together with scope.

In the final analysis prayer is your double-barrel weapon. First, always take additional time to pray when directly working on the scope of the vision. Second, prayer becomes one of the best litmus tests. Craig Groeshel tweeted one time, "If prayer isn't necessary to accomplish your vision, you're not thinking big enough." The question to pose to the group at the end of the conversation is, "Will this vision keep us on our knees in dependence on God?"

Take some time now and think about God-sizing your vision. What did you write down at the end of the previous chapter? What new thoughts do you have?

One Final, Practical Note

When finalizing your vivid description, don't do the final wordsmithing with the entire team. Take them through the four imperatives of making vision move that we have covered over the last two chapters. Get their input from the additional exercises mentioned in chapter 11. From there either the senior leader or the lead pastor may assemble a smaller team of three or four who are particularly skilled to help with final articulation.

Use the examples as provided as further illustrations of the four imperatives we have unpacked and illustrated. Go to appendix A for additional illustrations.

Chapter 14
Developing Your Background Vision

Context creates reality and the reality it creates is the content. Most managers manage the content, and only during a major strategic shift is the context brought into question. An operating budget or a two-year plan mainly provides content with a given an unquestioned context. The function of the ten-year plan is to provide context. An organization's leadership will have implemented the long-range strategic plan when they manage the context, not the content.

—Business consultant Stanley Davis

This chapter will look three years into the future and help you decide on the top four things your ministry should be focusing on. I call this three-year time frame the background horizon (see figure 14.1, perhaps also review figure 5.2). It's still long-range but not as far away as your beyond-the-horizon work.

Think of the following picture as a way of visualizing the overall Horizon Storyline. Imagine that you are driving a car in Colorado and heading directly toward the front range of mountains. You are just beginning to see the majestic peaks in the distance. While driving, you have three places for your eyes to focus: the dashboard of the car (foreground), the road immediately in front of you (midground), and the mountains way ahead of you (background). Your beyond-the-horizon view, by the way, is what your eyes can't see on the other side of those mountains. While you can't see it, you are thoughtful and excited about what's there—it's so important that I've focused on the topic for the last seven chapters!

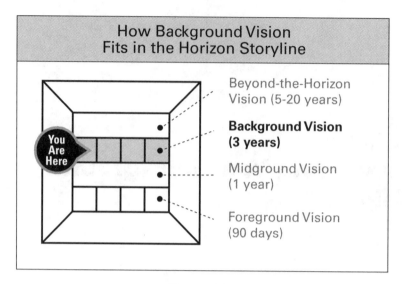

Figure 14.1

As you drive, how much time do you spend staring at the distant background? Not much, right? Typically when driving, you glance up frequently to the farthest horizon to get your bearings. You recalibrate your orientation, and you gauge your sense of progress against the background. But you don't drive the car by constantly looking that far away (which would guarantee a crash).

That's exactly how we will use the background vision for your church or organization. We won't fixate on it, but we'll regularly look up and glance at it to sense progress.

While beyond-the-horizon vision is intended for inspirational purposes, the background vision is not. Therefore you don't have to spend additional time wordsmithing your background vision.

Let's revisit the definition of *background vision* before we explore its benefits and jump into developing it.

The Big Rocks of Background Vision (3 years)

Your background vision contains four ideas, primarily qualitative, that clarify the four most strategic emphases in the next three years in order to fulfill your beyond-the-horizon vision. Each background vision emphasis can be stated in a short phrase with an amplified sentence explaining it. The background vision is not designed to inspire but to clarify.

Years ago Stephen Covey made a simple time-management illustration famous using rocks and jars. The presentation starts with a gallon-sized Mason jar and a set of things to place inside: seven fist-sized rocks, a small bucket of pebbles, and a small bucket of sand. His first approach is to put the more granular items in the jar first—the sand and then the pebbles. When he tried to put the rocks in the jar afterwards, there was not enough room. In the second part of the illustration, he reversed how the ingredients are added. If he put in the big rocks first, everything else can still fit inside because the smaller pebbles and sand flow around them.

The critical life lesson becomes obvious: schedule the most important "big" items in your life first, and then let all of the day-to-day minutiae fill in. "Big rocks first" becomes the mantra so the trivial doesn't triumph in your life by pushing out the most important priorities.

One easy way to think of your background vision is this big-rocks illustration. I often call the background vision your "four background big rocks." These are the four biggest things that must happen if you are going to realize your beyond-the-horizon vision. If you don't keep your team's mind-set and planning process aware of them, the Sunday's-a-coming urgency of day-to-day ministry will eclipse your dream.

Classic strategic planning might label these "big rocks" as strategic objectives or just strategies, but I find that more people relate better to these ideas by visualizing them on a horizon—just like the driving illustration. Here are ways to help people quickly relate:

- These are the four things to see on the distant horizon (visual metaphor).
- These are the four "big rock" priorities for the next three years (time-management metaphor).
- These are four mountains we must climb and conquer to get to our destination (journey metaphor).
- These are the four biggest obstacles—tensions to overcome to reach the climatic scene (story metaphor).

For those comfortable with strategic thinking, see figure 14.2 (which is a repeat of figure 5.4). If you want to describe the "big rock" priorities in the language of strategic thinking, you could call them:

- The four strategic objectives in the long-range plan
- The four-part plan to get to achieve our vivid description
- The long-range strategy to reach the long-range visionary
- The four big "hows" to get to our one big "what"

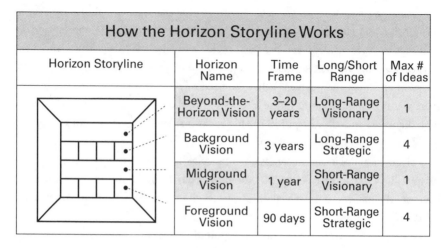

How the Horizon Storyline Works				
Horizon Storyline	Horizon Name	Time Frame	Long/Short Range	Max # of Ideas
	Beyond-the-Horizon Vision	3–20 years	Long-Range Visionary	1
	Background Vision	3 years	Long-Range Strategic	4
	Midground Vision	1 year	Short-Range Visionary	1
	Foreground Vision	90 days	Short-Range Strategic	4

Figure 14.2

Benefits of Background Vision

Now that I have defined background vision, let me highlight four benefits.

Benefit 1. Creates a broad-level road map to approach the future.

Since you have now painted an amazing picture of your church's beyond-the-horizon vision, the background vision helps with the large sweeping perspective of how you will get there. This is simply a summary of the various ways you just outlined above. Once you have locked these ideas into your team's thinking and planning process, you will wonder how you ever led without it!

Benefit 2. Directs long-term allocation of church resources.

One practical benefit of seeing the background vision so clearly is that you can constantly monitor resource allocation. Imagine how quickly special requests can be vetted when you see them through the filter of the long-range priorities. Imagine having simpler criteria for annual budgeting for what stays and what goes. Imagine having crystal clarity when raising funds and accepting or not accepting designated gifts.

Benefit 3. Limits blind spots that would inhibit progress.

A friend of mine was in the final month of a several-year project of building a plane from scratch. With almost all of the plane assembled—cockpit in place, engine and props ready to run—he began to mount the wings. To his great dismay, what was supposed to be a seamless final step proved to be a nightmare. The wing assembly did not align correctly due to using a wrong part in one of the first months. It set him back in dollars and time, but most of all it took a toll on his emotional energy.

Wouldn't it be completely awful, having set out to achieve your five- or ten-year vision, to find that you left out a major component three years prior? Imagine the horror! Engaging your team on the background doesn't guarantee you hit your vision, but it almost promises that you won't miss a big step on the way there.

Benefit 4. Provides context for short-range goal setting and all ministry activity.

Three laborers were making bricks in the hot desert sun. Someone came by and asked them what they were doing. The first answered, "Can't you see that I'm making bricks?" The second one said, "I am building an important wall." The third one paused, looked out into the distance and replied, "I am building a beautiful cathedral. And it's going to be one of the most beautiful cathedrals of all time."

Why did these workers answer the same question differently? Because they all have a different context although they are doing the same mundane job.

One of the most important functions of the background vision is to provide context for shorter-term goals and all ministry activity. The word *context* means a "together weaving." The word is most commonly used regarding an event, a word, or an archeological artifact. To understand the true meaning of an event or word or artifact requires understanding its surroundings, circumstances, and settings. One must "weave together" the bigger picture. What does a lady screaming mean? I don't know without context: maybe she is being attacked or maybe she stubbed her toe. The context can in fact completely change our understanding of the meaning of the event.

The same is true with the meaning of ministry events, personal time management, staff team goals, and the shorter-term horizons of your visionary plan. You name it. It all has some context. From your church's perspective what is that context? Hopefully it is your two long-range horizons working together. If your church is operating with a generic vision, it's safe to say there really is no context.

With little context it's not just easier; it's inevitable that people will slip into the daily grind. Your leaders will be making bricks not building cathedrals. At Kingsland Baptist Church (introduced in chapter 11; see also appendix A), what does a family meal really mean? It may be an amazing feat for a dad who is stepping into the role of primary faith trainer. It may be the catalytic meal where the gospel works in little Johnny's heart like never before. It may be one of ten thousand intentional families seeing the image of God in the home restored.

How to Develop Your Own Background Vision

I use a relatively simple facilitation exercise that takes approximately three hours to develop with a team of fewer than twelve. It's a slight adaption of a construct created originally by Tom Paterson.[1]

Using a whiteboard or large white sheets, create the following "table" for the entire team to engage in a discussion. See figure 14.3.

Background Vision Whiteboard Facilitation

Our Background Vision – Three Years		
Where We Stand	Where We're Headed	How We'll Get There

Figure 14.3

First column of figure 14.3: Take thirty to forty-five minutes and brainstorm fifteen to twenty-five statements that describe where your church stands today. Record these in the "Where We Stand" column. Use both qualitative statements (our staff feels too busy, our church enjoys a strong reputation in the community, etc.) and quantitative statements (we have twenty-three life groups averaging eleven people each, our budget is $1.3 million, etc.). Express them as bullet points.

Here's a sample of what bullet-point phrases look like. While this is a larger church example—I will refer to it as Journey Church—the exercise is the same for any size church:

- 1,900 in worship attendance at two campuses
- 1,450 Maple Avenue campus and 450 Southside campus
- Staff and lay leaders are excited about what God is doing
- No conflict, high-trust culture
- More than five years of strong attendance growth
- Twenty-three staff with 50 percent under age thirty-five
- 320 new members (big surge) last year
- Fifty-five sermon-based small groups (35 percent of worship attendance)
- Strong disciple-making culture (strategy, measures, tools)
- Age-graded attendance—187 preschool/180 elementary/215 students
- Student ministry has most opportunity to grow
- $2.9 million budget, 1,400 giving units
- We've outgrown our systems and processes
- Good leadership development culture but not great
- Need to "rebuild our leadership process"
- 110 people involved in nine mission trips
- Two hundred baptisms
- 160 consistent viewers of our church service online
- 444 volunteers serving at least once per month (23 percent of attendance)

This should be a relatively easy brainstorming exercise. Encourage your team to be honest, and model this with a fun and opportunistic spirit.

Middle column of figure 14.3: Take forty-five minutes to an hour to do the same exercise anticipating and imagining what your church will look like three years from now as you track toward the fulfillment of your beyond-the-horizon vivid description. Record as many as twenty-five to thirty ideas in the "Where We're Headed" column.

Be sure everyone on the team is familiar with your vivid description or at least your one picture idea (from chapter 11). The idea is to have your vivid description completed, but sometimes I conduct discussions of long-range horizons in a retreat setting where I move from the beyond-the-horizon vision to the background vision using the one-picture idea.

Help people at the start get their minds around the month and the year it will be three years from now. Sometimes I have a team remember three years back in history to get a sense of the "distance" in time forward that we are imagining.

The next forty-five minutes usually spurs some of the most valuable interaction I ever see among church leaders. It brings unprecedented clarity to so many things in church life. Keep in mind that some of these conversations may be challenging. (But they are always good.) You may want to mirror some of the statements that were made in the "Where We Stand" column. I usually start by guiding the team to plan on worship attendance and giving projections. What will be started, and what will be stopped in the next three years? What will be added and increased? What will be minimized and decreased? Will we launch a new service or campus or plant? Will we add new staff or change our leadership structure? Here is a sample list, again from the hypothetical Journey Church:

- *Ramp up our leadership development.*
- *Twenty-five hundred worship attendance total.*
- *We will have three campuses plus an online service.*
- *The online service will become an online "campus."*
- *Southside campus adds a third service.*
- *Video venue added at Maple Avenue campus (for next campus core team development).*
- *Growth across all ministry areas.*
- *$3.8 million budget, 1,850 giving units.*
- *Leadership involvement grows by a greater percentage than worship (20 percent).*
- *Gulfport church plant running two hundred in worship attendance.*
- *Permanent facility secured for Gulfport church plant.*
- *We become the church-planting pacesetter for our denomination.*
- *Church-planting intern process designed and operating.*
- *Double the number of students involved in student ministry.*
- *Significantly lower barriers to volunteer recruitment.*
- *Five partnerships in five countries for international missions.*

Third column of figure 14.3: Take thirty minutes and record fifteen to twenty-five statements that answer the question "How We'll Get There" in the last column. Encourage the team to think about broad strategic ideas, and don't let them get caught in the minutiae or distracted in problem solving. Drawing again from the hypothetical Journey Church:

- Help people come more consistently to worship (more than once per month).
- Change how we communicate to our culture today (social media).
- Transition the mind-set of our congregation from "addition" to "multiplication."
- Reevaluate how we count and reach people (systems).
- Attract church planters to our planting intern process.
- Prayerfully seek and launch third campus.
- Identify beachheads for next three campuses within our saturation radius.
- Communicate our new long-range plans with high intensity.
- Continue maximizing our core discipleship strategy and tools.
- Launch a new information system, website, and church app.
- Increase our capacity for people development (vs. program development).
- Direct more staff time on leadership development.
- Build a critical mass in Gulfport plant.
- Strengthen engagement in Gulfport church plant.
- Find new avenues and develop new skills to recruit people.
- Add new staff leaders for multiplication efforts.
- Clarify precisely what makes a "Journey Church" campus.

Organizing the third column of figure 14.3: Take fifteen minutes to organize the "How We'll Get There" column into four clusters or common themes. Suggestion: use different colored markers and symbols on the whiteboard to group ideas. For example, use a red triangle and mark all of the ideas having to do with leadership development and a blue circle for communication.

During a break either I or someone else I assign will synthesize and clean up these statements and articulate a clear, amplified sentence summary of the four top ideas. (I call this "scrubbing" the whiteboard work.) It's fine to let the content itself shape how you express these. A short phrase is fine. Two summary sentences also work, but don't try to say more. These become the four background vision ideas. Not everyone around the team has to articulate the summary statements as long as they are given the opportunity for input and feedback. In other words, while a facilitator takes the lead in summarizing, it is always important to allow the group to give a verbal sign-off of their agreement with the summary.

Note: People are typically surprised by the efficient power of summarization and clarification of this exercise.

How I Summarized and Organized Ideas for Journey Church

Let me offer an example of the four summary statements for the background vision based on the illustration above. Every bullet in the "How We'll Get There" column is bundled or clustered into one of the four ideas below. Sometimes a bullet point or two does not get summarized. That is okay. You are looking for the four *most important* background ideas.

As you read through a long list like this, it can feel mind-numbing. Remember that when a team produces a list like this in group dialogue, the exercises feel easy and energetic.

Background Vision Idea 1

Increasing our leadership capacity for future multiplication. We will sustain 10 percent involvement growth across all ministries with 20 percent increase of our leadership core.

This idea includes from the "How We'll Get There" list above:

- Help people come more consistently to worship (more than once per month).
- Continue maximizing our core discipleship strategy and tools.
- Increase our capacity for people development (vs. program development).
- Find new avenues and develop new skills to recruit people.
- Spend much more staff time on leadership development.

Background Vision Idea 2

Transform how we communicate to be simple, social, system based, and vision saturated.

This idea includes from the "How We'll Get There" list above:

- Change how we communicate to our culture today (social media).
- Transition the mind-set of our congregation from "addition" to "multiplication."
- Reevaluate how we count and reach people.
- Launch a new information system, website, and church app.
- Communicate our new long-range vision with high intensity.

Background Vision Idea 3

Successfully launch our third campus with a clearly defined replicable model for the next three campuses.

This idea includes from the "How We'll Get There" list above:

- Prayerfully seek and launch third campus.
- Identify beachheads for next three campuses (four, five, and six) within our saturation radius.
- Add new staff leaders for multiplication efforts.
- Clarify precisely what makes a "Journey Church" campus.

Background Vision Idea 4

Champion the Gulfport church plant to viability as a model for our church-planting internship.

This idea includes from the "How We'll Get There" list above:

- Build a critical mass or core people for the Gulfport plant.
- Strengthen the engagement of our congregation in Gulfport plant.
- Attract church planters to our intern process.

Translate Your Four Top Ideas into a Background Vision

Figure 14.4 shows the final result of the summary ideas from the hypothetical Journey Church being translated into four columns of background vision. Please do the same with your four big ideas as you sketch out your own Horizon Storyline grid (similar to figure 14.1 or 17.1). In this example, done in a retreat setting, the team has not developed its vivid description yet, but they have completed their one picture idea from the twelve templates. As you will see, they chose "leadership multiplication for the sake of gospel saturation."

I have provided a one-page Horizon Storyline form tool for you to use at GodDrea. ms/HorizonStoryline. It is designed to capture your whiteboard work and redistribute to your team.

Will's Processing Tips

I always remind leaders that you can easily draw the Horizon Storyline on a napkin or whiteboard with shorthand notes from summary statements. For example, after this church's retreat I wrote the following phrases on a napkin, quickly drawing the Horizon Storyline grid:

For the beyond-the-horizon-vision I wrote, *"From + to x: bring the gospel to our 125,000"* ("+ to x" is shorthand for "addition to multiplication.")

For the four background vision ideas, I sketched quickly: *"Increase Leadership / Transform communication / Launch #3 / Champion Gulfport"*

By summarizing in this way, I showed the team how portable the vision is. Voicing the long-range "1:4" in eighteen words made it meaningful and memorable.

Journey Church Long-Range Vision Example

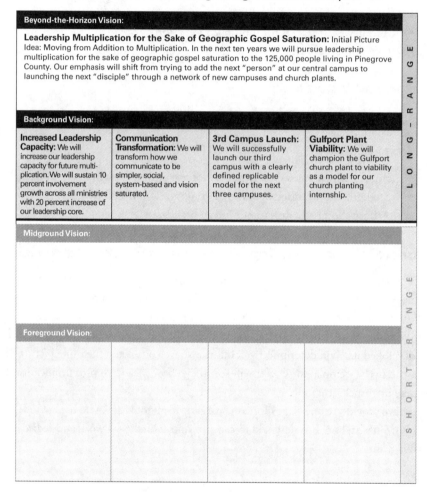

Beyond-the-Horizon Vision:

Leadership Multiplication for the Sake of Geographic Gospel Saturation: Initial Picture Idea: Moving from Addition to Multiplication. In the next ten years we will pursue leadership multiplication for the sake of geographic gospel saturation to the 125,000 people living in Pinegrove County. Our emphasis will shift from trying to add the next "person" at our central campus to launching the next "disciple" through a network of new campuses and church plants.

Background Vision:

| **Increased Leadership Capacity:** We will increase our leadership capacity for future multi-plication. We will sustain 10 percent involvement growth across all ministries with 20 percent increase of our leadership core. | **Communication Transformation:** We will transform how we communicate to be simpler, social, system-based and vision saturated. | **3rd Campus Launch:** We will successfully launch our third campus with a clearly defined replicable model for the next three campuses. | **Gulfport Plant Viability:** We will champion the Gulfport church plant to viability as a model for our church planting internship. |

Midground Vision:

Foreground Vision:

Figure 14.4

What's Next

Now you have completed your background vision. The next chapter will help you know how to apply your long-range vision to your leadership. Then the next section will walk you through how to frame a midground vision and a foreground vision.

Chapter 15
Leading the *Long-Range* Vision

Twenty years from now you will be more disappointed by the things that you didn't do than by the ones you did do. So throw off the bowlines. Sail away from safe harbor. Catch the trade winds in your sails. Explore. Dream. Discover.

—Author and lecturer Mark Twain

As an eager-to-drive sixteen-year old, I started my lessons with the bland basics of how to start the car. My dad taught me the three essentials that make the engine fire: fuel, air, and a spark.

Likewise learning to "drive" as a leader by using long-range vision starts with keeping the vision engine running. The three essentials are see it, talk it, and fund it. That is, you must keep the vision visible (see it), keep it conversational (talk it), and keep it financial (fund it). If any of these essentials are missing, you can forget about any advanced driving techniques.

This chapter creates a short pause before completing the rest of your Horizon Storyline. It finishes part 4: Focus Your *Long-Range* Vision (see figure 15.1). Remember, your long-range vision is the top two horizons we have just walked through in chapters 13 and 14.

One Christmas I received a waterproof radio to listen to in the shower. Installing it made a marked difference in the singing coming from my shower. The point is, I saw the radio every day. You must ensure that you see your vision every day.

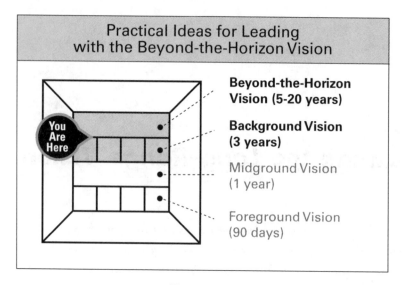

Figure 15.1

I use the shower metaphor intentionally: seeing the vision is not about transmitting the vision to the world. I have been warning you against going "old-school vision." When I say to keep it visible, I'm not referring to a formal written presentation. Don't think first about your website or wall décor plaque with a framed statement. Think about you. Preach the vision to yourself. A vision state of mind is more important than a vision statement.

Last year I was consulting at Calvary Baptist Church in Winston-Salem, North Carolina, pastored by Dr. Rob Peters. His senior associate pastor is Gary Chapman, author of the incredibly popular book franchise, *The Five Love Languages*. Dr. Chapman released the book in 1992, and almost twenty years later the book was reporting increased sales year over year, passing the ten million mark in 2015.[1] Needless to say, Dr. Chapman has a lot of time and expertise helping others speak the language of love. Therefore I couldn't resist the learning opportunity as we chatted at a break. I asked him to share the single most important lesson after helping couples for over two decades. His reply, "People need a visible reminder of their spouse's love language, like writing it on your mirror."

Two years ago our staff team at Auxano renewed our own Horizon Storyline. For some reason I enjoy the original whiteboard drawings from our review session. For six months I hung the white sheet from our team collaboration on the most prominent wall in my home office. At first I read over the board every time I walked in, paying particular attention to the background vision. I didn't take down the sheet until it was seared into my memory.

You must do the same. And until you have something better, you might consider laminating your Horizon Storyline's 1:4:1:4 and making it vision-on-a-rope in your shower (like my radio on a rope). Or screen-save it, windshield it, whiteboard it, or table-tent it. Tape it, stick it, glue it, or hang it until you see it every day.

Keep It Conversational: "Super-Size Your Small Talk"

You must be a fountainhead of chitchat for the vision engine to fire. The primary reason you need to see it each day is to make it a part of daily conversation. It has been said that out of a hundred diets, there is one foolproof way of guaranteeing success: get on the scale and note your weight every twenty-four hours. Likewise there are a hundred ways to communicate vision creatively in your church. All of them succeed when the vision is talked about in the hallway or coffee shop before and after the meeting.

We have multiple mantras at Auxano. The one I say a lot is, "The conversation is the win." It's not earth-shattering but it's instructive. Because vision travels through people, not paper, dialogue is everything. We also say, "Vision dripping is more important than vision casting." People expect an annual message or two on your church's vision. On vision Sunday a pastor is like a fire hose spraying the vision on the congregation at thousands of gallons per minute. As important as that moment is, some-

> "Vision dripping is more important than vision casting."

how it's not that big of a deal to your people. Most of the water runs off, and the people are totally dry thirty minutes later. It doesn't become real—it doesn't saturate—until it's talked about in the unexpectedness of small talk. This hallway vision moment is like the sprinkling from the watering bucket of a careful gardener. Imagine a soaking hose; there is no runoff.

Keep It Financial: "Fuel Your Dreams"

The easiest way to kill your long-range dream is to make sure the finance committee never hears about it and thus never builds it into the budget. I have seen visions articulated with smashing success that never get mentioned in the budgeting process. This happens for two primary reasons: a "deaf" budgeting system or a strong personality—finance chair, business administrator, or executive pastor—who doesn't own the vision.

Most of the time the disconnect between dollars and dreams is unintentional. It's easy to understand this with the financial systems. The church runs its tried-and-true (yet never fun) process to allocate ministry budgets. Most of the systems don't "listen" to the vision. The budget-planning process needs a decided pause to interject the new implications of long-range vision into the preexisting flow of decision making.

Even with the person managing the purse strings, there's rarely ill intent toward the vision. Yet I often notice a simple and unspoken dichotomy: the pastor preaches the vision, and the business administrator orchestrates the finances without considering the vision. How does this happen? Most good financial leaders tend to be realistic and risk-averse operators. By nature they're inclined to relegate the topic of vision to the senior pastor and "more creative functions" of the church. This is reinforced to the degree that the church also struggles with well-managed implementation. The dichotomy "gap" widens over the year. In these conditions the long-range vision, never supported financially, gets reduced to a nifty tagline and dies at the bottom of the gap.

Your vision's launching pad must become the bottom line of your budget.

Immediate Action Steps to Use Your Long-Range Vision

Even though you are still working through your Horizon Storyline, I want to share some immediate action steps for using your long-range vision. Think of these as driving tips now that you have the engine running.

Action Step 1. Use your long-range vision to cultivate personal passion.

I want you to become a casual fanatic. Imagine a person who is fun to be around and starts conversations in a casual way. Yet at the same time there is a clear, big dream burning in his soul. He doesn't force it down anyone's throat, but he can't wait to talk about it. A casual fanatic is pleasantly passionate. He has the fire of John the Baptist and the poise of the president.

A great spiritual visionary will have a deep spiritual conviction, but the depth of conviction—and the passion it produces—doesn't happen overnight. Rather, it is cultivated like a farmer working a field. I recommend that you get your long-range vision into your devotional life. Journal it. Doodle it. Google it to find and learn from others with similar vision. Don't just pray about it; wrestle for God's blessing on it. Beg Him for His favor on it. Find Scriptures that illuminate it and move your soul. Know those pieces of sacred text better than anyone on the planet. Do you want a real secret weapon to develop your passion? Make a personal sacrifice for the vision that no one else sees.

People who know me describe me as bold and tenacious, sometimes to a fault. I have hundreds of stories about the benefits of living with passion. Yet the passion for me didn't develop in a vacuum, and I wasn't born with it. To the contrary, I was pretty introverted through my high school years and suffered from a lack of confidence. My passion developed by ruminating on my dreams. When I see a generic vision, my heart gets troubled, and I allow myself to feel the passion again. When I started Auxano, I hoped to pay my bills, but I daydreamed about the day I would spend 100 percent of my vocational hours helping church teams achieve breakthrough clarity. I really believe God wants to do something cosmically significant and locally specific through your church.

> God wants to do something cosmically significant and locally specific through your church.

When people hear my vision, they also feel my passion. That's what I want for you. Howard Hendricks used to say, "No one will bleed for your vision unless *you* are hemorrhaging." Become the vision owner you were meant to be. When you get out of bed in the morning, let your vision be your springboard. Be fanatic enough about your vision that people feel your passion.

Action Step 2. Use your long-range vision to anchor team prayer.

Some days when I drive by the Egret Bay campus of Clear Creek Community Church (introduced in the preface), I choke up. One year our midground milestone was a financial goal connected to our "Build It" campaign for our first permanent campus. We prayed as a team every Monday morning that God would provide the millions of dollars we would need to achieve the next big dream. And He did.

This week, how many group prayers will you lead or participate in? When you add it up week after week, it's probably a pretty big number. Imagine your team asking for prayer requests and getting to the end of a personal item list only to have someone say, "Most importantly, let's lift up our five-year dream and our four background vision big ideas." You know you're moving in the right direction when people lift up the long-range vision (or a specific aspect of it) just as spontaneously or frequently as they do other prayer requests. Of course you will need to be the instigator and model what it looks like to keep the vision a prayer agenda item.

Action Step 3. Use your long-range vision to saturate church communication.

Saturation means involving every person possible in every ministry "vehicle" possible with every medium possible. In the first month after developing your long-range vision, design not an event but a one-year communication strategy.

Start by expanding your awareness of potential mediums. A list to get you started includes:

- Verbal communication (storytelling, training, testimony, conversation, prayer)
- Video
- Pictures
- Music and interactive worship
- Art (painting, sculpting, dancing, photography, graphic design)
- Social media (Facebook, Twitter, Instagram, Periscope)
- Digital (website, mobile, apps, PDFs, infographics)
- Print (brochures, worship bulletins, bookmarks, table tents)
- Environmental graphics (posters, bulletin boards, banners, signage)
- E-mail
- Letters
- Thank-you cards
- Public relations tools

You also want to influence every ministry vehicle possible. By *vehicle* I mean ministry environment. A group of adults serving in the nursery is an environment. A bunch of couples in a family room for a small group is a ministry environment.

Action Step 4. Leverage your long-range vision in leadership settings even more than in church-wide preaching events.

Your temptation will be to see the worship service and preaching event as the *only* important environment for underscoring your long-range vision. If that's your approach, you will severely diminish the delivery of your vision. Do you want to deliver your vision in a wheelbarrow, an eighteen-wheel truck, or a C-130 cargo plane?

Instead, the preaching event must work in harness with two other major vehicles: your church's connecting environment (small groups, classes, adult Bible fellowships, or Sunday schools) and your leadership pipeline (leader gatherings, training classes, elders meetings, teacher training). The preaching event by itself merely illuminates the vision. There it is substantiated, defined, and celebrated but not much more. I assert, to the surprise of most pastors, that the weekly preaching event is your smallest vehicle. It feels counterintuitive, I know. You think of it as your biggest vehicle because the most people attend and you spend the most time preparing for it.

But your connecting environment and leadership pipeline are the larger vehicles in the sense that more vision understanding, appreciation, passion, and ownership are transferred. Leader gatherings allow people to ask questions and wrestle with the vision.

They provide time for dialogue and interpretation of the vision. Connecting environments allow everyday people to see other everyday people embody the vision. When group life leaders share their excitement for the church vision in their kitchen while pouring a cup of coffee, the vision is validated and transmitted in its purest form. Why? As stated earlier, the vision is much more contagious when the person who shares it isn't paid to do so and does so out of passion and excitement.

> Your connecting environment and leadership pipeline are the larger vehicles in the sense that more vision understanding, appreciation, passion, and ownership are transferred.

Use every medium and every ministry vehicle, but don't forget every person. The word on the street is the icing on the cake. Think of every person as a carrier of the vision. You want them to sneeze it everywhere they go. To do this:

- Use simple and sticky phrases people can use to share your beyond-the-horizon vision in their own way.
- Train people to share it and include modeling moments and time to practice.
- Find a way to make a napkin sketch out of it.
- Invite and enlist volunteers to share it (live or video) in different ministry environments.
- Celebrate people when they do share the vision.

Action Step 5. Use your long-range vision to deliver meaning daily.

Like the postman, you and your core team must deliver meaning daily in packages both big and small. This is an incredibly simple yet profound habit: weekly, as a leadership team, have each person decide in advance on at least three meetings to share or "drip" the vision. It may be a volunteer training event or a one-on-one recruiting event. It may just be lunch with a good friend or an informal hangout at the coffee shop.

The moment can be as seemingly inconsequential as, "You know, after we rolled out the new ten-year vision, I've been thinking about doing something different for our vacation this year." Or, "So have you thought much about the ten-year vision that was launched this last month? Why or why not?"

At your next weekly meeting, debrief the times leaders have communicated the vision and then "lock and load" the next top three deliveries for the following week. Again this simple accountability step will create more learning, more camaraderie, and more progress than you can imagine.

Action Step 6. Use your long-range vision to practice blessed subtraction.

Now we are getting to the toughest discipline of all. It's a practice for which many thinkers—from negotiators, counselors, business gurus, and artists—have coined unique terms. It's the notion that focusing on a great vision means subtracting what doesn't belong.

- William Ury calls it "the power of a positive no."
- Jim Collins calls it the "the stop-doing list."
- Peter Drucker calls it "systematic abandonment."
- Greg McKeown calls it "essentialism."
- Henry Cloud calls it "necessary endings."
- Michelangelo calls it "purgation of superfluities."
- Mies van der Rohe calls it "less is more."
- Andy Stanley calls it "narrow your focus."

When Jesus sends the twelve in Luke 9:3, He says, "Take nothing for your journey." To the degree that you are unwilling either to let things go or make things go away, you will eventually suffocate the long-range vision. It doesn't matter how many experts you quote; there is no substitute for the grit of conviction.

Your long-range vision is a powerful magnet. Its ability to attract comes with the ability to repel. That's a good thing. Immediately look for ways to let that dynamic work.

What do you need to subtract?

- Anyone who works against the vision
- Leaders who disagree with the general direction of the vision
- Activity that siphons energy from the vision
- Programs that don't propel vision

A whole book could be written on how to handle these situations with love and grace. My point is to remind you to start practicing the elimination of forces that wage war against your vision. Implementing the vision is not a walk in the park; it's a dynamic process under the leadership of the Holy Spirit.

Listen to the senior pastors of high-growth churches talk about the necessity of letting people and programs go. Keep in mind these are voices coming from some of the fastest growing churches in America:[2]

> We killed Sunday school, and it saved our church. We killed men's and
> women's ministry and it saved our church. We found that you can't have

competing ministries and build intimacy. —Jeff Clark, Venture Church, Hattiesburg, Mississippi

We limit our programs. By saying "no" to additional church programs so we can say "yes" to resourcing outreach. —Stuart Hodges, Waters Edge Church, Yorktown, Virginia

I wish I had been told how pitiful and unproductive it is to worry over whom you retain and whom you don't. —John Beukema, King Street Church, Chambersburg, Pennsylvania

In the larger scheme of things, I think we pastors would do well to become okay with people leaving our church. —Benji Kelly, Newhope Church, Durham, North Carolina

If people are unhappy, I would rather help them find a church that "fits" them than have them stay unhappy and possibly quit going to church altogether. —John McKinzie, Hope Fellowship, Frisco, Texas

No one ever told me that if you lead well people will still leave the church. —Kerry Shook, The Woodlands Church, Woodlands, Texas

Keep voices like this around when you are faced with the tough calls you *will have to* make in order to see dramatic impact with your vision.

You Can Drive the Long-Range Vision!

You are most likely an effective communicator as one called to ministry. Even if you are still practicing, you really can bring the long-range vision to life. This chapter has suggested a number of practical ways to use long-range vision to show spiritual and visionary leadership. Remember the three essentials are see it, talk it, and fund it. Don't underestimate how the tyranny of the urgent always wants to steal attention away from the big picture (which is why I devoted all of chapter 3 to the tendency to obsess with "now"). Likewise don't underestimate the motivational power and unity that comes from a constant focus on the long range.

Now that we've covered some immediate action steps with the long-range vision, please turn the page to part 5 of the book on how to develop and execute your short-range vision.

PART FIVE

Execute Your *Short-Range* Vision

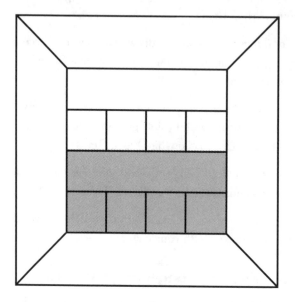

Chapter 16
Developing Your Midground Vision

There are no results without a concentration of resources.
—Renowned management consultant Peter Drucker

We now shift gears from the long-range part of the Horizon Storyline (the top 1:4) to the short-range part (the bottom 1:4), which figure 16.1 shows. Nazi General Erwin Rommel was a military genius working for an evil regime. His brilliant navigation tactics in World War II illustrates the relationship of these two parts of the horizon storyline.

Rommel is considered to be one of the greatest warfare tacticians of all time. He earned the nickname the Desert Fox as he led the elite tank formation, the Seventh Panzer Division of Germany, also known as the Ghost Division. Rommel surprised his enemies with tactics of superior speed and maneuverability as he mobilized hundreds of tanks across the ocean-like sands of North Africa.

Imagine the difficulty of reaching an objective hundreds of miles away (long-range) when there is nothing in the desert landscape to sense progress; a soldier could drive all day and not know visually how far he had traveled. While Rommel could plot the distant objective on the map, he wanted his troops to have a continual notion of forward movement. To achieve unprecedented speed, he innovated. Rommel had a lead jeep drive in advance of the tank formation and place a fifty-five-gallon oil drum in the sand with a giant flag waving above it. Every tank driver saw at least one short-range objective marker in order to "feel" progress. In this case the leader created a way for his troops to have visceral sense of movement with every rotation of the Caterpillar tank tread.

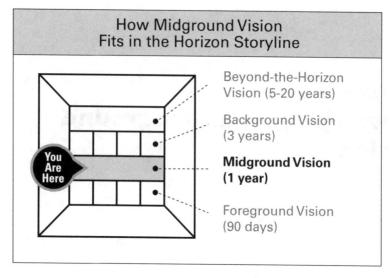

Figure 16.1

As a church leader you have your own desert to lead people across. It's the undifferentiated landscape of one Sunday after another. Like those tank treads, the weeks turn round and round and round.

How do you know if you are making any progress toward your long-range objective? The answer is your midground vision.

Your Midground Vision (1 year)

The midground vision is a single emphasis stated as a one-year goal.[1] The goal is both an inspiring picture (qualitative) and a measurable number (quantitative). They accompany one another. I also refer to midground vision as a midground milestone. The term *milestone* is useful as it keeps the picturesque dynamic within our Horizon Storyline. It's what the team—or the "the eyes of the organization"—is looking at practically just like Rommel's tank drivers.

Like the beyond-the-horizon vision, the midground vision is designed to inspire people and stretch their thinking about what might be possible. It can be stated in one sentence and adapted regularly for communication every day. While one year is a natural starting point for discussion, it can be flexible, covering anywhere between six and eighteen months.

The midground vision:

- Shows a big and visible next step toward your long-range horizons.
- Generates excitement for what God is doing in the next year.
- Focuses the attention, prayers, and resources of the church in a dramatic way.
- Reveals progress that can be celebrated (or recalibrated).
- Highlights one shared priority for all ministry areas.
- Cuts through the complexity of life and ministry with one focus.

Some examples of midground milestones:

- Before Vince Antonucci launched his first public service for Verve Church in Las Vegas, Nevada, he aimed to have eighty adults on his core team engaged in regular city service.
- Grace Point Church in San Antonio, Texas, led by Jeff Harris cast a vision to put 30 percent of the congregation on foreign soil within one year.
- The Bridge Bible Church in Bakersfield, California, recently committed to reestablish a leadership core of 360 people over a nine-month period.
- Northwest Bible Church in Dallas, Texas, challenged their congregation to know the unexpected joy of service measured by a thousand people from their congregation taking the "three-mile drive" to see the world. The three-mile drive is the distance to Vickery, an area densely populated by refugees.
- The Multiply Group led by Mac Lake plans to train twelve transformational coaching guides in the next six months to address the twelve top challenges of church planters in their first year.
- Asbury United Methodist Church in Raleigh, North Carolina, hopes to engage 65 percent of people who call Asbury "my church" in Life Groups next year, a 50 percent increase in current Life Group attendance.
- First Baptist Church in Kettering, Ohio, envisions 100 percent of people in Sunday school becoming active "Jesus speakers" who regularly invite people to the church, evidenced by twelve first-time guest families per week at the Pastor's Welcome.
- 100 Movement's led by Alan Hirsch is launching "Leap Year" with the goal of recruiting one hundred churches to take a one-year journey to apply more deeply one component of "apostolic genius" (from his book *Forgotten Ways*).
- Hope Church, Las Vegas, Nevada, led by Vance Pitman decided to shoot for 75 percent of their regular attenders engaging in a shared experience of visible

commitment to their new "5 percent disciple-making" strategy within eleven months.

- Brushy Creek Baptist Church, Easley, South Carolina, hopes to see more alignment around "living the gospel toward a lasting priority" with the goal of doubling families who consistently give and serve once a month.

- Salem Lutheran Church in Tomball, Texas, ignited their congregation with a "one campaign" based on their mission as imperfect people risking it all to make Jesus real, one life at a time. Their goal was 100 percent of worship attenders to invite at least one person to worship or a special event designed for unchurched people.

The Simple Hard Thing

The greatest obstacle to developing your midground goal is not your ability but your willingness. We ministry types have difficulty appreciating the power of radical simplicity. I hope you can see how simple it is—based on the illustrations—to state the goal itself. You have probably heard of S.M.A.R.T.[2] goals before. That acronym means your goals should be **s**pecific, **m**easurable, **a**chievable, **r**elevant (to the long-range), and **t**ime-based. You can do that. The hardest thing is to apply yourself to one big goal at a time. Keeping it simple has never required more guts.

> The greatest obstacle to developing your midground goal is not your ability but your willingness.

May I try to persuade you? Here are the top ten reasons you should advance toward your long-range horizon with one midground milestone at a time. Think like a military mobilizer helping the entire body of Christ move toward one giant flag in the sand. As you do, keep in mind the two main reasons church leaders miss the power of one: having none or having too many. That is, churches either have no clearly stated aspirations (no flags) at all, or they have too many goals (multiple flags) in an overwhelming strategic plan or cumbersome dashboard. The sweet spot is a rare yet priceless in-between: one highly visible, broadly supported goal.

The Trend Toward Radical Simplicity

In the last decade many organizational gurus are touting the benefits of the radical simplicity of one goal as a team. Let's peek into the thoughts of a few of them as they give their reasoning and coin their own language for dealing with the problem.

Advantages of Focusing on One Goal at a Time		
Reason	**Benefits**	**Why**
1	Focuses the attention of staff and leaders.	If you have no goal at all, there is no focus. If you have many goals, people will be playing for different teams, focused on different things.
2	Creates greater energy among the congregation.	Having no goals leaves the church's potential underactivated. With too many goals, people deplete their energy.
3	Directs everyone's prayers as a concert of dependence on God.	Having no goal leaves prayers random at best. Having too many goals dramatically lowers the likelihood of any goal having the congregation's full prayer attention.
4	Helps leaders think bigger about what God might be doing.	When there are no goals, teams tend to drift into smaller thinking. When there are too many goals, team thinking is susceptible to fragmenting.
5	Your church will see goals for disciple-making outcomes, not just financial goals on the way to the long-range vision.	Even when churches don't like to use goals, a financial goal will pop up eventually, probably for a capital campaign. With too many goals, people may never see the importance of disciple-making goals elevated within the church community.
6	Makes it easier to generate momentum.	If the church has no goals, leaders will define success any way they want. If the church has too many goals, the sense of momentum easily evaporates because people aren't working together for the same thing.
7	Helps leadership build toward bigger and bigger goals. Think of this as a snowball effect or the impact of compound interest on your money.	By not having goals, your church never creates an "on-ramp" to bigger goals. You completely miss out on a snowball effect. By having too many goals, the scope of each goal stays smaller and misses the opportunity to point to something bigger.
8	Fosters healthy risk-taking.	With no goal, there is little if any reason to risk. There is no stretch factor. With too many goals, the church likely lowers their risk threshold for any one of them.
9	Connects people to God's larger story of redemptive history.	With no goal, we risk leaving people to live in their smaller story. With too many goals, we disconnect people from the bigger picture of God's epic working.
10	Demonstrates God-honoring unity.	If you never have a goal, you miss the opportunity to show people a grand "togetherness." With too many goals, as you might expect, it may show how easy it is for leaders in the church to have their own agenda.

Figure 16.2

The first is Patrick Lencioni who encourages leaders to develop one shared rallying cry as a team that he calls a "thematic goal." Listen to him build his case:

> Most organizations I've worked with have too many top priorities to achieve the level of focus they need to succeed. Wanting to cover all their bases, they establish a long list of disparate objectives and spread their scarce time, energy, and resources across them all. The result is almost always a lot of initiatives being done in a mediocre way and a failure to accomplish what matters most. This phenomenon is best captured in that wonderful adage, "If everything is important, nothing is."[3]

As Lencioni reflected on the fact that emergency response teams never have silos and always know what's most important, he concluded that all teams should have an urgent shared goal.

> As I thought about the power of a rallying cry, I wondered why all organizations couldn't replicate the benefits of achieving that kind of focus (short of creating false crises, which is never a good idea). And I decided that there is no reason that every organization couldn't have a rallying cry, even when it is not in crisis. I called this rallying cry "a thematic goal" because it needs to be understood within the context of the organization's other goals, at the top of the list. And so, the thematic goal is the answer to our question, "What is most important, right now?"[4]

Another group that promotes radical simplicity in goal setting is the team at Franklin Covey, who wrote the book, *The Four Disciplines of Execution*. The contribution to the conversation is the first discipline: focus on the wildly important. The nifty term "WIG" has been adopted and stands for "wildly important goal." Here is their rationale:

> Basically, the more you try to do, the less you actually accomplish. This is a stark, inescapable principle that we all live with. Somewhere along the way, most leaders forget this. Why? Because smart, ambitious leaders don't want to do less, they want to do more, even when they know better. Isn't it really difficult for you to say no to a good idea, much less a great one? And yet, there will always be more good ideas than you and your teams have the capacity to execute. That's why your first challenge is focusing on the wildly important.
>
> Focus is a natural principle. The sun's scattered rays are too weak to start a fire, but once you focus them with a magnifying glass they will bring paper

to flame in seconds. The same is true of human beings—once their collective energy is focused on a challenge, there is little they can't accomplish.[5]

What Lencioni calls a thematic goal is the same idea as what the Franklin Covey guys call a WIG. Both of these are the same idea as what I call the midground milestone. It's one goal in the next year that defines your midground vision.[6]

Having dealt with the "why one goal" as the primary obstacle, let's cover two important how-to steps. This is not a comprehensive list but two valuable tips as you develop your midground milestone.

Use Collaborative Genius to Generate Creative Milestone Ideas

Create a fun brainstorming environment and invite the team to speak into the midground vision. I recommend keeping the group to twelve or fewer people. Keep the conversation focused on the beyond-the-horizon vivid description and the four big rocks of your background vision. With the context of your long-range vision clear, begin a conversation on "what's important now."[7] I like the question, What is the single most important thing that will demonstrate and motivate progress toward our long-range vision?

The key is to generate an unexpected, creative, and mind-stretching range of ideas as a team, before the team picks one.

For example, I was recently with the Hope Church team in Las Vegas. Their midground emphasis is encouraging the investment of time around a newly articulated "5 percent strategy." The four-step strategy is to spend God time (fifteen minutes a day), Group time (two hours every other week), Gather time (one hour a week), and Go time (one week per year). Here are some of the creative milestones or goals they came up with in the brainstorming time:

- Create a "shared experience" to show a visible, Group-time investment decision for 75 percent of the church.
- Develop a tool where 50 percent of our people show they have actually calendared the 5 percent strategy for one year.
- Count cumulative Go-time minutes of the church in one year if 75 percent invested 2 percent of their time. It would equal thirty-four years of missions service in one year.
- Count the cumulative God-time minutes if 75 percent invested 1 percent of their time. It would equal ten million minutes with God.

- Count the total number of people trained via online training aiming for 75 percent of regular attenders trained.
- Double the number of baptisms.
- Move 415 people through a leadership pipeline that will deeply embed the new strategy.

Two of the numbers on this brainstorm were so powerful and mind-blowing to participants that we had to stop the process as people gasped in amazement. They were the ten million minutes of God time and the thirty-four years of missionary service in one year. When that happens, you know you have engaged a most successful team time!

Use Key Questions to Select the Best Goal

When a group lists a strong set of potential milestones for their midground vision, the following questions can help them narrow it down to one. Someone may read the questions and conduct a group vote asking each person to champion a favorite goal for sixty seconds or less.

1. Which one of these milestones gets me personally excited the most?
2. Which one of these milestones sparked an immediate positive response from our vision team?
3. Which milestone could create the most energy for most of the people in our church?
4. Which one of these milestones represents the biggest step toward our beyond-the-horizon vision and background vision?
5. Does the milestone give us an inspiring step of faith and risk-taking posture without sounding unrealistically absurd?
6. What milestone will keep us engaged even after the first six months?
7. What milestone can we see translating creatively into all of our ministry departments?
8. What milestone would provide our congregation with a deep abiding sense of accomplishment and really get us excited to engage another milestone?

With few exceptions the teams I have worked with can effectively narrow their focus and decide on one midground milestone within two to three hours from the beginning of brainstorming to the final selection.

What's Next?

In this chapter I have emphasized the quantitative nature of the midground vision. As we conclude the chapter, don't forget that there is qualitative aspect as well.

Once the leadership decides on a measurable goal, I encourage them to develop three- to five-minute vision casting moments (vision dripping). You can use the four imperatives for making vision move from chapters 12 and 13 in exactly the same way you did with your vivid description. In addition, chapters 17 and 18 in *Church Unique* treat this subject further and provide a vision-casting spider diagram.

Once you have selected your midground vision singular goal, it's time to work on the next and final horizon: the foreground vision. The next chapter does just that.

Chapter 17

Developing Your Foreground Vision

People don't tend to wander around and suddenly find themselves at the top of Mount Everest.

—Motivational speaker Zig Ziglar

Every church I visit is pretty busy. I see lots of activity, but I also see frustration with getting something done together *beyond* the next weekly production cycle of worship services. This scenario raises an important question: how much of your leadership team's time is allocated to something *other* than programming next week?

For most churches it's not nearly as much as desired. You might have a leadership rally scheduled for three months out, a facility addition coming online next year, or a Woman of the Word conference coming up. But most hours of the typical staff are consumed almost completely by drop-dead deadlines surrounding Sunday morning worship.

If that's not enough, the weekly unexpectedness of being in the "people business" creates further havoc on time management. Marriages are unraveling, children are rebelling, cancer is spreading, and automobiles are colliding. And none of these events bothered to get on your calendar for the upcoming week.

Given this challenge—and the noble calling associated with it—how do you begin advancing a long-range vision in the midst of weekly worship preparation and daily relational demands?

The answer is with *foreground vision*. We now "put our feet to the ground" with the Horizon Storyline. What started at thirty thousand feet; we now apply at thirty feet.

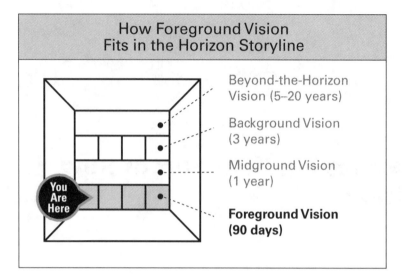

Figure 17.1

Foreground Vision (Ninety days)

The foreground vision contains up to four specific initiatives that must be started within ninety days, as needed. The foreground initiatives are typically led by cross-functional teams in larger churches or by ministry departments or individuals. The initiatives should support the midground vision directly or indirectly. Think of these initiatives as the four most important next steps in order to complete the single, midground vision.

Why do you need a foreground vision? The ninety-day horizon:

> The foreground vision contains up to four specific initiatives that must be started within ninety days.

- Clarifies weekly action-steps and daily priorities for leaders.
- Sequences short-term projects, tasks, and goals.
- Activates the unique gifts and abilities within the body.
- Provides regular, positive accountability for individuals and teams.

I have waited more than a decade before writing on the topic of execution. Why? I like to create tools that are model neutral—that is, they work in any faith tribe, ministry philosophy, or church size. This is extremely difficult in churches when it comes to execution, as "getting things done" can and must look different church to church. The nature of execution must flex to account for each church's unique polity, decision-making process, leadership style, and congregational expectations.

Therefore this chapter has two parts: five key essentials to embrace and a menu approach to adapt. You can really sink your teeth into the few essentials. They are core no matter how big your flock or what theological stripes you wear. You can have fun with the menu approach; experiment, practice, and refine it until you find your right recipe to get extraordinary things done.

Five Execution Essentials to Embrace

Essential 1. Embrace ninety days as a "season of success."

The foreground horizon forces us to think about the next ninety days, a special unit of time. Ninety days is like a long sprint. It's short enough to sustain focus, even urgency, yet long enough to accomplish something significant. It's the rhythm of creation we know as the season. It's the basic quarterly reporting cycles of business and the semester cycle for many schools and churches.

Ninety days was more than enough time for Nehemiah to rebuild the walls of Jerusalem. It's enough time to read the Bible at twelve pages per day, to turn a sloppy civilian into a lean Marine, or to become a world-class salsa dancer. It is enough time for your team to become an unstoppable force as you implement your vision.

In referring to the foreground as a ninety-day horizon, the point is that something must start in the next ninety days. Some things might be started and finished. Other initiatives might take multiple ninety-day cycles. The key insight is that ninety days is an optimal frame for human growth and organizational development. And it works perfect too for a church team to "look above" the immediate horizon of this weekend.

> Ninety days is enough time for your team to become an unstoppable force as you implement your vision.

Essential 2. Embrace the power of four.

Why am I encouraging no more than four initiatives in your foreground? For the first ten years of consulting, I started with a blank slate. I resisted any forced boundaries like a preset amount of initiatives to have. But the beauty of four just kept showing itself over and over again. It's simply the best way I know to direct a team's time and attention when facilitating churches of all sizes. I bet you will find that the 1:4:1:4 cycle is incredibly simple and simultaneously robust. Think of the four foreground initiatives as the table legs of your immediate future.

Essential 3. Embrace a rhythm of review.

The key to success for any short-range goal is a weekly review cycle as a team. Again, every church I know has weekly meetings, so the key is to introduce a review of the foreground initiative beyond the demanding weekly stuff. Some teams do this by adding extra time in their weekly meeting routine or by adding an additional short and sweet meeting every week dedicated to the foreground initiatives alone. Consultant Patrick Lencioni advocates daily stand-up meetings (the meeting time is so short, everyone stands up), which I have seen a few churches do with great success. As we move toward defining three kinds of initiatives for the foreground vision, a weekly review minimum is critical for each one. In fact, let me warn that if you don't conduct a weekly cadence of review, you might as well not have ninety-day initiatives at all.

> If you don't conduct a weekly cadence of review, you might as well not have ninety-day initiatives at all.

Essential 4. Embrace a visual scoreboard.

Shortly after Hurricane Katrina, Friday night football resumed in a small Texas town for a big game. At kickoff the fans were stoked. But shortly afterwards there was a strange lack of attention on the game. Fans weren't cheering the players but were distracted, chatting with one another. It turned out the scoreboard had blown down in the hurricane. It's almost impossible to hold peoples' interest when you don't know the score.[1]

That's another reason Sunday worship demands almost all of the staff's attention. Every week the number of people in worship is a visual scorecard for the preacher and other staff.

Your short-range initiatives are kept alive by the eyeballs of your team. It may be as simple as a color graph printed each week and taped above the office copy machine. Or it may be a number updated on a dedicated whiteboard or digitally designed for a flat screen. In one church the team measured the number of conversations with leaders by putting a marble in a huge glass jar for every conversation initiated. Another adds a flower to a prominent hallway board, prompting ongoing buzz as the cluster of flowers grows over the weeks.

What form of visual scoreboard will you use to hold everyone's attention?

Essential 5. Embrace a bias for action.

I'm not sure how it happens in the church, but I regularly see a crazy variation of the "get-'er-done" factor. Some teams have enough self-starter spirit to light a small city while others float from day to day like driftwood in the open sea. It's entirely possible to have a godly, smart, and educated ministry staff person who has no bias for action.

Without some team members who embody personal momentum, trying to implement your short-range 1:4 is challenging. It's not that everyone has to be a superstar. But there ought to be enough spark-plug people around the team to keep it revving.

If you have some sluggish team players, encourage them to step up their game as you implement your Horizon Storyline. Assign them work with people from whom they can catch some energy. Also, consider providing personal coaching or extra management direction. Initiative can be learned.

Flexible Approach: Three Kinds of Foreground Initiatives

Now it's time to tailor and adapt your foreground initiatives to your situation. The flexibility is gained by having three kinds of initiatives to choose from for your foreground vision. Remember you will have four of them.

Let's imagine the following *midground* milestone (see figure 17.2):

Example of a Midground Milestone

Increasing small group involvement
by 50 percent in one year
starting on June 1
by going from four of ten
worshippers in small groups
to six of ten worshippers
in small-groups.

Figure 17.2

Now what are some possible *foreground* initiatives to support it?

Cross-functional Emphasis

A cross-functional emphasis is an initiative containing many smaller action steps that require a team from multiple ministry areas. For example, imagine a team that's tasked with redesigning and launching a new assimilation process (*foreground initiative*) that has a small-groups pastor, welcome team leaders, children's ministry leaders, and the communication director.

A cross-functional team will usually consist of three to nine people with a clearly designated leader who can define and sequence action steps, assign action steps to team members, and report progress weekly to a lead team or ministry supervisor. For larger churches (over eight hundred in worship attendance), Auxano uses the Paterson Center StratOp methodology to build out "Action Initiative Plans" for a cross-functional team emphasis.[2]

Ministry Area Subgoals

A ministry area (or department) subgoal is an initiative owned by a ministry area team or an individual leader. Usually a departmental goal has fewer action steps than a cross-functional emphasis (as they are less complicated). There is always a clear time frame, and progress toward the subgoal is reported to a lead team or ministry supervisor. Some examples of departmental goals for our example midground vision are:

- A student ministry recruits and trains twenty students by the September kick-off to provide free child care for small groups, a common obstacle to group involvement.
- The small-groups leadership team implements a ninety-day turbo-group training class to launch fifteen additional leaders by the September kickoff.
- The worship team decides to recruit and video record twenty-six people to give testimonies about the life-altering value of a small group. They will complete all of the recording and editing to have a year's worth of every-other-week worship-service testimonies.

Note that all of these subgoals are clear and measurable with a time frame. Keep in mind the "SMART" acronym from the previous chapter.

All-staff Drivers

A driver is an initiative that's a little different from a goal. It's an actionable theme or factor on a weekly basis that your team has control over that will impact the church's ability to accomplish the midground vision. The best way to clarify the nature of a driver is to illustrate. To increase small group attendance by 50 percent, possible drivers include:

- **Intentional inviting:** We will intentionally invite people to small groups every week, especially in the "ten-minute mingle" before and after worship services.

- **Dropout connecting:** We will initiate relational "check-ins" with people who have stopped attending a small group to see how they are doing and learn what caused them to leave.
- **Leadership modeling:** Staff will engage weekly storytelling about their personal experiences in small groups.
- **Responsive follow-up:** We will quickly respond to any person's interest in a small group.

There are two ways to structure and provide feedback on these drivers. A fun, informal way that creates positive accountability is to conduct a team check in regular leadership meetings. As the team leader you might say something like, "Okay team, let's spend a few minutes reporting in on the *intentional inviting* driver this week. How did you do inviting people to a small group this week? What stories do you have? What are you going to do different this week to invite people?" Don't miss the last question in the sequence—the strength of the driver is how it redirects new activity and focus *this week*. If the church has no mechanism to affect *next week* based on the vision, the church fundamentally will not achieve the vision.

Another way to use drivers that dials up the intentionality quite a bit—some churches can do this and some can't—is to create what's called a "lead measure" kind of driver. The language of "lead measure" is used to contrast it with a "lag measure."[3] Unfortunately, the way most people think about goal setting is a lag measure. The goal is something that is not directly controlled but something that "happens" or "lags." For example, the number a church reports for worship attendance or the amount they raised in a capital campaign is a "lag measure." The church leaders don't have direct influence over this number.

> Unfortunately, the way most people think about goal setting is a lag measure.

A lead measure, however, is one you do directly influence. For example, a lead measure is meeting with five leaders a week, one-on-one, to share the capital campaign vision seeking their commitment to it. In this sense the lead measures foretell and influence the goal (lag measure) you want rather than just reporting it after it has occurred.

Let's look at the four drivers we mentioned earlier and turn them into "lead measure" drivers:

- **Intentional inviting:** Every staff person (or volunteer leader) will invite three people to a small group every Sunday before, in between, and after worship services.

- **Dropout connecting:** Every staff person (or volunteer leader) will have one lunch per week with someone who used to attend small group but no longer does.
- **Leadership modeling:** Every staff person (or volunteer leader) will share a testimony of the impact of a small group in their life with five people every week.
- **Responsive follow-up:** Our team will respond to 100 percent of "connect card" small group requests within twenty-four hours.

Lead measure drivers like these are incredibly powerful, but they do take a higher level of management energy on the team.

Also, don't miss the importance of the "all staff" aspect of using a driver. This dynamic creates a leadership blitz. While the midground milestone ensures that every ministry area is focused on a singular goal for the year, a ninety-day driver can additionally focus your entire team on one key result leading toward it. When this happens, every ministry team leader is in essence putting on the "small-group pastor hat" for part of the leadership role. The nursery director is inviting three people to small group every Sunday—not their typically assigned task—along with the student director and the worship leader. When a team is excited about the driver and they focus on it together, I promise you'll see ministry results like you never thought possible.

Let me summarize what we have covered so far in figure 17.3:

Use Different Initiatives Based on Church Size

Mix and match the types of initiatives based on your level of organizational complexity and management resources. Generally speaking, the larger the church, the more you can and should use cross-functional emphasis. For smaller churches the ministry area subgoal is the easiest to implement. Drivers can be used at any size level.

Figure 17.4 gives an example of how to adjust the use of different initiatives based on church size. It is a general guideline and certainly not a hard, fast rule. The number-one learning after using these three types of foreground initiatives is that churches have a difficult time using cross-functional teams. It's not how they typically function, and the "tyranny of Sunday" is hard to fight. Therefore, use them only to the extent that you have the leadership capacity and people who can manage the team well.

Using the model of the church size of four hundred to twelve hundred, here is the completed short-range 1:4, based on our working example (figure 17.5):

How to Involve Everyone, Every Week

Foreground Initiative Type	Number of Smaller Action Steps	Responsibility	Complexity	Review
1. Cross-Functional Emphasis	Many (5–15)	Team	High	Direct report or leadership team
2. Ministry Area Subgoal	Some (3–8)	Team or individual	Variable	Direct report or leadership team
3. All Staff Driver	One	Individual	Low	Peer to peer in staff meetings

Figure 17.3

Customize Your Foreground Initiatives by Church Size

Church Size by Attendance	Initiative 1	Initiative 2	Initiative 3	Initiative 4
4,000 +	Cross-functional emphasis	Cross-functional emphasis	Cross-functional emphasis	All staff driver
1,200–4,000	Cross-functional emphasis	Cross-functional emphasis	All staff driver	All staff driver
400–1,200	Cross-functional emphasis	All staff driver	Ministry area subgoal	Ministry area subgoal
0–400	All staff driver	Ministry area subgoal	Ministry area subgoal	Ministry area subgoal

Figure 17.4

First Church Short-Range Vision Example

	LONG-RANGE
Beyond-the-horizon Vision:	
Background Vision:	

Midground Vision:	SHORT-RANGE
Better Life, Together: We see more people in our church being loved and loving deeply in strong bonds of covenant community. Life is too short to not have real spiritual friendships. We will see an increased small group involvement by 50 percent by May of next year so that six out of ten people who worship at First Church will belong to their own smaller circle of fellowship.	

Foreground Vision:			
(#1 Cross-functional Emphasis) **Revise Group Connect Process:** We will design and launch a new assimilation process by September 1.	(#2 All Staff Driver) **Invite Three Weekly:** Every staff will invite three people to a small group every Sunday before, in between, and after services between now and September 1.	(#3 Ministry Area Subgoal) **Train 15 Leaders:** The small groups leadership team will implement a 90-day turbo group training class to launch fifteen additional leaders by the September kick-off.	(#4 Ministry Area Subgoal) **Create 26 Videos:** The worship team will create twenty-six video testimonies about the life-altering value of small group to use every other week starting on August 1.

Figure 17.5

Making the Horizon Storyline Work

As you complete the building of your Horizon Storyline, follow four guidelines in implementation:

Guideline 1: Involve Everyone

Ensure that everyone plays a part. As you use the different kinds of initiatives, make sure no one "falls through the cracks" when it comes to a ninety-day horizon action step. Drivers can guarantee that everyone plays a role, but the other initiatives may or may not. Orchestrate the whole.

Guideline 2: Block the Calendar

Start calendar blocking the renewal process of updating your Horizon Storyline. Like a drive through the countryside, the Horizon Storyline assumes you are getting somewhere and ultimately arriving at your future destination. You will arrive somewhere (or not) every ninety days, one year, three years, and sometime between five and twenty years. Each one of these checkpoints in the future is an opportunity to update the tool. For example, on September 1 in our example, all four initiatives may be reevaluated. Some may continue and some may change. Don't miss this exciting feature of your new visionary planning tool.

Guideline 3: Tell the Story

The Horizon Storyline is your story. Now you can practice piecing together the entire plan as a story itself (one of the key features of the Horizon Storyline we covered in chapter 5 and in figure 5.1).

Here is how to create a story: first, think of the beyond-the-horizon vision as a climatic scene and the background horizon as the four giant obstacles on your epic journey in order to arrive there. Then think of the midground milestone as an inciting incident that creates focus, attention, and energy with the foreground initiatives as specific next steps.[4] It's not that hard to imagine great stories or favorite films with this structure in mind. (It's called dramatic or plot structure.) The "inciting" is the event or situation that creates tension or initiates a problem that drives the story forward. The climatic scene is the resolution (or not) of that initial problem.

For example, the inciting incident in *The Wizard of Oz* is Dorothy being hit by a tornado in Kansas. The climatic scene is finally getting to see the wizard with her three friends only to discover that it is just a man standing behind the curtain. In the original *Star Wars,* the inciting incident is Darth Vader's attack on Princess Leia's rebel ship, and the climatic scene is Luke Skywalker exploding the Death Star with the surgical shot from his X-wing fighter.

The same features that make a story worth retelling and keeps you on the edge of your seat in a movie—dramatic structure—also makes your Horizon Storyline easy and even fun to share.

It might sound something like this (see figure 17.6):

Using this script, you invite the listener into the immediate action of your midground vision as an inciting incident. And you create a massive sense of "wow" and anticipation for a climatic scene in your church's future.

Sample Horizon Storyline Script

May I tell you about where God is taking us as a church?

In the next ten years we dream of:

_____

_____.

In order to reach that destination, we first have to accomplish these four big things in the next three years:

- _____,
- _____,
- _____,
- _____.

Our focus for the next year is:

_____

_____.

The four immediate steps to make this happen are:

- _____,
- _____,
- _____,
- _____.

Figure 17.6

When you blow people away with your stunning clarity, please be sure to send me a note! (See "About the Authors" for how to contact me.)

Guideline 4: Draw It

Look for ways to draw your Horizon Storyline quickly and frequently. (See figure 17.7.) Don't miss the simple, quick napkin sketch you can draw at any time. It's a great, quick tool you can put the key words of your vision in.

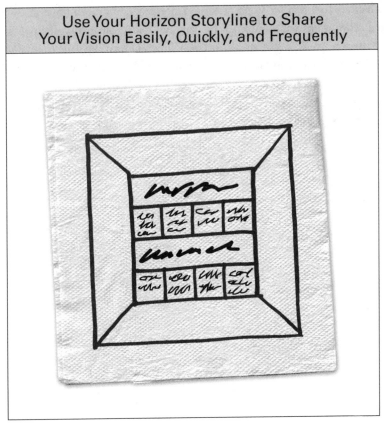

Figure 17.7

Guideline 5: Adapt But Be Careful

If you feel like you just can't limit yourself to four ideas on the background and four initiatives on the foreground, you can add more. But do so only at the risk of losing focus. I recommend it only if you have successful completion, with the enthusiasm of your team with the 1:4:1:4 first.

Don't Merely Read This Chapter

This entire book is intended to be something your church can put to work, chapter by chapter. This chapter in particular is extremely practical in hope that so many potential action steps will bubble up for you and your team that you'll pause to put some of them to work (or on the calendar) before you turn the page to read the final chapter. Draw the Horizon Storyline on whiteboards or white-pad easels both as you are building it and after you have completed it. You'll want to keep it before your volunteer groups and leadership teams. You'll be surprised how often you can use it in training settings (see figure 17.8).

Figure 17.8

PART SIX

Lead with Freedom

Chapter 18
The Greatest Benefit of Stunning Clarity

I glorified you on earth, having accomplished the work that you gave me to do.

— Jesus Christ (John 17:4)

My freedom thus consists of moving about within the narrow frame that I have assigned to myself for each one of my undertakings. I shall go even further: my freedom will be so much the greater and more meaningful the more narrowly I limit my field of action and the more I surround myself with obstacles. Whatever diminishes constraint diminishes strength. The more constraints one imposes the more one frees oneself of the claims that shackle the spirit.

— Igor Stravinsky, *Poetics of Music in the Form of Six Lessons*

When I started consulting in 2001, I wanted the church to be better. But since then my passion shifted. Today I want pastors to be freer. Specifically I hope pastors feel freer, confident of what God is calling them to do, and, as a result, accomplishing more with their short lives on the earth. Jeff Harris on our Auxano team, and senior pastor of Grace Point Church in San Antonio, has a personal tagline: "one life, one lifetime." Have you ever asked the question, "What has God set me free to do with my one life?"

This personal freedom is a rare commodity in the churches I serve. It seems displaced by personal frenzy. Almost every pastor I know is running on a ministry treadmill. The more people you reach, the faster the treadmill turns. But when people leave, the treadmill runs faster too. After hundreds and hundreds of Sundays, the next one arrives even faster.

Sometimes our hurriedness is driven by an internal dynamic. In my earlier years as a pastor, I thought "forty days of no rest" was unwritten code for maximum kingdom impact. I was naïve and inflicted with a driven self-importance.

Most of the time, however, our busyness is carried by a lack of clarity. Like a heat-seeking missile, our lives endlessly swerve by redefining the next hottest target and the new melting urgency. We desperately need to "target lock" to fly straight and true, like Jesus who steadfastly set His face to go to Jerusalem rather than letting the approval of the Samaritans or other influences blow Him off course (Luke 9:51–54).

Ministry without clarity is insanity.

Leading with a long view has many advantages, but the one I want most for you is *freedom*. I want you to have a long-term target lock that guides the days, months, and years of your one life—your one lifetime. Ministry without clarity is insanity.

The *Unimportance* of Practically Everything

It has been said that you can't overestimate the unimportance of practically everything. Don't miss how Jesus understood and lived from this dramatic perspective. Be amazed as you think about what Jesus did *not* do after walking on the earth for three years—which in some ways is just as amazing as what He did accomplish. Jesus didn't heal every person in His geographic sphere of influence. With the screaming needs of one village still audible, He went to the next. Jesus didn't indulge the "opportunities" that peeked around every corner. Platform building didn't distract Him.

Within the limitations of His humanity, Jesus gives the final debrief of His planet-walking mission, "I accomplished the work you gave me to do." He glorified the Father by giving His life for all and investing His life primarily in twelve. That was His long-range vision. His background vision, a three-year horizon of public ministry, was guided by a long-range revelation. And each short-range footstep was anchored by a vivid sense of destiny. Don't miss the stunning clarity Jesus demonstrated.

While He accomplished *His* vision, it is also the one that was *given* to Him. Jesus understood the unimportance of practically everything—that is, everything else other than what the Father gave Him to do.

Don't miss the stunning clarity Jesus demonstrated.

If you read *God Dreams* and miss this emphasis to focus on God's calling, I have failed you. Everything written is designed to dial you into the work God has given *you* to do. That's the point of the title: they are your dreams, but they are really God-given dreams to you.

Vision received from God and discerned together illuminates your essence in a way that makes the most of what we think of as "important" or "good" actually nonessential. That's what freedom is. It's not the ability to do anything you want. It's the opportunity to give all of yourself to what God has given you to do.

> Freedom is the opportunity to give all of yourself to what God has given you to do.

Being a visionary means living free, free to give yourself *to* something and freedom *from* everything else. And not giving yourself to the gospel or God or ministry generally but in a specific way—in your place and time, with your gifts, your people, and the passions you wield, together. The Horizon Storyline is a waste of time if it doesn't inject a sense of freedom in your soul.

Freedom = Confidence, Courage, and Progress

Knowing what to abandon is one thing, and doing it is another. Clarity needs courage behind it, or it doesn't lead to freedom. Will you act on the clarity God gives? Will you make more room for the essential? Will you rethink and reorder your comfortable ministry pathways toward the brighter, bigger destination God shows you? Freedom, when fully grasped—when acted upon—will bring a new confidence, unexpected courage, and unimaginable progress.

> The Horizon Storyline is a waste of time if it doesn't inject a sense of freedom in your soul.

There is strange beauty and power to a ferocious focus. It's not more rigid; it's more loving. It's more honest. It brings God more glory. This is the greatest gift this book can give: to alert you to and guide you in the freedom anchored in the big-yet-specific calling of God for your church.

My prayer is that you know a freedom that brings surprising joy on the way and dramatic contribution on your final day. To God be the glory—the God of your wildest dreams!

Acknowledgments

I am grateful for my coauthor Warren Bird who pushed me to be more accessible to church leaders through his extensive writing experience and masterful skill in bringing clarity to ideas. As a consummate researcher and story collector in the church world, he was the perfect partner to shape and validate the templates themselves. His orchestration was essential to bringing this work together, allowing me to write and continue to lead Auxano undistracted. Most of all, his heart to serve the Lord always burned bright through his encouraging spirit and prayerful diligence. Thank you, Warren!

I also thank my wife, Romy, to whom this book is dedicated. Her contributions and support were ever present from art classes that shaped the core ideas in the book to allowing me the freedom to travel frequently for church consultations. She gave me many nights to work late into the evening. My favorite symbol of her support was keeping the original cover design on her iPhone screen over the months of work. I love you, darling!

The Auxano team was indispensable to this book as they helped me field-test the material reflected in *God Dreams*. The team includes Jim Randall, Clint Grider, Todd McMichen, Mike Gammill, Bryan Rose, David Putman, Bob Adams, and Cheryl Marting. My amazing executive assistant, Tessy Rice, has handled countless details; our campaign coordinator, Andrea Kandler, has proofed numerous drafts; and my two favorite artists on the planet, Jessica Arrendell and James Bethany, crafted the excellent graphics you see.

I am also indebted to Eric Geiger whose support and strategic insight were integral to *God Dreams* becoming a reality. He is one of the most anointed leaders I know and serves with Auxano and as a vice president at LifeWay. The team at LifeWay has been a delight to work with. This book would not have happened without their partnership on many levels and their belief that thousands of churches will be helped by *God Dreams*.

Examples of Beyond-the-Horizon Vivid Descriptions

The following are examples of the vivid descriptions of the beyond-the-horizon vision. They come from many different churches, some smaller and some larger, and from many sections of the United States. The final example is not from a church but from Auxano.

1. Waves of Transformation
Church: Newbreak Church, San Diego, California
Pastor: Mike Quinn
Vision Templates: Leadership multiplication that results in targeted transformation

In the next decade we will raise up hundreds of guides who will in turn take thousands of people on the journey of a lifetime. Not a vacation but a transforming adventure: a biblically fueled, Spirit-inspired, and relationally charged leadership-development process. The adventure will focus on Jesus and our twelve marks (the twelve marks are our definition of a disciple, taken from the mission measures side of the vision frame) following Him.

Why leadership development and why now? By God's grace thousands of men and women call Newbreak home. We now have five campuses—strategic mission posts spread throughout our region.

But San Diego County is a place with hundreds of unique community identities. From refugees on the run to displaced transplants to an always mobilizing military, our corner of California is dying from spiritual starvation, and it's increasingly adrift on a sea with no rudder.

Therefore our leadership development itinerary will not stop until thousands of people become agents of bold change, serving their surrounding communities with authentic love. We imagine dads enjoying their children, marriages welded together, and coworkers radically concerned for one another. We see neighborhoods turned upside down by the unexplainable kindness of Newbreakers. We envision hundreds of small groups as life rafts pulling people from an ocean of crowded loneliness. We see dozens of beachheads in our city's niche neighborhoods, with platoons of skilled and loving Newbreakers moving in to start new campuses and empower new causes. The impact of each campus will be measured by positive community transformation. And we won't stop until we blanket our city with an ever-growing network of campuses on mission.

What's the Newbreak vision when you boil it all down? It's a wave of leadership development that brings a wave of community transformation that brings a larger wave of leadership development that brings an even bigger wave of community transformation. There's nothing like watching a swell build from the vantage point of the cliffs in Ocean Beach. That's what we see as we look at communities from a development perspective. Can you see it?

What we do through Newbreak in our lifetime will shake the planet, from here to the farthest points in the world.

Let's make some waves.

2. Rural Relevance across the Mountain West

Church: Harvest Church, Billings, Montana
Pastor: Vern Streeter
Vision Templates: Institutional renovation that brings geographic saturation

Within the next ten years, Harvest will establish, renew, and strengthen the tangible value of "the local church" in communities within the five-hundred-mile radius of Billings, Montana.

Harvest is fueling the rural relevance of the local church across the mountain west by overflowing into rural communities especially where local believers perceive there is a lack of a viable, life-giving church. Harvest started in response to community planners who wanted to give the boot to the presence of the local church. Today we are ready to reboot the reputation of what God's people mean to a community when we actually live life as though Jesus were living through us. We will accomplish this through culturally relevant worship and tangible community focus, so tangible that people are surprised by the love of Jesus through us.

We started in Billings, which is the trailhead of Montana. Now the Harvest brand will be the trailhead for hundreds of believers to start Christ-centered communities of hope and purpose across our vast landscape.

3. An Invitation for Everyone in the "4B Area"

Church: Clear Creek Community Church, Houston, Texas
Pastor: Bruce Wesley
Vision Template: Geographic saturation

We hope to establish ten campuses of Clear Creek Community Church in the 4B area. The 4B area is from the Beltway to the beach, from the Bay to Brazoria county, home to 500,000 people, 55 percent of whom consider themselves "nones." That means when more than half the population checks into the hospital or talks religion around the water cooler at work or completes their census form and they are asked about their religious preference, they choose "None."

How does a person who claims "none" come to love and trust Jesus Christ? We believe hope swells for people who consider themselves "nones" when they have a trusting relationship with a person of genuine faith who is fluent in the gospel. That's when a self-identified "none" is most likely to consider the gospel of Jesus Christ.

So we are committed to see everyone who claims a religion of "none" to have no more than one degree of separation between them and a gospel witness who attends a Clear Creek campus in the 4B area, who will invite them into a community of faith where they will have repeated opportunities to hear and experience the amazing love of God in the gospel of Jesus Christ.

The only way this saturation of trusting relationships will happen in our lifetime is through planting campuses and churches in close proximity to where people live, shop, work, play, and go to school; where followers of Jesus see themselves as missionaries sent to build bridges into people's lives with God's life-changing love rather than religious people judging others or seeking refuge from the world.

We start campuses in the 4B area, we multiply groups into every neighborhood, and we collaborate with other churches. We also plant new churches in the greater Houston area as launching pads for the people who are running into every dark corner of our city with the light and love of Jesus Christ.

As a result, God's redemption can spread like a wildfire of hope across our coastal plains. And at the tipping point where one person in ten is a genuine Christ follower, then the culture will change: mommas and daddies will stay together, our children will thrive with a spiritual and moral compass to find their way, and people will hold their heads high in the marketplace because they do business as unto the Lord, and generosity will abound so people have what they need and no one will go to bed hungry. If God moves this profoundly in our area in our lifetime, then other followers might take responsibility for people in another part of the city and cry out to God with faith, "Do it again, Lord. Do it here among us, too."

4. Christ-Centered Parenting
Church: Brushy Creek Baptist Church, Easley, South Carolina
Pastors: Jim Spencer, Lead Pastor, and Nick McClellan, Teaching Pastor
Vision Template: Spiritual formation

Over the next five years, we dream to inspire hundreds of upstate South Carolina families to make Christ-centered parenting their greatest achievement and highest priority.

Brushy Creek's sense of urgency for the spiritual formation of families is stirred by our culture marked by a fanatical obsession with pleasure and prosperity. Upstate families consistently sail with misguided rudders; they have unknowingly gone off course in the name of recreation and have led themselves toward destructive crosswinds and unforgiving waves.

In the next five years, we will provide our community with gospel-centered, family-friendly, and application-driven programs matched by welcoming, clean, and state-of-the-art facilities. We will be a safe harbor for families to rest at port, as they will find restoration, supplies, and training needed to set sail again. We see an upstate armada of strong parents navigating together through the rough seas of daily living. We envision this fleet of Christ-centered families carrying a gospel banner that will introduce even more misguided men, women, boys, and girls to the good news of Jesus.

God Himself has promised life in His Son Jesus Christ; therefore, we know that the time is now for us to raise our sails, reclaim these wandering vessels, and bring them into port.

5. Slavic Village Restoration
Church: Cuyahoga Valley Church, Cleveland, Ohio
Pastors: Chad Allen, Lead Pastor, and Rick Duncan, Founding Pastor
Vision Templates: Targeted transformation by means of crisis mobilization

Summary: *In the next five years we will pursue the radical transformation of Slavic Village, one of America's hardest-hit foreclosure markets, through a kaleidoscope of missional initiatives with the dream of a complete renovation of an entire neighborhood block.*

God is graciously allowing us to participate in His work to see a city block in a decaying community restored. Our city-block restoration vision is guided by our mission of inviting people to new life in Christ. We are motivated by the message of Isaiah 61:4: "They shall build up the ancient ruins; they shall raise up the former devastations; they shall repair the ruined cities, the devastations of many generations."

We have adopted an urban area just north of us, Slavic Village, as a community where we want to focus our resources for restoration. In the words of Acts 1:8, it's our Judea. Why Slavic Village? In the summer of 2007, according to RealtyTrac, Cleveland's 44105 zip code, Slavic Village, was the hardest hit community for foreclosures in the entire United States.

We will seek a holistic approach toward restoration in Slavic Village and issue a full-court press of ministry partnerships, church planting, missional engagement, and community enrichment from tutoring kids to job training for parents to fruit-and-vegetable giveaways for all. We collaborate with many others and mobilize our people to bring stability and hope for the future for hundreds of families in the name of Christ.

In 2016, we hope to be working with many area churches to renovate two to three houses on a city block in Slavic Village. In 2017, our dream is to restore five to six houses. Ultimately we want to see an entire block restored, renewed, and filled with the hope of Christ.

6. Speaking the Peace of God into the Brokenness of Life—a Renaissance of Reconciliation

Church: Calvary Baptist Church, Winton-Salem, North Carolina
Pastor: Rob Peters
Vision Templates: Institutional renovation that leads to geographic saturation

Calvary has a rich heritage as a church that is nearing its centennial anniversary. For this heritage we are grateful and humbled. Yet over time our efforts have splintered, and our impact has diffused. Despite our active ministries a penetrating assessment recently revealed significant challenges in evangelism, discipleship, and leadership—issues that can and must change.

How will Calvary make these changes? We will come together as one and engage our One Mission "Vision Pyramid Strategy." Imagine a giant pyramid with one stone on the top and ten thousand stones on the bottom, with layers in between: one, ten, one hundred, one thousand, and ten thousand. At the top is our one mission, pointing up to Jesus' Great Commission. This is our ultimate guide. At the bottom is our lives— you and me, the people of Calvary—five thousand members connecting each week with ten thousand lives in our community. We are the grassroots. We are the church. We are the living stones of God's house, and the movement must begin with us.

The layers of our pyramid strategy look like this: one mission, ten initiatives, one hundred plants, one thousand salvation stories, and ten thousand lives touched.

Our ten initiatives will be the ten-piston engine powering a spiritual renaissance. A renaissance is a renewal of life, vigor, and interest. Our community is experiencing more vigor today in the arts, medicine, and technology than ever. We must bring the power of the gospel to this cultural renewal. It's not simple, but God can do it through us, His church. Some initiatives will focus on the "inside" of the church: from clearing room for a discipleship pathway and a leadership pipeline, to igniting generational mentoring, to refreshing our campus, to building a pastoral school of ministry. Other initiatives will focus on blessing the city: from alleviating childhood hunger and poor reading, from addressing racial tension to economic development, from spurring community health to spiritual health. With this engine and the limitless power of gospel fuel, we will speak the peace of God into the brokenness of our world.

From our ten initiatives we will plant or revitalize one hundred churches over the next ten years.

In turn we will witness one thousand stories of life transformation through salvation: people rescued by Jesus, men and women made whole again, boys and girls freshly redeemed, tears of joy at every celebrative baptism.

Finally, we will see God touching ten thousand people each week through intentional initiatives of our church body. Imagine five thousand worshippers each engaging at least two people outside of Calvary with a smile, prayer, hug, gesture of generosity, unexpected blessing, or total availability at an inconvenient time. We will do this. We can speak the peace of God into the brokenness of the people and the world around us. We will see a renaissance of reconciliation in our lifetime.

7. Welcome Home, Restoring the Whole Family of God

Church: Saint Andrew's Presbyterian, Newport Beach, California
Pastor: Richard Kannwischer
Vision Templates: Spiritual formation that includes need adoption

By the year 2020, we will see Saint Andrew's transformed from a house of God to a home in Christ. In order to make this dream a reality, we will be putting our house in order, creating space to belong, extending the family, and renovating lives, one disciple at a time.

By putting our financial house in order, Saint Andrew's can move forward in the freedom of a fresh start and new opportunities to welcome others to a home in Christ.

As we create space to belong, those we are welcoming feel at home. When you feel at home, you become free to be yourself. You relax, you get comfortable, and you want to stay and talk about what really matters. Our 2020 vision is that our campus feels like home and becomes home to many more families in our community.

Saint Andrew's has a rich history of starting new ministries that have flourished and leveraged our reach for Christ—here, near, and far. By extending the family, our 2020 vision includes a new wave of mission innovation—planting new churches, extending our impact through technology, and giving more than one hundred home-less children in Orange County a permanent home.

By renovating lives through a discipleship institute, we will create a robust and replicable model for growing believers, guiding countless others in our mission of *following Jesus Christ to lead lives that reveal God's goodness.*

8. Coasting or Difference Making?

Church: Asbury United Methodist Church, Raleigh, North Carolina
Pastors: Terry Bryant
Vision Templates: Need adoption in harness with geographic saturation

Summary: *In the next five years, every person who calls our church home will be link-ing arms in difference-making relationships. We will focus efforts on two needs—hunger and education—in the three concentric-circle ministry areas (in the geography of Acts 1:8).*

We live in a highly educated, thriving, and dynamic culture in North Raleigh. What we experience far too often is that while we are constantly busy, we often feel like we are coasting through life. We always have stuff to do but seldom feel like we are making a difference. So we will move from coasting to engaging gears, moving past meaningless self-centered activity and accelerating new and practical ways of living out our faith. We will be salt and light to our neighbors (Matt. 5:13–16).

Strengthened through our common worship and group engagement, we intend to be difference makers in our local community and world through two key areas of focus: First, being on mission to end hunger, recognizing the call of our Lord, "For I was hungry and you gave me something to eat" (Matt. 25:35 NIV). Second, being on mission to improving underresourced education centers, recognizing the call of Scripture to "train up a child in the way he should go" (Prov. 22:6). We are going to become a place where it becomes inescapable that to be part of Asbury is to respond relationally and tangibly to these needs in our community and world.

*We intend to do this specifically through relational involvement and service with the Asbury Preschool, Lynn Road Elementary, and our partners in Haiti (Hearts and Hands for Haiti). We will accomplish this through mentoring children, encouraging educators, improving school campuses, and engaging with parents. We see hundreds of unchurched parents and children from the Asbury Preschool finding new life in Christ at Asbury. We see thousands of pounds of fresh produce donated locally. We see not only hundreds of Asbury's people visiting Haiti and engaging with children there but also sending millions of meals to Haiti. We see hundreds at Asbury serving as lion pals in our mentoring program for children. We see hundreds of backpacks filled with food for children on the weekend. That our Lord might proclaim, "You loved me when you packaged that meal, you walked with me when you grabbed the hand of an underresourced student and served, you blessed me when you received that family into my church" (Matt. 25).

*Jerusalem and Judea (Asbury Preschool), Samaria (Lynn Road), ends of the earth (Haiti) (Acts 1:8).

9. Transforming Ten Thousand Homes

Church: Kingsland Baptist Church, Katy, Texas
Pastor: Ryan Rush
Vision Templates: Spiritual formation that creates targeted transformation

The family has been ordained by God as the foundational place for faith to take root and grow. The decline in a healthy home life, then, is a crisis with far-reaching implications that must not be taken lightly. This cultural decline of a healthy home life is a problem too great for political or educational efforts for change. We must turn instead to spiritual revival, and we are convinced that God has prepared Kingsland for this important moment in history.

We believe that the only hope for family restoration is the power of the gospel of Jesus Christ. God has uniquely positioned Kingsland with the passion, resources, and leadership to make a significant impact on home life in the next decade. We envision ten thousand homes transformed as they are:

- Invited to enjoy five intentional meals each week with the entire household.
- Invited to live the Twelve Habits of True Fulfillment in Jesus (our mission measures from our Vision Frame).
- Invited to embrace the grace offered through Jesus.

We see mealtime as the catalyst for facilitating systemic change in the lives of all ten thousand homes and will endeavor to use those meals as the first step in transformation.

10. The 20/20/20 Watershed Year

Church: Auxano Consulting, Houston, Texas
Leader: Will Mancini
Vision Templates: Need adoption addressed through leadership multiplication

Summary: *The year 2020 will be a watershed year marked by having served leadership teams in 20 percent of North America's evangelical churches; that is, forty thousand church teams will have tasted breakthrough clarity of vision.*

Every church unengaged by a strategic outsider is stuck somewhere. Somewhere in the fog of busyness and stupor of "done-for-you resources," vivid vision is lost.

Yet we envision a watershed year in 2020 for our team's contribution to the local church in North America. We will have seen God's favor open so many doors to work with churches that a tipping point will have occurred. The story of these churches will be unstoppable. They will report about the new armies of everyday visionaries and renewed strategies for redemptive movement.

Our dream is that the good news of clarity will multiply. We see pastors sharing their Vision Frame on a napkin with other pastors. We see Horizon Storylines on whiteboards creating questions and conversations that stretch the imagination and stir the heart. Because of the widespread use of our tools, the year 2020 is the year we lock our legacy. Most church leaders will be helped in our lifetime—some directly and many indirectly—as a result of the first 20 percent becoming more clear, focused, and free in their ministries.

The influence of our Auxano name in 2020 will ensure an "I can't believe we get to do this" career for dozens of staff navigators. We will have maximized our six-service toolbox in order to maximize the potential of every church we serve. The team of servant-oriented thought leaders we have formed today will then be forged into a collaborative world-class team.

While difficult to measure, we will put our hand on the pulse of our tipping point impact: 20 percent of evangelical church teams (forty thousand teams) will have tasted breakthrough clarity of vision. One out of every five churches will be free from the cage of photocopied vision and instigating a jailbreak for others.

The fingerprints will be seen from tools downloaded, blog posts devoured, books written, training conducted, nonemployees certified, and most importantly, teams served on-site. With God's favor this watershed year will ensure overflowing blessing to the churches we serve and families that support our calling.

Appendix B
The Story behind the Horizon Storyline Tool

People who have tracked with me over the years might be curious about the history and development of the planning process I've taught. In short, the Horizon Storyline tool of *God Dreams* is the further development of the vision proper tool in *Church Unique*.

Figure B.1 is the original Vision Pathway I published in 2008 in *Church Unique*. It involves three steps. The first is the process of discovering your Kingdom Concept, which is the ability to discern and define your primary strengths as a church. It involves answering the question, What can your church do better than 10,000 others? The second step is developing your Vision Frame, the core tool explained in *Church Unique*. It is a visual representation of the need to ask and answer five irreducible questions of leadership (listed in figure B.4). The third step is delivering your vision daily, which is aided by a tool I call the Integration Model.

Since 2008, I have made three significant updates to this visual guide. I built these into figure B.2, called The Vision Framing Process.

First, I changed the name of the process from The Vision Pathway to The Vision Framing Process because that's what pastors I work with tended to call it.

Second, I added an icon at the far left for the important step of "recasting vision." The icon, although in *Church Unique*, was not embedded as a part of the process itself. Now it is. The icon itself represents pumpkin jars from a story I retell in the Preface of *God Dreams*. In the planning context the pumpkin jars story is a constant reminder to look, before the vision process begins, for barriers and obstacles that limit what God is doing. It includes debunking mediocre approaches to vision that also limit good thinking. Therefore I refer it as recasting vision or simply the need to *rethink*.

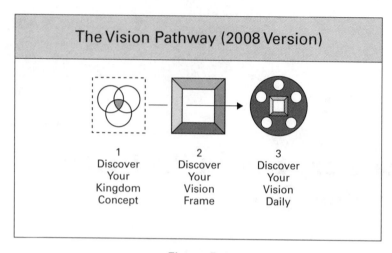

Figure B.1

Third, and most importantly to *God Dreams*, I created a separate icon for vision proper. In *Church Unique* vision proper didn't have a separate icon, as it was just the middle or inside of the Vision Frame. But as people asked more and more questions about it and we at Auxano developed more tools, it became important to distinguish it as a separate step. In fact, the bulk of *God Dreams* drills down further with vision proper by providing the Horizon Storyline. In the vision-framing process it is represented by a mountain image with a road and mile marker inside the Vision Frame. This is to reinforce the idea that Vision Proper answers the question, "Where is God taking us?" as a snapshot or travel brochure of a better future.

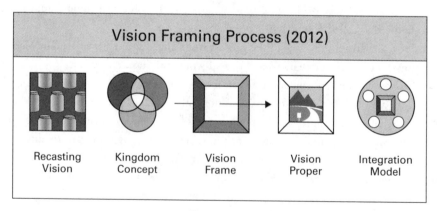

Figure B.2

The most important deliverables of the updated vision process are the articulation of a church's identity and direction using the Vision Frame and the ability to do so within a missional reorientation.

I summarize my understanding of the missional reorientation in chapter 3 of *Church Unique*, "The Iniquity of Church Growth," by panning popular perspectives of the church in the latter half of the twentieth century. In a nutshell the missional reorientation represents the shift from viewing mission as one of many functions for the church (a church with mission) to become the *only* thing the church exists to do (the missional church). Mission moves from *an activity* of the church to *the identity* of the church.

Church Unique highlighted how to discern and define your church's unique mission, values, strategy, and mission measures first—the four outside parts of the Vision Frame (see figure B.3)—and then encourages you to develop vision proper inside the frame. In some ways I was using language that leaders have been familiar with for a long time. In other ways it was bringing a new clarity and transferable tools to experienced and emerging church leaders alike, all designed to take into account the opportunities of the missional conversation.

As the preface of *God Dreams* explains, whether you are familiar with Vision Frame or not, *God Dreams* is a stand-alone work. However, by introducing—or reintroducing—you to the Vision Frame of *Church Unique*, you will better appreciate how the Horizon Storyline tool works.

Figures B.3 and B.4 depict the supporting shorthand definitions and visual icons for the Vision Frame. Mission is represented as a compass. Values are portrayed as flames. I often say that great leaders have a compass in their heads and a fire in their hearts. Strategy is visualized as a flashlight representing "to show the way." And mission measures are pictured as a bull's-eye to represent when a church is successful, fruitful, or "winning" in its mission. This issue of "winning" is seeking a more substantial definition than the typical metrics of attendance and giving track to gauge success. Finally, similar to figure B.2, the mountain scene visualizes where God is taking a church as the next big dream.

Figure B.4 summarizes the various components of *Church Unique*'s Vision Frame. In the far right column I use a superscript "m" for the term *missional*. For example I refer to values as "missional motives" represented for simplicity and shorthand as "ᵐmotives."

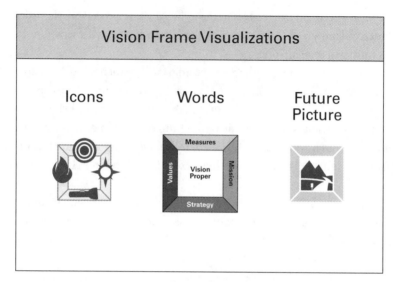

Figure B.3

Components of the Vision Frame

Frame Component	Icon	Irreducible Question of Leadership	Missional Reorientation
Mission		What are we doing?	ᵐMandate
Values		Why are we doing it?	ᵐMotives
Strategy		How are we doing it?	ᵐMap
Measures		When are we successful?	ᵐMarks
Vision Proper		Where is God taking us?	ᵐMountaintop + Milestones
superscripted m=missional			

Figure B.4

The Problem with Vision Statements and Further Advice about Defining Vision

Vision is the most talked about and least understood term in the leadership lexicon. As I wrote in *Church Unique*:

> Why, after so many books and conferences on the subject, is it true that "less than one out of ten senior pastors can articulate what he believes is God's vision for the church he is leading"?[1] How can it still be said that "the most important problem in the church today is a fundamental lack of clear, heart-grabbing vision. The church in America has no vision. It has programs and institutions and property and ministers and politically correct hymnals, but no vision"?[2] How do we account for this gap between prolific writing about vision and the floundering practice of vision? Is there something wrong with how we think about vision? The answer is both yes and no.[3]

I affirm the many excellent books and consultants who teach that vision is a "mental image of a preferred future" or a "memorable picture of what tomorrow will look like." Every leader wants to do a better job as a visionary.

What concerns me are the results. Too often I find the vision statement trapped in one of two ruts. I call them the "compelling page dump" and the "lofty one-liner."

Problems with the Compelling Page Dump

The page dump is a roughly one-page statement that describes the future of the church with vivid and compelling language. Typically:

- One person wrote it.
- The document remains static over time.
- No one other than the originator uses the document.
- The vision is used only in formal vision-casting settings.
- The vision is primarily read, not heard, by the vision receiver.

The compelling page dump rose in popularity after Rick Warren published his "I have a dream" vision statement in *The Purpose Driven Church*. Several books on ministry vision have underscored this type of expression, including Aubrey Malphurs's *Advanced Strategic Planning*.

Where do you find the compelling page dump most frequently? It is usually somewhere on a church's website, framed on the wall, or filed away as a handout for the new member class or a prospective staff member.

Although the effort to produce the page dump vision is worthwhile and noble, this approach has limitations. The primary problems are that the statement is static rather than dynamic, it is reserved for formal communication and not daily use, and it tends to be used by the primary vision caster and not the leadership team.

I can remember reading a compelling page dump prior to signing on with my first church after seminary. Two years later I remember pulling out that same vision statement and reading it with discouragement. It had not changed, but our church had changed. It glamorized what we were doing, but it was never revisited in any staff meeting or planning retreat. I was not taught how to use it. In a nutshell it felt, to borrow a term from Eugene Peterson, like ecclesiastical pornography: it presented something scintillating without the possibility of real relationship.

Problems with the Lofty One-Liner

A second kind of vision statement attempts to express a picture of the future as a noble, future-oriented ideal and boil it down into a short phrase or sentence. Typical attributes:

- It is usually developed as a group.
- It is intended to be motivational.
- It looks to the future by presenting an unreachable, transcendent concept.
- It never changes.
- Most leaders in the organization wouldn't repeat it day to day.
- The vision is primarily read and not heard by the vision receiver.

Examples are "Making disciples globally by mobilizing every generation locally," or "Quenching the thirst of every man, woman, and child with the good news of

Jesus," or "Growing a diverse community of passionate worshippers who will love people toward Jesus." These statements may contain some important vision elements for the church, but by themselves they are incomplete. First, they don't paint a vivid description of a future reality or any of the intermediate steps to get there. In fact, the intent of the statements is to present something unattainable, like a North Star that guides you but that you can never reach. The problem with this idea is twofold: first, who wants a vision you can't reach? Second, to the extent that it provides directional value it becomes redundant to mission.

Most of the current confusion between a mission statement and a vision statement has arisen because of this misapplication. People create a vision statement that competes for attention with the mission as a loftier or more eloquent generic restatement of it.

> These statements may contain some important vision elements for the church, but by themselves they are incomplete.

Another limitation is that it's difficult to use on a daily basis. It is so lofty that it would not roll off the tongue; one feels forced to say it because it sounds so formal. Additionally, it is too generic to be useful in real ministry decisions.

I remember working with a large parachurch ministry. I noticed they not only had a lofty one-liner but used it everywhere. During our first meeting we reviewed all of their vision equity. I asked each of them to write anonymously the most meaningless or empty part of their vision language. Half of the team wrote the lofty one-liner. It was so removed from their vernacular and so unnecessary to the leadership that they had actually begun to resent it. Once I showed them it was redundant to the mission, it was happily discarded.

What Is the Solution for Today?

Church leaders need a way to think about vision articulation that is at the same time more primitive and more sophisticated. By primitive I mean it must be hearty and raw, connected to reality. It is powerful because it is first authentic. By sophisticated I mean it must take into account the complexity of teams, the messiness of change, and the sensitivity of spiritual guidance without compromising boldness. Sophistication allows true collaboration toward God-sized dreams.

The definition of *vision* can be nuanced to accomplish this: *vision* is "the living language that anticipates and illustrates God's better intermediate future." (In *Church Unique*, I use the term Vision Proper for this definition.) Here's what I mean by these terms:

Living language: The importance of living language is that the vision is always a developing Polaroid picture. Never static, vision is always evolving. Like a sequence of smaller mountains that give view to larger mountains on reaching the summit, today's new accomplishments give view to tomorrow's possibilities. Our definition moves us away from vision as statement to vision as dynamic vocabulary. Picture a treasure chest of phrases, ideas, metaphors, and stories that is the container of vision vocabulary. The beauty of a treasure chest like this is that the whole team can put words and dreams into it, and the entire leadership can pick ideas and stories out of it. It empowers a shared vision in a unique way that the compelling page dump and lofty one-liner do not. Living language also reminds us of the importance of verbal communication and eyeball-to-eyeball exchange of dialogue. Because communication is primarily nonverbal, personal presence in vision casting is everything. In other words, the posture, tone, voice inflections, and facial expressions of the person communicating convey more meaning than the words themselves. A vision should never be designed to be read. What would have happened to Martin Luther King Jr.'s "I Have a Dream" speech if he made it a PowerPoint presentation or decided just to send out flyers? People do not follow your compelling page dumps; they follow you! The vision cannot be separated from the vision caster, and the vision caster cannot separate his message from his life as a model. What Charlie Parker, the legendary jazz saxophonist, said of music is true of vision: "Music is your own experience, your thoughts, your wisdom. If you don't live it, it won't come out of your horn."

Anticipating God's future: The use of vision has so emphasized a static snapshot that communication risks becoming information, not inspiration. Therefore the idea of anticipating becomes larger than just describing or painting the picture. It pulls in conviction, passion, and emotional commitment. It's not what the leader thinks can be or even should be but what must be. Vision that does not engage the heart and touch the emotions is nothing more than flowery words on paper. Simply put, a shared anticipation fuels participation in a shared vision. Because the visionary embodies the anticipation of the future, he or she brings more to the table than just a picture; he or she brings a contagious longing for what God wants to do.

God's better intermediate future: This language is a reminder that a church's vision is one of many in the course of redemptive history. It reminds us that God is the Chief Visionary who is bringing us into a final Utopia, our final rescue to the joy of His undiluted presence. Until that day we push forward, not with arrogance but with confidence, because we know we are a part of a divine chain reaction. The inherent accountability in this definition is that the leader must know the vision is from God.

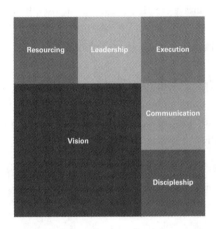

What Auxano Can Do for You

Where do you need breakthrough?

This question is at the heart of Auxano, the ministry that Will Mancini founded in 2004.

The core work of Auxano (which means "to cause to grow") is Vision Framing, an on-site consulting process developed to help church leaders achieve God-given clarity and articulate well-defined vision. This team-centered experience builds on the principles outlined in both Will's celebrated previous book, *Church Unique*, and his newest book, *God Dreams*. As a result, hundreds of churches and ministries from every major faith tribe now possess an unprecedented understanding of God's calling as well as actionable plans for leading, integrating, and casting vision in their unique culture.

Auxano is a national team of thought leaders and consulting practitioners. It is the only nonprofit consulting group dedicated to developing a unique vision for every local church. Auxano's mission is to create breakthrough clarity with church teams to realize their vision.

If you resonate with any of these thoughts, Auxano is here to help you (through these key services):

- Leaders do not completely agree and lack total excitement about our next big directional decision (vision).
- Our ministry is limited by the quality and quantity of leaders we reproduce (leadership).
- Deep down we know our programs aren't creating a culture of discipleship (discipleship).
- Our design, messaging, and social media engagement could be improved (communication).
- Our relational team would benefit from more focus and accountability on a weekly basis (execution).
- The giving of our congregation is not what it could be, and we are tired of typical campaign approaches to address it (resourcing).

To learn more about how Auxano can serve your church or ministry, visit auxano. com, e-mail info@auxano.com, or phone (800) 894-0991.

Go Ahead

About the Authors

Will Mancini wants you and your ministry to experience the benefits of stunning, God-given clarity. As a pastor turned vision coach, Will has worked with a wide variety of churches from megachurches and missional communities to mainline congregations and church plants. He is the founder of Auxano, creator of VisionRoom.com and author or coauthor of three previous books including his celebrated guide, *Church Unique: How Missional Leaders Cast Vision and Create Movement.*

Will lives in Houston, Texas, with his wife, Romy, and their three children, Jacob, Joel, and Abigail. When not in Houston, he loves mountain biking and snowboarding. His pastoral experience includes leadership development responsibilities at two greater Houston congregations: Clear Creek Community Church in League City and Faithbridge Church in Spring.

Will's style blends the best of three worlds: process thinking from the discipline of engineering, communications savvy as a former ad agency executive, and practical theology as a pastoral leader. His education includes a ThM in pastoral leadership from Dallas Theological Seminary and a BS in chemical engineering from Penn State.

For more on Will, visit his blog at willmancini.com, or follow him on Twitter @willmancini, on Facebook at claritywill or on Instagram at will_be_clear.

Warren Bird, PhD, is director of research and intellectual capital development at Leadership Network, the nation's leading organization to help entrepreneurial church leaders in growing churches move from ideas to implementation to increased influence and impact. Warren has also served as church planter and staff pastor and as a longtime teacher in the doctor of ministry program at Alliance Theological Seminary.

Warren is also the award-winning author or coauthor of twenty-eight books for church leaders, more than two hundred magazine articles, and several dozen groundbreaking research reports. Widely quoted in national media, he is one of the nation's leading scholars on megachurches, multisite churches, high-visibility pastoral succession, and large-church compensation.

Warren and his wife, Michelle, live in metropolitan New York City. They have two adult children.

For more on Warren, see leadnet.org/warrenbird or follow him on Twitter @warrenbird.

Notes

Foreword

1. Joseph Mangina, *Revelation* (Grand Rapids, MI: Brazos Press, 2010).

2. Stephen Covey, *The Seven Habits of Highly Effective People* (New York: Simon & Schuster, 1989).

Chapter 1: Pursuing God Dreams

1. Sam Gamgee in J. R. R. Tolkien's *The Lord of the Rings*, chapter 4, book 6. See also http://www.redeemer.com/learn/resources_by_topic/suffering_and_tragedy/service _of_remembrance_and_peace.

Chapter 2: The Problem of Generic Vision

1. "Atherosclerosis & Coronary Artery Disease," WebMD, Heart Disease Health Center. http://www.webmd.com/heart-disease/atherosclerosis-and-coronary -artery-disease.

2. A. H. Rabinowitz, "Commandments, the 613," in *EncJud*, 5:760–83.

3. Auxano Campaigns, http://www.auxano.com/services/resourcing.

Chapter 3: Obsessing with Now

1. Quoted in Amy Julia Becker, "Why Bloggers Are Calling It Quits," *Christianity Today*, June 12, 2015. http://www.christianitytoday.com/women/2015/june/why -bloggers-are-calling-it-quits.html?paging=off.

2. "The 10,000 Year Clock," The Long Now Foundation, http://longnow.org /clock.

3. Ibid.

4. Stewart Brand, *Clock of the Long Now: Time and Responsibility: The Ideas behind the World's Slowest Computer* (New York: Basic Books, 2000), 2.

5. James Lane Allen, *As a Man Thinketh* (Charleston, SC: CreateSpace, 2014), 20.

6. Amazon.com, *2014 Annual Report*, page 2, accessed June 9, 2015, http://phx.corporate-ir.net/phoenix.zhtml?c=97664&p=irol-reportsannual.

7. Ibid.

8. To learn more about the "younique" personal vision journey, go to willmancini.com/younique.

9. Angela Watercuter, "This 23-Ton, 5.3-Million-Brick X Wing Is the Biggest Lego Model Ever," *Wired,* http://www.wired.com/2013/05/largest-lego-x-wing.

10. Mark Twain, *A Connecticut Yankee in King Arthur's Court* (New York: Harper and Brothers, 1889; digitized by the University of Michigan, 2008), 422.

11. John Eldridge, *The Sacred Romance* (Nashville, TN: Thomas Nelson, 1997), 41.

Chapter 4: Solving Your Planning Problems

1. Andy Stanley, *Visioneering: God's Blueprint for Developing and Maintaining Vision* (Portland, OR: Multnomah, 2005), 158.

2. Ramesh Richard, *Soul Vision* (Chicago, IL: Moody Publishers, 2004), 86–87.

Chapter 5: Introducing the Horizon Storyline

1. See Merrill D. Bowan, "Integrating Vision with the Other Senses," http://simplybrainy.com/wp-content/uploads/2011/01/2008-Int-Vis-Other-Senses-All-Illustrations.pdf.

2. Ibid.

3. See Wikipedia, "Accommodation (eye)," http://en.wikipedia.org/wiki/Accommodation_(eye).

4. This horizon is the only one discussed in *Church Unique* as the "missional mountaintop plus milestone (^{m}Mountaintop + Milestone), symbolized by a superscripted m. The "Mountaintop" is a vivid picture based on the one-year goal and "Milestone" is a measurable dimension to the goal. I often teach the importance of combining qualitative (mountaintop view) and quantitative (measurable milestone). The midground horizon is the most important one to combine both.

Chapter 6: Imagining beyond the Horizon with Four Starting Points

1. "We think in pictures. If you wish to change what you think, change the picture." See http://greece.mrdonn.org/aristotle.html.

2. Erik Calonius, *Ten Steps Ahead* (New York: Portfolio Penguin, 2011), 3.

Chapter 7: Vision That Advances

1. Steve Addison, *What Jesus Started* (Downers, Grove, IL: IVP Books, 2012), digital edition.

2. "All the World My Parish," Journal of John Wesley, Christian Classics Ethereal Library, accessed July 26, 2015, http://www.ccel.org/ccel/wesley/journal.vi.iii.v.html.

3. *Saturate,* accessed July 26, 2015, http://www.saturatetheworld.com/vision.

4. Saturation Church Planting, accessed July 26, 2015, http://scpglobal.org.

5. Jeff Vanderstelt, *Saturate: Being Disciples of Jesus in the Everyday Stuff of Life* (Wheaton, IL: Crossway, 2015), digital edition.

Chapter 8: Vision That Rescues

1. Warren Bird, "Church Makes a Community Splash, Literally," *Leadership Network,* accessed July 26, 2015, http://leadnet.org/church_makes_a_community _splash_literally.

2. "Paris Basis—1855," YMCA, accessed July 26, 2015, http://www.ymca.int /who-we-are/mission/paris-basis-1855.

3. You Version, https://www.youversion.com.

4. Rick Warren, *Purpose Driven Life* (Grand Rapids, MI: Zondervan, 1997).

5. Celebrate Recovery, accessed July 26, 2015, http://www.celebraterecovery.com.

6. Warren Bird, "Colorado Churches Change the Adoption Equation," Leadership Network Advance, September 3, 2013, http://leadnet.org/colorado _churches_change_the_adoption_equation.

7. J. Mack Stiles, "Nine Marks of a Healthy Parachurch Ministry," *IX 9 Marks,* accessed July 26, 2015, http://9marks.org/article/journalnine-marks-healthy-parachurch -ministry.

8. Frank Decker, *Brooklyn's Plymouth Church in the Civil War Era: A Ministry of Freedom* (Mount Pleasant, SC: The History Press, 2013), 98–99.

9. "Ready Church Challenge," SBC of Virginia, accessed July 26, 2015, http:// www.sbcv.org/ready-church.

10. "Disasters and the Local Church," Tearfund, http://www.tearfund.org/-/media/Files/TILZ/Churches/Disasters%20and%20the%20local%20church/Disasters_and_church_web.pdf.

Chapter 9: Vision That Becomes

1. Elmer Towns, Ed Stetzer, and Warren Bird, *The Ten Most Influential Churches of the Past Century: How They Impact You Today* (Shippensburg, PA: Destiny Image, 2014), 95–106.

2. See "Conversations: Watermark's John McGee on the Marriage 'Health Club, Hospital and University' Approach," http://leadnet.org/conversations-john-mcgee-on-the-marriage-health-club-hospital-and-university-approach.

3. Donna St. George, "Couples Who Share Religious Practices Tend to Be Happier Than Those Who Don't, Study Says," *Washington Post*, August 12, 2010, http://www.washingtonpost.com/wp-dyn/content/article/2010/08/11/AR2010081101961.html.

4. Collin Hansen and John D. Woodbridge, *A God-Sized Vision: Revival Stories that Stretch and Stir* (Grand Rapids, MI: Zondervan, 2010).

5. Ibid., 69.

6. Quote from rear cover of James MacDonald, *Vertical Church Bible Study* (Nashville: LifeWay, 2012).

7. Tim Stafford, "The Pentecostal Gold Standard," *Christianity Today*, July 1, 2005, http://www.christianitytoday.com/ct/2005/july/18.24.html?share=%2bGoPBn7g6Lff%2f%2buaZ7x%2bcXQhswVoNz8X.

Chapter 10: Vision That Overflows

1. Dave Ferguson and Jon Ferguson, *Exponential: How You and Your Friends Can Start a Missional Church Movement* (Grand Rapids, MI: Zondervan, 2010).

2. Bill Easum and Bill Tenny-Brittian, *Effective Staffing for Vital Churches* (Grand Rapids, MI: Baker Books, 2012), 77.

3. Cru, "1951–1959," http://www.cru.org/about/what-we-do/milestones.html.

4. "America's Top 25 Multiplying Churches," *Outreach Magazine*, 2007.

5. Todd Wilson, *Spark*, Exponential eBook, https://www.exponential.org/resource-ebooks/spark.

6. Len Wilson, "Top 25 Fastest Growing Large United Methodist Churches, 2015 Edition," http://lenwilson.us/top-25-fastest-growing-large-umc-2015.

7. Donald E. Miller, *Reinventing American Protestantism: Christianity in the New Millennium* (Oakland, CA: University of California Press, 1999).

8. Bill Easum and Bill Tenny-Brittian, *Effective Staffing for Vital Churches* (Grand Rapids, MI: Baker Books, 2012), 75.

Chapter 12: Making Vision Move

1. Will Bourne, "The Most Important Social Media Company You've Never Heard Of," *Inc.*, accessed July 26, 2015, http://www.inc.com/magazine/201504/will-bourne/banjo-the-gods-eye-view.html.

2. John F. Kennedy, "Moon Speech," National Aeronautics and Space Administration, accessed July 26, 2015, http://er.jsc.nasa.gov/seh/ricetalk.htm.

3. Banjo, http://ban.jo.

Chapter 13: Transforming Your Picture Idea into a Vivid Description

1. John Adair, *The Leadership of Jesus and Its Legacy Today* (Cleveland, OH: Pilgrim Press, 2002), 125–26.

2. "Watershed-Based Management Plan for the Upper Illinois River Watershed, Northwest Arkansas," Illinois River Watershed Partnership, accessed July 26, 2015, http://www.irwp.org/assets/PDF/UIRW-Watershed-Based-Plan-2012-11-30-Final.pdf.

3. Charles Arn, "Pastoral Longevity and Church Growth," Wesley Seminary, http://wesleyconnectonline.com/pastoral-longevity-and-church-growth-charles-arn.

Chapter 14: Developing Your Background Vision

1. Auxano is currently the largest team of full-time, nonprofit-based Paterson Centered certified facilitators in the country. If you would like to learn more, please see our "execution" service at Auxano.com. The vision tool is part of the StratOp process, Copyright Paterson Center, LLC. All rights reserved. Used with permission.

Chapter 15: Leading the Long-Range Vision

1. Gary Chapman, *The 5 Love Languages, revised edition* (Illinois: Northfield Publishing, 2015).

2. "2012 Outreach 100 Largest and Fastest-Growing Churches in America," 2012 Special Edition of Outreach Magazine, http://www.outreachmagazine.com/2012-outreach-100-largest-fastest-growing-churches-america.html.

Chapter 16: Developing Your Midground Vision

1. As mentioned previously, this is the only horizon discussed in *Church Unique* chapter 17 as the "missional mountaintop plus milestone (symbolized as *ᵐ*Mountaintop + Milestone)".

2. The SMART goal concept is commonly attributed to Peter Drucker and was first used by Tom Doran in 1981. People interchange the meaning of "A" and "R" which I have selected based on what works best in the Horizon Storyline. http://en.wikipedia.org/wiki/SMART_criteria.

3. Patrick M. Lencioni, *The Advantage* (San Francisco, CA: Jossey-Bass, 2012).

4. Ibid.

5. Chris McChesney, Sean Covey, and Jim Huling, *The 4 Disciplines of Execution* (New York: Free Press, 2012).

6. As the architect of the Horizon Storyline, I need to identify two notable exceptions. First neither of these tools has a long-range component. The last major treatment in the business space I am aware of is Jim Collins's 1994 work from *Built to Last* on BHAGS (big hairy audacious goals). Second, the Horizon Storyline is handcrafted especially for the local church.

7. For those familiar with the Vision Frame from *Church Unique* or Auxano consulting, this is where your Vision Frame itself can give categories for the midground vision emphasis. The Vision Frame, as your identity, "pushes" you into the future while your long-range vision pulls you. I call the Vision Frame the "wind to your back" and the beyond-the-horizon vision, the "bungee cord tied to your heart."

Chapter 17: Developing Your Foreground Vision

1. Chris McChesney, Sean Covey, and Jim Huling, *The 4 Disciplines of Execution* (New York: Free Press, 2012).

2. Read more about Auxano's relationship with the Paterson Center at Auxano .com/execution.

3. This language is used at large, but I was introduced to it by McChesney, Covey, and Huling, *The 4 Disciplines of Execution.*

4. I was introduced to the idea of using dramatic structure in a planning context through Donald Miller's storyline materials (blogs, conferences, and workbook), which he uses for personal planning.

Appendix C: The Problem with Vision Statements and Further Advice about Defining Vision

1. George Barna, *The Power of Team Leadership: Achieving Success through Shared Responsibility* (Colorado Springs, CO: WaterBrook Press, 2001).

2. Mike Regele and Mark Schulz, *Death of the Church* (Grand Rapids, MI: Zondervan, 1995), 229.

3. Will Mancini, *Church Unique: How Missional Leaders Cast Vision, Capture Culture, and Create Movement* (San Francisco: Jossey-Bass, 2008), 167.